Codex59

PORSCHE

DOUBLE WORLD CHAMPIONS
1900 ~ 1977

RICHARD VON FRANKENBERG
WITH MICHAEL COTTON

ISBN 0 85429 171 7

First published September 1977, Reprinted May 1978

© Haynes Publishing Group 1977, 1978

The Haynes Publishing Group
Sparkford Yeovil Somerset BA22 7JJ England

Distributed in North America by
Haynes Publications Inc.
861 Lawrence Drive Newbury Park California 91320 USA

a FOULIS Motoring book

The first part of *PORSCHE – DOUBLE WORLD CHAMPIONS – 1900-1977* was written by Richard von Frankenberg and was published under the title *Porsche The Man and his Cars*. It was translated from the German by Charles Meisl. Motor-Presse-Verlag GmbH of Stuttgart published it originally under the title *Die ungewohnliche Geschichte des Hauses PORSCHE.*
Mike Cotton edited and amended Part 1 and wrote the whole of Part 2 for this new title adding many new photographs, the majority of which can be credited to the Porsche company and to *Motor Sport*

Printed and bound in England
Editorial production Tim Parker with Annette Cutler
Jacket design Edward Piper

Contents
Part 1

Part 2

Part 1

Ferdinand Porsche, engineering genius, and the very beginnings of the legend created in the twentieth Century

1 Paris Exhibition–Lohner– First racing 'Porsche'

THEY called it the exhibition of the century, and it far excelled its predecessors of 1878 and 1879; pavilions were bigger, more visitors came, more countries were represented, and more specialized groups of exhibits were shown. Without doubt, science and engineering were the focal points of this Paris exhibition in the year 1900. The Eiffel Tower, built in 1889, stood proudly above it all, a powerful symbol of technical progress. This time the entire exhibition was lit by the new-fangled electric arc-lights and there was even an 'Electricity Palace'. All branches of engineering were on show: rapid-firing guns and machine guns, multi-spindle lathes, enormous cranes, the Edison X-ray camera, electric conveyors, a 2,500hp steam engine by Borsig, an 18 ft high stationary engine by Lanz, and, of course, there were also motor-cars.

In 1894 the first motor race had taken place. It was a long-distance run from Paris to Rouen, and a Daimler-engined car had been declared the winner. Then came a race from Paris to Bordeaux. Through these events the motor vehicle became popular and the demands made by these races advanced the early designs. In those days talk was only about the French and German makes. Germany had seen the production of the first cars, while France staged the first competitions; other nations only started to produce motor vehicles worthy of competition at the turn of the century.

In Austria the first self-propelled vehicle, which could be properly called a motor-car had been built in 1875. This, the Marcus car, had actually been driven a short distance on the road, but to Marcus fell a typical inventor's fate, he was not in a position to improve his invention nor to popularize it to the extent of putting it into production. The first firm in Austria to take up car production in a proper commercial way was Jacob Lohner & Co.

This company had been founded in 1891 and was one of the oldest coach-builders in Austria. They built beautiful horse-drawn carriages some of which were very luxurious, and Jacob Lohner became 'K.u.K. Hofkutschenbauer' – in other words, Coach-builder to his Imperial Majesty. On 1st December 1896 Lohner decided to build motor-cars in emulation of such great ones as Daimler, Benz, and Panhard of France. Yet Lohner wanted to plough his own furrow; he thought that electric power would be preferable to the internal combustion engine. As supplier to the Imperial Court, he considered that it would be necessary to build motor-cars acceptable at Court and worthy of being driven to a theatre premiere. Internal combustion engines were too noisy and complicated, and therefore he pinned his faith on electromobiles.

At that time competition between electric and internal combustion engined vehicles was still rife, and the petrol engine was by no means winning. Even the steam-engine manufacturers were competing seriously. One must not forget that the first absolute speed records had been achieved by steam (Serpollet) and electric cars (Jeantaud). Also, one must not overlook the fact that the population, especially in the country, was very much opposed to these new stinking monsters.

Lohner, being the first motor-car manufacturer of the monarchy, received gracious permission to exhibit his newest designs in the Austrian Pavilion of the World Exhibition in Paris in 1900. The Lohner car was *the* Austrian vehicle in Paris and, because of this, was viewed with exceptional interest. Not only the potential buying public but also the experts were astonished at the individualistic design that Lohner exhibited. On the sign-boards that surrounded the stand was stated clearly for all to see 'Electric Chaise', 'System Lohner-Porsche'.

Jacob Lohner & Co. was quite a well-known firm at the time; but who was Porsche? A completely new name; was it perhaps this Mr. Porsche who had invented the curious drive system with which the Lohner Chaise was equipped? The inquisitive ones pushed forward to see everything at close range; they asked questions and were astonished at the replies. If we look up the technical journals of the period in which the Paris Exhibition was described, we read comments like this:

'The radically new designs which were to be expected at the Paris Exhibition had effectively stopped the motor-car enthusiasts of Europe for a whole year from ordering or purchasing. Everyone looked forward as if hypnotized to the opening of the Exhibition and disappointment was great when the verbal and written reports stated, more or less in unison, that broadly speaking only well-known designs with small constructive improvements had appeared.'

One can gather from this that the well-known automobile manufacturers of the period had not bothered to show anything particularly outstanding. For instance another two years were to elapse before the house of Daimler appeared with the basic design for a motor-car as we know it today, which finally severed the automobile from the carriage: engine in front together with the gearbox, inclined steering column, seats side by side in the direction of travel, and a normal steering wheel.

The appearance of the vehicles at the Paris Exhibition still resembled the carriage. 'Among the two or three real innovations,' so says the report on the show, 'probably the most outstanding is the sole Austrian automobile, an electric car on the Lohner-Porsche system built by Jacob Lohner & Co. of Vienna and exhibited by them.'

Then follow technical details: 'The epoch-making novelty of the car consists in the entire elimination of all intermediate gearing such as pinions, belts, chains, differentials, etc. In fact the first car without transmission has been built. This is achieved by the fitting of the electric motors of the Porsche design into the hubs of the front wheels which thus become the driven and steered wheels.'

The contemporary reporter then exaggerates the disadvantages of the internal combustion engine although in principle his judgement was correct: 'The advantages so gained are manifold. By eliminating the transmission, power loss through friction is eliminated, the latter amounting to 40% or even 60% in some of the best-designed petrol-engined vehicles, whereas the losses with electric drive amount to only 20%.'

And now he pleads for front wheel drive: 'The suitability of the front wheels both for steering and driving eliminates in one fell swoop the unpleasantness of the vehicle with rear wheel drive, which is pushed, whereas front wheel drive plus steering are identical with horse production in that the vehicle is being drawn, and pulled, when a corner is being taken, is always and immediately in the new direction; thus skidding on sharp corners or on slippery paved roads is eliminated, or at least only happens briefly, exactly as if the vehicle were drawn by a horse when skidding is very rare, and when it occurs, is soon over.'

When one reads these sentences it is very apparent how at that time automotive thought was still allied to the horse-drawn carriage. The reporter in this sentence could not know, of course, that the designer Ferdinand Porsche was due to abandon front wheel drive in the years to come. But up to 1903 Porsche always designed the Lohner cars with the electric motors in the front wheel hubs. Also at that time he drove in various races with 'front wheel drive' cars (but, of course, the latter expression did not exist then).

The Lohner-Porsche Chaise exhibited at the Paris show was said to have an output per motor per wheel of 2.5hp at 120rpm, and an efficiency of 83%; 120rpm is of course today a laughable output. 'The electric motors, however, were overloaded up to 7hp for periods of 15-20 minutes without noticeable heating-up, and this was undoubtedly due to the excellent cooling that resulted from the revolving motor housings being placed in the front wheels.

'Otherwise the construction of this vehicle tends to be over-shadowed by the sensational manner of its driving mechanism. The weight of the complete machine amounts to 2,160 lb of which 914 are attributable to the accumulators built into the frame and 253 lb to each wheel and motor.' From these weight indications the disadvantages of pure electric drive is quite apparent; accumulators are extremely heavy and have only a limited range, and the necessary charging of them (or their possible exchange) takes longer than the refuelling of the internal combustion vehicle. If we add these weights together we find that only 740 lb were left for the chassis and body of the Lohner-Porsche Chaise, which shows that (in 1900) this vehicle was designed with lightness in view.

Further description shows other modern features: 'to use the vehicles to the greatest advantage on the generally poor Austrian roads, the centre of gravity has been kept as low as possible, the lower edge of the case containing the batteries (this case was below the driving seat and just above the axles of the vehicle) being only 18in. from the ground, and the track reduced to 45in.' The external appearance was naturally even then old-fashioned and similar to a horse-drawn chaise. There was a central lamp in front and two little carbide side-lamps on the right and left of the seats: the mudguards were typical carriage ones and vestigial in form: the wheels were wooden-spoked and had solid tyres and a little servant-seat perched behind the driver and passenger who were provided with a hood. Further technical details are delightfully old-fashioned: 'The hand lever of the small controller is fitted at the right-hand side of the driver; it is used for all forward movements, and for the electric short-circuit braking: a change-over switch serves the purpose of reversing: a foot-pedal is for the brakes on the rear wheels and cuts the electric current at the same time.'

All contemporary vehicles had only rear wheel brakes and this applied also to the Lohner-Porsche Chaise; but apart from the mechanical brakes there were also short-circuit electrical ones for the hub motors in the front wheels and this meant in fact, that four-wheel brakes were available. But the expression 'four-wheel brakes' did not exist then and the fact that brakes could be applied to all four wheels was not even particularly mentioned.

It is stated in the contemporary report that the vehicle exhibited was the first of its type and, inclusive of the electric motors, had been built in the remarkably short time of ten weeks in the workshops of Messrs. Lohner. From this it can be deduced that at their works the change-over from building horse-drawn carriages to self-propelled vehicles was very thoroughly done. This was obviously one of the reasons why in 1898 they engaged young Ferdinand Porsche.

The 'forward positions' of the controller had a low and a high speed. In the low speed 17kph (11mph) could be reached and 37kph (about 23mph) in high. And then follows the most remarkable sentence of this entire report: 'and for racing purposes this speed can be increased to about 37mph.

Even then, in the first car constructed by Ferdinand Porsche, a sporting purpose had been envisaged and a racing version was planned.

Throughout his entire career as a motor designer we shall always find that sport was Ferdinand Porsche's guiding motive; 37mph was a considerable speed at that time, especially for a car offered for sale. The absolute world record at the beginning of the Paris Exhibition stood then at 105.8kph (about 65mph) established by Jenatzy in his electric car.

Thus far we have quoted from the first 'road test' of Porsche Number One. The car created such a furore in Paris that naturally Lohner was asked by the experts how old was the designer of this unusual automobile. Mr. Lohner was not too keen to answer and only hesitatingly admitted the designer's age: for Porsche was just twenty-three when Lohner gave him the job in his newly established car manufacturing department. The vehicle with the hub-mounted motors had been designed in the autumn of 1899 when he had reached the age of twenty-four. 'He is very young,' said Lohner at the World Exhibition, 'but he is a man with a big career before him. You will hear of him again.' And Mr. Lohner was certainly right.

2 Porsche's origins

IN all probability the name Porsche is derived from the Slavonic one of Borislav; but a family from East Germany need not necessarily be of Slavonic origin even though it may have a Slav name. At the time of the colonization of East Germany, quite a number of Slavonic names became accepted among German families. Parish records from the fifteenth to the seventeenth century containing the name of Porsche are found in the vicinity of Gorlitz, Bautzen, Zittau, and Forst in the Lausitz district, but they have no relationship to that branch of the family to which the great Ferdinand Porsche belonged. His great-great-grandfather is known with certainty: he was Wenzel Porsche, messenger to the local Squire of the Manor in the district of Reichenberg in Northern Bohemia. From him his genealogical tree can be traced directly and without gaps; all of his eight great-grandparents are known: not only the names but also localities and occupations can be clearly established. Ferdinand Porsche's ancestors all came from a region close to the northern Bohemian frontier. The kingdom of Bohemia belonged, during the days of the old Austrian Empire, to the Hapsburg dynasty; Vienna was not only the centre of power and administration but also the goal for anyone with ambition. Ferdinand Porsche's grandparents and great-grandparents all lived in the region between Reichenberg and Bohmisch-Leipa, in other words within a sector of some 25 miles. Their occupations also did not differ very much: artisans, weavers, coopers, carpenters, tailors, clothworkers and tinsmiths: some were even working directly for the many squires and noblemen in the castles and manor houses in their vicinity. The baptismal certificates of some of the Porsches record the fact that several owned their own houses, though without land.

The father of the man whose path to fame we are about to trace, Anton Porsche, was born in 1845 in Altharzdorf, today a suburb of Reichenberg. After finishing his apprenticeship, he established himself in Maffersdorf on the other side of the river Neisse and east of Reichenberg, as a tinsmith. There he married in 1871 Anna Ehrlich, born in 1850, who came from a similar family to his own. She originated from Ruppersdorf close to Reichenberg.

They had five children: first a son who was called Anton and who obviously one day was going to inherit the paternal business. But as a young apprentice he met with an accident which, due to the insufficient medical knowledge of the times, caused his death very shortly afterwards. The second eldest child was a daughter, Hedwig, and the third was a boy again, born on 3rd September 1875, and called Ferdinand; it was he who was now destined to learn the family craft and to carry on the business—a business it was, for now father Porsche was a very competent tinsmith with enough work to warrant the engagement of assistants. Furthermore, he had the gift of the gab and was made vice-mayor of the village.

To fill in the family tree at least in outline: the fourth child was another son, Oscar, who later had to become a tinsmith in order to continue the family business, for Ferdinand was destined for higher things; number five was a daughter, Anna who later married an innkeeper from a village near Reichenberg; the elder daughter Hedwig married an employee of the carpet factory belonging to the Ginzkeys, a family about which we shall have something else to say a little later.

There was nothing extraordinary about the brothers and sisters of Ferdinand Porsche and nothing to indicate that they were different from others. All the more was it obvious that Ferdinand did not conform to this pattern.

He was hardly 15 and an apprentice at home when the first serious row flared up between father and son, for Ferdinand spent a lot of time making electrical experiments. To understand this attitude one must imagine oneself in peasant surroundings; after all, they did not even have electricity in Reichenberg! No one understood why this 15-year-old son of a tinsmith wanted to experiment with electricity, or, indeed, how he even knew that electric current existed. He explained to his father that he wished to produce this current himself by means of a battery. But his father was furious about such nonsense, as he called it, and was very sharp with him. From his point of view this was understandable. Anton Porsche was a very strict and harsh father and taskmaster; he ran his family in a patriarchal manner. He forbade Ferdinand everything that did not belong to the tinsmith's craft.

But to people who have a career in their mind obstacles are there to be overcome; the determination to 'become somebody' usually develops early in life and grows unconsciously. Anyway, Ferdinand Porsche continued with his experiments up in the loft of the house, despite the daily 12 hours' stint of work which was not unusual in those days, and he managed to remain undetected, for his father was often away working in distant villages. His mother tacitly let him carry on with his experiments.

But one day his father did find out about them. Greatly enraged, he stamped on all the batteries without thought that they contained acid. This squirted out and burnt his boots and skin, which only gave him more cause to deal very severely indeed with his renegade son, who considered this sort of play more important than his craft.

On the other hand this event did produce some good, for mother Porsche brought up the subject of the talents which obviously seemed to lie in young Ferdinand. And one day they discussed quite openly whether it might not be better to send him to a special school in Vienna. No, said his father, that would be going too far. After all he could travel to and from Reichenberg and take evening classes at the Imperial technical school there—then one could find out whether he really had any talent. He thought that Ferdinand should become a tinsmith — a good one; that would always be a safe job, and in the meantime he should remain apprenticed to him.

This compromise of taking evening classes in Reichenberg was more than Ferdinand had dared to hope for. At home his father did not watch over him quite so closely. And then he produced a surprise which persuaded even his father of his worth. Anton Porsche came home one evening from working in a neighbouring village and from afar he saw a strange light—his house was electrically lit. Young Ferdinand, by himself, had built the complete installation, generator, switchboard, wiring and everything! No one in the neighbourhood had electric light except for the large carpet factory belonging to the Ginzkey's. A few days later the owner of the factory spoke up for the boy so that father Porsche could no longer refuse permission for him to go to Vienna. Ginzkey's help extended to the offer of a very useful job as a student employee at Bela Egger—the firm that later became Brown Boveri. In Vienna Ferdinand would have the opportunity to be a part-time student at the Technical University, and to acquire the theoretical knowledge which he lacked.

At the age of 18 he went to Vienna, was independent, and his career began.

3 At Bela Egger—Lohner-Semmering record —War vehicles

THE Bela Egger concern manufactured electrical equipment and machinery. Ferdinand Porsche advanced very quickly, for they recognized that this young man had something akin to a sixth sense for technical problems; he always came up with his own ideas and these were respected. After barely four years he became manager of the test department and first assistant in the calculating section. Jacob Lohner was looking for such a man, for he wanted to build electric cars. His designer, he specified, should come from the electrical industry, should be young and adaptable to new and progressive ideas.

To be quite honest, this very gifted young engineer Ferdinand Porsche cost the house of Lohner a considerable sum of money over the six years he worked there. Not because he earned a lot of money himself, or that he was extravagant: no, his demands were for more money to spend on experiments and for testing experimental prototypes; series manufacture interested him very little.

At the time of the World Exhibition, the 'marriage' between Lohner and Porsche was still a happy one. Everyone talked about the Lohner car because its exceptional design created world-wide interest. Ferdinand Porsche was also a very good driver and on 23rd September 1900 he established a record on the Semmering road near Vienna with a racing version of the Lohner-Porsche car. At that time a section of road of exactly 10km length from the 70km stone to the Hotel Erzherzog Johann at the top of the Semmering at the 80km stone was used for races and record attempts. In these 10km the height differential was exactly 400m, equal to an average incline of 1 in 25, which was considerable for the motors of the period. These 10km were dusty and contained a number of sharp bends, and the 'Semmering record' was at that time in Austria the best known test for cars and motor-cycles. There was an official record list in the offices of the Austrian Automobile Club and the following categories were entered there: motor-cycles, touring cars, racing cars, electromobiles, and voiturettes.

On 23rd September 1900 Ferdinand Porsche started at exactly 6 o'clock from the 70km stone. Two official timekeepers were present, two officials from the Automobile Club took care of the start, having previously carefully weighed the car. This machine was a little heavier than the Chaise exhibited in Paris. It weighed exactly 1,120 kilos, but was devoid of a body and only boasted two seats in tandem above the box containing the batteries.

It is remarkable that Porsche designed for this, his first racing car, a kind of bonnet which could be considered as a precursor of aerodynamic ideas. The front of the car was pointed and from there to the steering wheel was fitted a curved, windcutting smooth sheet-metal housing.

Ferdinand Porsche took exactly 14 minutes and 52 1/5 seconds to the finish, at the Hotel Erzherzog Johann, and this time was recognized by the Austrian Automobile Club as a 'record for all types of electromobiles.' The car had the same hub-mounted motors in the front wheels as the model shown in Paris. The record time previous to Porsche's was 23 minutes and 27 seconds; for Porsche to cover the Semmering track at a greater average speed than 40kph was a sensational achievement in the year 1900.

The next technical step consisted of 'mixed' drive. Already at the time of the Paris World Exhibition Porsche showed some projects to Jacob Lohner. The limited range of pure electric drive was a great disadvantage, yet on the other hand he did not want to give up his idea of the hub-mounted motors. Electric drive had many points in its favour, so why not combine it with the petrol engine! Why not fit a petrol engine instead of the heavy batteries, then couple a dynamo to the petrol engine so as to convert mechanical energy into electric and thus have a power source for the hub motors; in that manner the pleasant electric drive was retained. Porsche called the vehicles powered in this manner 'petrol-electric mixed cars.' The petrol engines came from the Daimler Company in Germany.

The 'mixed' cars had front wheel drive. At the Exelberg races in 1902 Ferdinand Porsche won with such a car in the 'up to 1,000kg' class.

Racing cars of the period were distinguished from touring cars by not having any bodywork and sometimes not even a bonnet. Both seats were entirely in the open—yes, always two seats, for in those days regulations prescribed that even on a hill climb a passenger had to be carried, who had to lean out of his seat when cornering in the same manner as a sidecar passenger does on a motor-cycle.

On 8th November 1902 Ferdinand Porsche received a letter which made him proud indeed: 'His Imperial Highness, the most serene Archduke Franz Ferdinand graciously sends enclosed to your goodself a memento of the manoeuvres in West Hungary. The performance of your automobile and your safe conducting thereof have given every satisfaction to His Imperial Highness.'

For in the meantime Ferdinand Porsche had become a Reserve Infantry soldier and had even been issued with a uniform, but not, however, to serve in the infantry. The Archduke Franz Ferdinand — he who was murdered in 1914 in Sarajevo — had ordered this reserve infantryman into his own service, complete with a car of his own conception, and during the manoeuvres Ferdinand Porsche drove the Archduke around from the various staff headquarters to other positions. The car was a 'mixed' drive one.

Many engineers at that time were most sceptical of the 'mixed' system which Ferdinand Porsche had designed because they considered that the power transmitted from the petrol engine to the hub motors was going a long way round. But Porsche kept to his idea and the future showed him to be right. Although 'mixed' drive did not maintain itself in normal road cars, special vehicles still use it to this day.

Let us anticipate a little: 'mixed' drive was used in two of Porsche's designs in the First World War. For the Imperial army he created a 'wagon train,' made up of a traction engine with a petrol motor which pulled a number of trailers, up to ten of them. Each of these trailers had hub-motors which were powered by means of a long cable via a generator. Thus a relatively small traction engine could pull this entire 'wagon train' even over mountain passes, forward and in reverse. Steering was by an arrangement which Porsche invented for this purpose.

The individual trailers were light to medium weight, so the entire 'train' could even be moved over small temporary bridges. The traction engine went over first, laid a cable and

17

brought the trailers across one after the other, so that only one was on the bridge at a time, each moving by the power of its own hub-motors. In Volhynia and on the Isonzo front (during the 1914-18 war) where the transport of heavy goods had collapsed, the Porsche wagon trains still crawled across country, separating and coupling up as necessary.

On the principle of this 'train' of 1915 there is today in America a 'cross-country freighter' which is over a hundred yards long, fitted with two 500hp diesel engines and seven trailers. This is intended for the jungle or the arctic circle, in fact for the worst cross-country going: a wagon train with 'mixed drive.' Generators produce electric current which is conveyed to the trailers by electric cable and every trailer has hub-motors.

Porsche's construction which became best known during the First World War was the so-called C-train: by it the 42cm mortar made by Skoda became fully motorized, although previously this, the heaviest piece of artillery in the Imperial army, had only been fitted in fortifications or transported by rail. To this day there has not been a heavier motorized gun. Six traction engines of 150hp each pulled six enormous trailers with 8 wheels apiece — each wheel having a hub-motor. The barrel of this monster piece of artillery weighed 17 tons on its own and 26 with accessories. The gun carriage was just as heavy and the necessary foundation weighed another few tons. Yet even under poor cross-country going the transport of this gun was no major problem for the 'mixed drive' train. These 42cm mortars transported to the Isonzo front by the C-train materially influenced the 1917 Austrian offensive.

During the Second World War Porsche designed a number of tanks, and his 'Tiger' and the almost legendary 'Mouse' were equipped with 'mixed drive.'

The Lohner-Porsche car was not only used in the Austrian manoeuvres but also tried by the German army and described as working 'to the fullest satisfaction of the German military authorities.' The Vienna fire brigade was one of the first to become motorized and as early as 1904 had vehicles equipped with hub mounted motors of the Porsche system.

Porsche applied for patents for the hub-motors at the end of 1897 whilst he was working at Egger. In March 1903 he is described by a reporter of a Vienna newspaper as being 'full of technical dreams which strive for realization.... Mr. Porsche is a tireless creator and worker in the technical field....to dream and to act—that is the essence of people the like of Porsche; unfortunately there are not enough of these in Vienna....'

But his technical dreams could not be brought to fruition in the relatively small works of Jacob Lohner, and Ferdinand Porsche, now 30 years old, left to join the Austrian Daimler works in Wiener-Neustadt, in those days the biggest motor-car factory in Austria. In that same year he received the Poetting medal, a high distinction given only to Austrian engineers.

4 Austrian Daimler–Maja–Mercedes

WHEN Porsche took up his new employment as technical director of Austrian Daimler he had started on his way to success.

The company, later called Austro-Daimler, had been founded in 1848 as 'Fabrik fur Maschinenbau der Bruder Fischer.' It had been in existence 50 years when the owners decided to build motor-cars, and since they had no experience of their own in this type of work they went to Daimler in Stuttgart and negotiated construction under licence. This turned out to be a clever move.

The first advertisement in a Vienna newspaper referred to a 'Daimler motor carriage for use on the road, powered by a petrol engine instead of horse drawn; it can be seen at Bierenz, Fischer & Co., Vienna 1, Giselastrasse 4.' The first leaflet stated: 'generally speaking the motor carriages are arranged to travel at speeds of 5 to 25km per hour and they can be put into motion within one or two minutes.'

During the negotiations about licences the company changed its name to Osterreichische Daimler-Motoren-Kommanditgesellschaft' and from 1901 to 1904 Paul Daimler, the son of Gottlieb Daimler, was chief engineer in Wiener-Neustadt. The works produced a very useful motor lorry as early as 1902 and from that date onwards they made strenuous efforts to bring about motorization of the army.

Under the technical management of Ferdinand Porsche the construction of passenger cars and of racing cars was intensely pursued and the standard type for years 1905 to 1908 was the 30hp Maja car. This name has a little history of its own.

In those days there was a certain wealthy man of Austrian origin who lived mostly in Nice; his name was Jellinek. Mr. Jellinek put his money into the motor industry for he saw a considerable future in it; and some of his money was invested in the Daimler works. He had two daughters, one was called Mercedes and the other Maja. Neither was particularly attractive but Mr. Jellinek was proud of them and, as things are when paternal money works behind the scenes, the Daimler company in Stuttgart christened a new type of car 'Mercedes.' This name pleased the purchasers and the name of Jellinek's daughter became the *marque* Mercedes. However, the Maja produced by the Austrian Daimler works did not achieve world renown.

In 1909 Ferdinand Porsche designed an entirely new passenger car of 32hp, equipped with a 4-speed gearbox and available alternatively with chain or shaft drive. It was able to climb 22% inclines and for long distance travelling the rear-mounted petrol tank held about 15 gallons. The emperor Francis Joseph had one of these as his private car and so did the Bulgarian queen. This new type took the place of the Maja and since then that name has disappeared from the realm of automobile *marques*. As was customary in those days Porsche received a medal for 'exceptional merit' from the Bulgarian court, because he had supplied them with a very good motor-car.

But let us return to the year 1907. Apart from a number of public service vehicles for the fire brigade and also trolley buses which continued to work on the 'mixed' principle, Porsche designed at the Austro-Daimler works an 85hp racing car which had mixed drive with hub-motors, but the basic design remained as originally laid down in Stuttgart, hence the name 'Mercedes-Electrique-Mixte.' This car had twin ignition by two separate magnetos, a system which became generally accepted in racing engines at a later date. Racing car brakes were already a problem in those days, and Porsche introduced a form of water cooling for the rear brakes and this was interconnected with the water cooling of the engine—a curious design which he later gave up. There were no front wheel brakes except electrical ones in the hub-mounted motors. The maximum speed of this racing vehicle was 77mph.

A contemporary report in an Austrian motor paper tells us that the Austrian Daimler company had built new factories and workshops in the summer of 1907. Their airiness and light was particularly emphasized. The reporter also mentions meeting the 31-year-old technical director Porsche who was very busy tuning a racing car, undergoing brake tests in one of the workshops. The reporter says that it was quite a job to get Porsche to leave the racing car and to give information about other parts of the works where dynamos and electric motors were being made....

It was no exaggeration to say that as early as 1900 motor sport was the 'leitmotif' of Porsche. To 'get him away from racing cars' during his entire life was most difficult.

In the year 1907 Austro-Daimler started building an entirely different type of engine, firstly for airships and a little later for aeroplanes. The people who flew in Europe in 1908 could be counted on the fingers of one hand, but even then Ferdinand Porsche was pioneering construction of aircraft engines. The first official engined flight in Europe, three years after the Wright Brothers first flew in the United States, was on 23rd October 1906, when Santos-Dumont, a Brazilian living in France, flew his double-decker, equipped with a 50hp Antoinette engine for a distance of about 26 yards. On 13th January 1908 Henri Farman won the coveted prize of 50,000 francs for the first full circuit flight in Europe.

The first aircraft engine made by Austro-Daimler was intended for the Austrian Parseval dirigible balloon, an airship built on the so-called non-rigid system—whereas the Zeppelin with its framework was constructed on the 'rigid' system. An Austro-Daimler 4-cylinder motor was mounted vertically in a steel tube nacelle under the Parseval airship. The Austrian Army authorities were most interested in airships and their engines and two further models in 1907 and 1908 were equipped with engines made by the Austro-Daimler works.

It was the habit of Porsche to grab hold of a screwdriver in the works to tune an engine when he deemed it necessary; in the same spirit he participated in the test flights of the airships which were fitted with his motors. On one occasion this might have ended in a serious accident because the airship, flying within a low lying cloud-bank, was caught by a gust of wind and a church tower built on the side of a mountain was seen too late by the crew. The airship only missed hitting the tower by the quick action of the crew in discharging ballast.

During this excitement too much ballast was released and the dirigible at the same time got into an up-current and as a result of both rose extremely quickly, well above the safe operating height, and threatened to burst. To cap it all the gas valve would not open and those aboard felt themselves in dire peril. Ferdinand Porsche with his manual skill and calm in critical situations finally managed to operate the gas valve, so that the airship lost height and finally landed according to plan.

In 1910 the first aeroplane engine left the works in Wiener-Neustadt, despite the fact that at the time not a single aeroplane existed in Austria; Porsche insisted that they should develop such engines in view of the future which aircraft were bound to have.

With the stimulus from the engine, we find that Austria possessed in 1913 no less than 120 aircraft—this small country had the sixth greatest number of aeroplanes in the world. Aircraft engines of the Austro-Daimler works became known all over the world before the First World War. England, classic home of aircraft engines, saw the firm of Beardmore take up licenses for the manufacture of the Austrian engine, and one of these is in the Science Museum, Kensington.

Porsche's first aircraft engine design was a water-cooled in-line engine with cast-iron cylinders and welded-on jackets; overhead valves were operated by leaf springs, for Porsche was experimenting. In 1912 he brought out an aircraft engine which has often been called the great-grandfather of the Volkswagen: it was an air-cooled flat-four with overhead valves—a design entirely removed from the engineering concepts of the period. The individual cylinders of this opposed engine were slightly in V towards one another.

He also designed a rotary engine which was lubricated through its hollow crankshaft, but this was manufactured only for a short time. Then came a series of V-type engines and at the end of the First World War he created a 300hp V12. Following this came a sort of W-engine where three rows of cylinders acted on a common crankshaft. This engine had a hollow overhead camshaft over the middle row of cylinders and not only could a machine-gun be fired through it, but it also drove the airscrew. The two overhead camshafts of the other rows of cylinders were also hollow and contained two further machine-gun barrels and these fired through the airscrew arc, a system which one would think originated in 1938 instead of 1918!

The standard series of aircraft engines consisted of in-line 6-cylinder ones, all with overhead camshafts and producing between 160 and 360hp. They were intended for fighter aircraft. An English technical journal in its analysis at the end of the First World War came to the conclusion, that the Porsche designed aircraft motors of the Austro-Daimler works were beyond doubt the best engines of the Central European powers.

Porsche had in the meantime become managing director of the Austro-Daimler company, and in 1916 the Emperor gave him the Officer's Cross of the Francis Joseph medal in conjunction with the military 'pour le merite' mention. The technical university in Vienna conferred upon him an honorary doctorate in recognition of his work in the field of automobile and aircraft engineering.

At this time he worked on designs for a helicopter. This extraordinary flying machine represented a combination of a captive balloon and aircraft and it was to be powered by means of a cable from the ground, but it was never built. Firstly because the form and type of helicopter rotor was not satisfactory and had to be constantly altered, and secondly because an electric motor giving 300hp for a weight of 250 kilos could not be coped with from the thermal point of view. The motor was designed for 6,000rpm.

With such futuristic plans which Porsche kept hatching within the framework of his constructive work one might wonder if he did not sometimes go beyond the bounds of the possible to create projects which, although undoubtedly showing the way, were certainly premature. But the 'technical dreams' which the reporter of the Vienna paper in 1903 so cleverly noticed were all hinged to reality. Let us then return to those designs which actually came into being. Austro-Daimler took part in the Prince Henry trials of 1909 with a car which was built to succeed the Maja. This event, one of the best known in Germany at the time, was in several daily stages from Berlin via Breslau, Budapest and Salzburg to Munich. Naturally Ferdinand Porsche had to take part himself, as well as

Fischer, one of the directors of the Wiener-Neustadt works. Those were the really heroic days of motor sport, when designers and leading directors personally tested their vehicles in competitive events. The third car of the team was driven by the Austrian sportsman Hugo Boos-Waldeck.

Success was small but noteworthy, the team arrived without loss of marks and had acquitted itself well in the special test; although they did not obtain a win they did gain a silver plaque. Fischer was satisfied, but not Porsche. On the evening of the prize-giving party, which was quite a social event, he was not to be found. Where was the technical director of Austro-Daimler? At last they found him in a small room, chewing a dry bread roll with two sheets of paper in front of him. He was drawing for all he was worth. Director Fischer was beside himself: 'What are you doing here? Everyone is waiting for you....' 'What am I doing? Designing a new car, of course,' Ferdinand Porsche replied. And Fischer could not but agree that a 32hp car would not get anywhere in the general classification in such a difficult event, it would be necessary to design a more powerful and modern vehicle.

In 1910 the team was again at the start. The Prince Henry trial—so called after the motoring enthusiast Prince Henry of Prussia who created it—had become extremely popular in the meantime. There were over 200 starters; seventeen special tests had to be taken, consisting of hill-climbs and speed tests. The car which Ferdinand Porsche had built at Austro-Daimler was equipped with a new 86hp engine, and the bodywork also was entirely new. Some thought it funny, some surprising. Porsche called it the tulip-shape: narrow down below where the chassis was and widening upwards, and the radiator was kept very narrow. This 'tulip shape' did not represent real aerodynamics because wind-tunnels did not exist to measure air resistance. Yet it was designed to bring about higher speeds by means of a small frontal area and a body form which adapted itself to the air-stream. In the special tests they even turned the headlights sideways so as not to present a flat vertical face to the wind but only the narrow side.

This vehicle reached a chronometer top speed of 87mph and this was almost 9mph faster than any other car participating, although it was by no means the most powerful one.

All cars had to be touring machines, fully equipped with mudguards, lights and four seats. And these four seats had to be occupied during the entire run. In those days regulations were taken very seriously; if a car was built for four people then it had to show in competition that it could be driven with four people aboard. Amongst the occupants of Ferdinand Porsche's car there was a first-class mechanic, just as in the other cars. But there was someone else: Porsche's wife. She was very enthusiastic for motoring sport and always wanted to come along when her husband competed in an event. In that year 1910 she already had two children, the eldest, a daughter, called Louise, and the second born in 1909 a son, named after his father, Ferdinand, the Ferry Porsche, who today is chairman of the Porsche board. Ferdinand Porsche's wife came from a family of artisans who hailed from Bohemia. Her father lived in Vienna and she herself was a working girl, most unusual in those days and a sign of emancipation. She was a book-keeper in an electrical works—this type of superior woman's work only became normally accepted after the First World War. Ferdinand met her in Vienna whilst he still worked for Lohner; her name was Aloisia Johanna Kaes.

Family feeling was a strong trait in the house of Porsche. He who had suddenly made such a career did not forget his origins and took great care of his parents, brothers and sisters and his friends of by-gone years. To give an instance: in 1902 he wanted to try the first Lohner car with hub motors and 'mixed' drive for a longish distance. This test run took him to Maffersdorf where proudly he made his father and younger brother get into the vehicle and took them for a drive. He was also married in Maffersdorf.

But back to the Prince Henry trial of 1910, Eduard Fischer, the director of Austro-Daimler who had also driven in 1909, was again in the team, and the third man this time was Heinrich Graf Schoenfeldt. Those three were known as the 'iron team', and they took first, second and third place in the general classification of the 1910 event. The Austro-Daimlers won almost all special tests and of the twelve cups they took nine home.

This Prince Henry model became a great sales success for Austro-Daimler all over Europe. One car of the series is still running in good condition in private hands in England. The 4-cylinder engine had a cubic capacity of 5.7 litres and the valves were operated by an overhead camshaft. The 86hp represented an output of 15hp per litre which was very respectable in those days when 3,000rpm was considered an extremely high rate of revolutions.

The Austrian Automobile Club arranged an international Alpine trial and the 'iron team' also took part in this. In 1911 and 1912 Ferdinand Porsche still took the wheel himself, and Graf Schoenfeldt continued until 1914. The sport was the thing and Ferdinand Porsche would have loved to go on with it. But the Austro-Daimler company became bigger and bigger and just before the war amalgamated with Skoda, so that he no longer had time for active competition.

His particular task at Skoda was to motorize the big 30.5cm mortar of the Imperial army. He designed a mortar traction engine which came in two types: either with an 80 or with a 100hp motor. For light cross-country going it had solid rubber tyres and for rough terrain enormous iron wheels with a diameter of 5ft 3in. The driver was enthroned fully 13½ft from the ground and the engine could pull 24 tons. Technically interesting was the fact that this mortar traction engine had four-wheel drive and the steered front wheels were not driven by universal joints as is usual today, but eccentrically through a series of bevel gears.

Porsche had tried experimentally before the First World War to equip a lorry with four-wheel drive to increase its ability for cross-country work. Presumably he was the first designer to arrive at a practical solution of four-wheel drive for heavy cross-country vehicles.

In the Book of Honour of the Austrian artillery there is a special chapter about this motorized mortar: 'The special significance of this piece lay less in its great power and range than in its extreme mobility, which enabled the mortar battery to follow the army of the field and to get into action with great dispatch. This was particularly decisive when attacking the Belgian fortifications.'

This was in the First World War. When Namur was taken the Austrian 30.5cm motor-mortar played a decisive role. Bulow had, by using the First, Second and Third German Army, pushed back the French and British at Namur and Maubeuge, but he could not take the fort at Namur, which now threatened his flank and rear. Heavy artillery had to be brought up quickly and by putting in the motorized mortar, General von Gallwitz took the fort in three days.

Porsche designed a traction engine also for smaller guns and this was called the 'Daimler-horse' or the 'motorized gun-carriage.' It was intended to replace the horse-drawn light artillery. This gun carriage had two big iron wheels and a spur at the back. It was also built in lighter form for field kitchens and baggage trains. They used it on the Italian front and in Galicia. In winter particularly the troops were pleased with this vehicle for it had an air-cooled engine. Porsche had provided steel claws on the outer edge of the iron wheels of these vehicles and the driver was able to control the amount by which they protruded. If the vehicle got into deep mud or snow the steel claws were more or less extended as necessary.

To design these adjustable claws had not been an easy task. The chief of the design office at that time, Otto Koehler, assigned an entire staff of technicians to deal with this problem and a whole series of solutions were put before Porsche. Porsche went from drawing board to drawing board and discussed the problem with the individual engineers (he used this system throughout his life). He provoked all of them by questions, always

23

probing, always scribbling with his pencil, always simplifying.

None of the solutions of the claw-problem pleased him. He was rough and tough in his speech and always got into a temper quickly; rubbish, stupid, too complicated, a fine lot of engineers in my office....No one can build claws such as you have designed them here....

Porsche was well aware of the difficulties of this constructive problem and suddenly an idea occurred to him: 'Five hundred kronen,' he yelled loudly, 'five hundred kronen to the man with a sensible idea by tomorrow!' Back they went to their places but despite the 500 kronen had no better ideas. Then a 20-year-old youngster came to Otto Koehler; Porsche had 'discovered' him in 1913 and, much to the annoyance of older experts, put him into the design office. His name was Karl Rabe and he brought along a surprisingly simple solution of the claw problem, which was based on the utilization of the centrifugal force of the wheel. The solution seemed almost too simple to chief designer Koehler and he hardly dared to call Porsche, for the latter's ire was greatly feared. But he came, stopped before Rabe's drawing board whilst the other engineers tiptoed closer. A deathly silence pervaded the design office. Ferdinand Porsche looked at the drawing without moving a muscle and suddenly called out: 'Pay him out, pay him out!' Without a further word he walked past the ranks of his other engineers. This self-same Karl Rabe was made departmental chief of the design office at Wiener-Neustadt in 1919, although he was only 24 years old and a great number of older engineers thought they had prior rights to the job. But Porsche was not very interested in 'rights', only ability counted with him and Rabe became his closest collaborator. When Porsche left Austro-Daimler to go to Daimler in Stuttgart-Unterturkheim in 1923, Rabe remained at Austro-Daimler for the time being and continued Ferdinand Porsche's constructive ideas in the automobile section.

When Porsche started his own design office at the end of 1930 at Stuttgart he asked Karl Rabe to join him as chief designer and he stayed on as chief engineer until the beginning of September 1966; he is a modest man, never seeking publicity. In an interview in 1950 he said: 'I cannot give any information about the early designs at Austro-Daimler. I am afraid they were before my time, because I only worked with Porsche since 1913....'

5 Nationality–Postwar designing–Sascha

THE end of the First World War brought about an unusual number of technical and social problems at Austro-Daimler. In 1918, 6,000 people were employed there and suddenly all armament contracts stopped. They had to change over again to passenger-car production and the market had to be conquered anew. The main task was export, for Austria had become a small country. The first car produced in 1921 was a 6-cylinder with a 4.4-litre engine developing 60hp. Once again it could not deny its sporting ancestry. It had an overhead camshaft engine, beautifully smooth in appearance and most attractive to look at. (Old Ferdinand Porsche always talked about a 'beautiful' engine when he meant a good one and he said often that the constructive solution of a technical problem also had to convince him from the aesthetic point of view.)

This 4.4-litre car was a good export seller, but in Austria it did not have a good market, nor in Germany; in those post-war years small and economic vehicles were more in demand, especially as in both countries economic reasons necessitated the use of smallish engines. The car had become an object of luxury.

At that time Porsche was a Czechoslovak citizen, for he came from a district which after the peace treaties of Versailles and St. Germain had become part of Czechoslavakia and in his words: 'Maffersdorf is my home, I do not change my nationality like my shirt.' Had he not opted for Czechoslovak nationality he would have had his home in Maffersdorf confiscated, nor could he have travelled to Paris after the First World War and Paris, or to be more specific, the Paris Motor Show, had always been an important place for him.

When young Ferry was 10 years old his father built him a car—no, not a kiddie-car, but a real two-seater with an engine from a rail-trolley. This had a maximum speed of some 30mph and little Ferry was allowed to drive this in the work's grounds. The police closed both eyes to the fact that he even turned up with the little car in the streets of Wiener-Neustadt. Indeed, he even participated in a gymkhana of the Automobile Club—even at the age of 11 he was quite a reasonable little driver.

Ferdinand Porsche also had his hobbies and that made him very human. He had had built at Austro-Daimler a special cross-country 'hunting car' which had two seats and a central one behind, on either side of which were capacious containers. When guests were being driven in it they sat on top of these containers, which held guns and food, the lot packed in large rucksacks. They used to go to Hochwolkersdorf in the Rosalie Mountains in lower Austria where Porsche had his hunting lodge, called after his wife, Louise.

Or they might go to the Worthersee in Carinthia, the traditional summer holiday place for the Porsche family, on the southern bank of which they stayed at a villa. Porsche had a big motor boat there, naturally powered by an Austro-Daimler engine, which he called the *Argonaut*. It was fitted with every conceivable comfort; galley, sleeping cabins and a sun deck. He loved sailing on the Worthersee. In those years he did a lot of the test driving himself, the roads over the alpine passes around the Worthersee being ideal as a testing ground.

He seldom went to a theatre but loved the cinema and often saw the same film two or three times; he also liked variety shows and the occasional operetta. Opera and drama, however, left him cold and—let us be frank about it—he seldom read books of a controversial nature: these could not relax him. The so-called intellectual world did not interest him. Without doubt he had a one-track mind. Yet in the same breath one must say that he was splendid in this single-mindedness because he saw the entire technical world as a whole. He never did content himself with one specialized field such as motor engineering or engine design. In engineering he was universally talented and aircraft and locomotives occupied his mind just as much as cars. This was the reason why later he designed turbines, tractors and wind machines.

His first small car was designed in 1921. At Austro-Daimler his ideas on that subject were viewed with scepticism, although Citroen in France, Austin in England and Tatra in Czechoslovakia were endeavouring to open Europe to the field of small cars. As a matter of fact Wanderer, with the 5/15 PS car had done some pioneering work before the First World War and so had Henry Ford with his Model T, the latter being a sort of small car in American eyes. Yet Austro-Daimler wanted to keep to the large and representative car, and they reached a compromise with Porsche which enabled him to build an 1,100cc car in small series in the guise of a sports and racing car.

It appeared in the spring of 1922 and Porsche called it the Sascha, which was the Christian name of Count Kolowrat, with whom he was friendly in Vienna. This gentleman was a film producer in what was at that time a new industry. He was rather tubby and very keen on Porsche's concept of a small car. Indeed, he it was whose impetus had brought about the idea of the small sports car.

The Sascha had a 4-cylinder in-line engine with overhead camshaft, the latter being gear driven. Engine power was probably between 40 and 50bhp and the fastest speed it reached in 1922 was just over 89mph over a flying kilometre in Holland. This, incidentally, is quite a respectable time even in this day. The sports car differed from the racing version only in having mudguards and headlamps. Thus the sports car could be transformed into a racing one in a very short time and with very little effort—which was quite customary in those days. Racing cars all had two seats then, the 'monoposto' only appearing after 1930. Three works Saschas were sent to compete in the Targa Florio of 1922 which then was being contested for the twelfth time on the so-called long Madonie circuit, no less than 66.5 miles long. (Until the last classic race was held in 1973, a Targa Florio lap was *only* about 47 miles long). The race was entirely on gravel roads with many potholes, and inclines of up to 1 in 8 had to be negotiated. Total race distance consisted of four laps, i.e. about 268 miles. There was a separate 1,100cc class, in which the two works cars were driven by Fritz Kuhn and Lambert Poecher. The third car had a slightly bored-out engine and this competed in the big racing car class, driven by a certain Alfred Neubauer, a former officer of the Imperial Army, and employed as a test driver by Austro-Daimler. Porsche esteemed him highly due to his exceptional talent for organization: this was the man who went together with Porsche to Daimler in Unterturkheim where, at a later date, Neubauer became racing manager.

Kuhn and Poecher won their class against powerful international competition, especially from France and Italy, achieving an average of about 33.5mph. From that day on the quite unknown Sascha became a famous vehicle. Neubauer put up quite a showing in the large racing car class, achieving an average of 34.7mph and managing to get into seventh place. The overall winner, the Italian Count Masetti on a Mercedes, averaged 39mph.

The press of all Europe commented on this success of Austro-Daimler. London's *Autocar* said that these interesting little cars from Austria were a positive attraction at the race, and Porsche as their designer was particularly mentioned. A Viennese motoring paper thought that this was obviously the basis for the car of the 'little man' in years to come, which was now undergoing its tests in motoring sport. The Italian paper *Gazetta dello Sport* stated on 3rd April 1922: 'Apart from the technical progress in general, we must also note the triumph of the smallest engines. Up to the evening before the race we did not rate the four Austro-Daimlers which Kolowrat believed in so implicitly, yet four laps of the Madonie circuit were enough to change the mind of even the most sceptical of us.... Until now one would have thought it virtually impossible to obtain such performance, speed and sturdiness from a 4-cylinder engine of such small cubic capacity.... To achieve this, every means had to be used to reduce weight, both by choosing higher quality materials and by the new design of a high-revving engine with its light but strong pistons and connecting rods. Furthermore, it was necessary to use fully the swept volume of the engine and to enlarge valves to the maximum, to arrange rational carburation, and ignition so as to achieve a final output of up to 50bhp from such a tiny car. This chassis is no less impressive.... Without fear or favour we declare that these Austro-Daimlers were the revelation of the Targa Florio.... They proved the quality of engines of maximum power output yet small swept volume and they were mounted in a chassis of most modern construction....'

Not only was the Sascha used for racing in 1922 but Ferdinand Porsche also developed for Austro-Daimler two larger racing cars of which one, with the 2-litre engine, was used by the works that autumn. His dream was to make the Austrian factory world-famous through motor racing.

The rest of the board of directors did not share Porsche's views. The development of racing cars was extremely expensive and at that time the production car business did not flourish to the degree that extensive finance could be diverted to the sport. But managing director Porsche argued like this: through sporting successes we shall popularize our *marque* and thus we shall sell considerable numbers of vehicles. The board of directors on the other hand considered that motor sport was a hobby and a very expensive one at that. The sums expended bore no relation to the propaganda value and sales results. As far as technical advancement through racing car construction was concerned this was not believed in by the board. This sort of conflict had often occurred before in other car firms and split them into two camps: the soberly calculating commercial people on one side, the technicians and sports fans on the other. The enthusiasm for future development tended not to admit the commercial calculations of the day.

Ferdinand Porsche pointed out the final balance of the year 1920: in 15 countries Austro-Daimlers had started in 51 events; they had won 43 times and been second 8 times. Did this not prove the quality of the design?

Then came that black day at Monza in the autumn of 1922 during the Italian Grand Prix, the last race of the year. Kuhn, the number one driver of the Austrian works was about to take a fast right-hander with the 2-litre car. Suddenly, and without skidding previously, the car slid out, touched the kerb, turned two somersaults and finished up with its wheels in the air. Kuhn was thrown out and killed at once.

The incident was investigated most thoroughly, and the cause found to be a fault in the material; one of the spoked wheels had fractured. And now the board of directors in Vienna really tore Porsche to pieces. Had it truly been the fault of the material or had the

27

design been wrong? Was it not clear from this accident how senseless the whole of motor racing was, a sport which not only consumed money but also men? The 51 successes of the season were forgotten, only the Monza accident was in their minds.

When the budgets of each department for the following year were established more and more voices were raised in complaint: Porsche spends too much money in research and development. They said he experimented too much, and even circulated a little anecdote about it. A man bought a new Austro-Daimler in the spring: in September he asked the service department for a spare. He was sent to the chief of the department who called all his mechanics together saying: 'Look at him, he has turned up with one of the old models. We have brought out four new models in the meantime.' So the customer is told 'for a long time we have been out of spares for your car.'

In stories of this nature there is always a grain of truth. Somehow Ferdinand Porsche was restless and unquiet. He was never entirely satisfied with his designs and kept on seeing possibilities for improvements, so that there really were many changes in the series-produced cars.

Porsche's impulsive temperament was well known and when the arguments got to a critical point and the board wanted to tie him down not only financially but also from the design point of view, he up and left the conference in a fury. A few months later he accepted an offer from Unterturkheim and became technical director at Daimler and a member of the board. Naturally, his decision was also influenced by the fact that the German works were enthusiastic about motoring sport.

Austro-Daimler lived for several years on the ideas and projects which Porsche had left behind, especially because Karl Rabe continued his work. The ADM, a sporting 2.6-litre with overhead camshaft, two carburettors, four-wheel brakes and centralized one-shot lubrication was continued for another four years. It was a most durable car with which one could participate in touring trials with considerable chance of success. (In 1924 and 1925 more than 70 successes were booked to the credit of the ADM). A motor sporting development of this rigid-rear-axle car which Porsche had designed, was the ADM-R. With this vehicle which Karl Rabe had in the meantime further lightened and improved, Hans Stuck began his hill-climb career, in 1927. For four years Stuck succeeded with this Austro-Daimler in all the European hill climbs, even against such internationally famous racing cars as Bugatti, Alfa Romeo and Maserati. Stuck, soon called the 'king of the mountains,' won 46 times for Austro-Daimler and achieved the fastest time of day on 40 occasions. Twice he was Austrian and once Swiss hill-climb champion. When they ran the European hill-climb championship for the first time in 1930 obviously Hans Stuck entered the racing car class and won, still at the wheel of the ADM-R with which he had developed a much admired cornering technique on the dusty roads of the mountain passes. This technique was particularly suitable for the rigid-axle car. Second man in this championship of 1930, again in the racing car class, was Laszlo Hartmann of Hungary in a 2.3-litre supercharged Bugatti, whereas the sports car class winner was Rudolf Caracciola with his Mercedes SSK in front of Burggaller in a Bugatti. Porsche had already been working a long time at Unterturkheim and was responsible for the development of the SSK; therefore one can say that both classes of the European championship had been won by Porsche designs.

The ADM was followed by the ADR, the birth of which had been helped along by Rabe, and the sporting version of which was called the 'Bergmeister' (master of the mountains). It had independent suspension by swing axles and a central tube chassis.

6 Porsche goes to Daimler–Stuttgart

THE small car of which Austro-Daimler had built a sporting version in the shape of the Sascha did not see the light of day in touring form although the designs were in existence. In the spring of 1923 Porsche joined the Daimler Motoren AG in Stuttgart-Unterturkheim, a company which became Daimler-Benz three years later. When Porsche got there, lorries used to transport the workers' wages from the bank because the enormous bundles of paper money could simply not be transported any other way, for this was the time of inflation in Germany. Despite this, Daimler in Unterturkheim were one of the few works whose economic situation, a little occasional local labour trouble notwithstanding, remained quite reasonable. War production, which included aero-engines had been cleverly transformed into peacetime work, yet research and development in the passenger car field had not lain dormant.

Motor sport was fostered immediately after the war and this became obvious by Count Masetti's win in the Targa Florio of 1922 in a Mercedes. Then it became known that an entirely new 4-cylinder 2-litre car was being developed which for the first time was to be equipped with a supercharger. Christian Lautenschlager had won the most important motor race of the day, the Grand Prix of France, in the years 1908 and 1914 and the works were not going to rest on their laurels. The new 2-litre design was being prepared for the famous American Indianapolis event, a race which was already quite well known.

When Porsche came to Unterturkheim these machines were ready crated for shipment to the States, but there the Daimler people met with no success. Indeed one can talk of a complete failure of the new supercharged car at Indianapolis, and it is said that Lautenschlager's furious comment was this: 'The 50,000 dollars which we could have won have got stuck in the car's exhaust system and inlet tracts.' In fact the inlet valves, the exhaust system and the new supercharger were not tuned to one another and, although the cars were being worked on constantly by the mechanics, they never did perform properly nor were they reliable. They probably had tried to race this design before it was fully ready.

Ferdinand Porsche was given the task of developing it fully and he spent nine months on the 2-litre supercharged car. He established himself in Stuttgart and engaged Professor Bonatz, an architect who had designed the Stuttgart main railway station, to build a large villa for him at the Feuerbacher Heide above Stuttgart and today this is still the private refuge of the Porsche family.

Porsche goes to Daimler — Stuttgart

As a matter of fact things were not too easy for him at Daimlers. His style was considered unusual and novel, especially in comparison with Paul Daimler—the latter had preceded him at Daimler just as he had at the turn of the century at Austro-Daimler—who was more orthodox in his outlook and had directed design from the top, and seldom set foot into the test department or design office.

Paul Daimler's way of working was to stand at a desk and listen to the problem put forward by the heads of the departments. Incidentally, Paul Daimler had left Unterturkheim to go to Horch.

Porsche's style was unusual in that he suddenly appeared in the experimental department just after a car in trouble had been taken there. Whilst the engineers in their white coats still stood around and discussed matters, Porsche would be given an oily works overall and would crawl under the car so as personally to discover the trouble. One day an engineer made the mistake of asking: 'Can you see anything, sir?' Porsche raked the assembled technicians with an annihilating look and yelled at them: 'Why don't you have a look yourself, you....' An insult which the engineers probably had not even heard in their own homes! Porsche banged the door shut and did not speak to his collaborators for days. There were opposing opinions about him in the various departments: 'This rude character, what does he want from us,' said some. Others, on the other hand, respected him unconditionally for his exceptional ability, quick action and sagacity. Porsche, however, really conquered Stuttgart in Sicily, but let us be more precise—by victory in the Targa Florio in the spring of 1924, the car being driven by Christian Werner. After the 2-litre supercharged car had been reasonably developed in the winter of 1923-24 (Ferdinand Porsche often drove the car himself on the test track even though he was now 48; he could still cope with the power output of the cars he designed), Daimler nominated three cars as a works entry for the 1924 Targa Florio, to be run on 27th April on the same circuit where the Sascha had been successful in 1922. Again four laps had to be covered measuring a total of 432km.

7 Targa Florio

THE first Targa had been run in 1906, and Count Vincenzo Florio, after whom this competition is named, has often been spoken of as the greatest motor racing benefactor and the father of the European sports car events. This first race of 1906 was organized by Florio when he was 23, and the roads of the Madonie circuit practically all belonged to his private estate. The Florios were a very wealthy family. Apart from their estates they had interests in shipping, railways and export. Vincenzo Florio's father was already dead, but his elder brother, really just as much an automobile fanatic, tended to dampen Vincenzo's enthusiasm to keep the prestige of the family on an even keel. At the age of 19, in 1902, Vincenzo had bought a racing car from Panhard-Levassor in Paris with which he won an Italian race at Padua. Even in 1909 he raced a Fiat in his own event and was second in the general classification! Famous names and *marques* were turning up for the Targa. To name just one, Vincenzo Lancia, who later founded the Lancia Works, came in second in 1907 and 1908 at the wheel of a Fiat.

The first Mercedes at the Targa Florio appeared in 1911. But the winning cars were Fiat, Isotto-Frachini, Lancia, Spa, Berliet and Peugeot. In 1920 one of the winners was an Alfa Romeo driven by a certain Enzo Ferrari, the very man who later founded the Scuderia Ferrari and then the famous car business of that name.

Unterturkheim had sent a works entry in 1921, driven by Max Sailer. This was the 1914 Mercedes Grand Prix car which had been improved in detail and equipped with a 4.5-litre engine. It got into second place close to Count Masetti's race-winning Fiat. At that time Masetti was Italy's best known and fastest private entrant, who was always being lent works cars and who also won the Targa in 1922 with a Mercedes painted in Italian racing red. In 1924 he drove an Alfa Romeo and was considered a potential winner apart from being the most powerful opponent for Mercedes. Unfortunately he met with a fatal accident in 1926 when driving a Delage.

Another competitor feared by Mercedes was Antonio Ascari, Alberto's father, who at that time was at the peak of his career. In 1923 he was second in an Alfa Romeo, and this time he wanted to win beyond everything. As a matter of fact in those days the Targa Florio was only eligible to racing cars and the sports-car class, as we know it today, did not exist.

Ferdinand Porsche was in complete agreement with the other directors of the Daimler board: if one enters a great and famous race, the preparations must be thorough. It would not be enough to send a single car to Sicily. A whole team must be sent and enough mechanics must go along with it. There was never any doubt that Ferdinand Porsche himself would travel to the Targa and there as team-chief supervise all preparation as well as decide racing tactics. The Mercedes team consisted of Christian Werner, the veteran Christian Lautenschlager who had just celebrated his forty-seventh birthday, and Alfred Neubauer, in those days an active driver.

In 1922 the Works team in Sicily consisted of Lautenschlager, Sailer, Salzer and Werner. They were to drive the heavy unsupercharged cars still based on the pre-war design. None of them had been able to get near the Italian competitors and most of the Mercedes had broken down due to mechanical troubles. Only Count Masetti who had privately entered a new and lighter Mercedes was successful. Yet the German drivers had at least got to know the circuit and the conditions in Sicily.

Christian Werner who was born in Stuttgart in 1892 was at that time considered the fastest man in the Mercedes team, but also the most taciturn. He had started at Daimler in 1911 as a mechanic and the works entered him for the first time on an international basis in 1922; he returned from the Rumanian trials as the overall victor. In 1923 he was part of the team that was sent with the 2-litre 4-cylinder cars to Indianapolis.

In the Targa Florio of April 1924 the cars took the start from 7 o'clock onwards at two-minute intervals. Starting times had been drawn for by lots and Ascari was lucky because he started two minutes after Werner. Therefore he knew that if he saw the Mercedes in front of him he had made up time against his opponent. When cars start one by one the further towards the end one starts the better it is for signalling on such very long circuits.

In the Mercedes pits they were expectantly checking the stop watches. On the first lap Count Masetti in the Alfa Romeo was fastest once again, but Christian Werner was close up — albeit with Ascari following within seconds. During the second lap Werner had got into the swing of things and put up a new lap record for the 57 mile circuit, thus leading the field. The Alfa Romeo pit was soon aware of this and signalled to Ascari to speed up. Masetti had slowed up a little in the meantime.

Ascari now really tried all he knew and on the third lap caught up a good few seconds but the last lap would obviously be the decisive one. The Italians now were confident, Ascari seemed to catch up more and more, soon he would have Werner in his sights and then overtake him, but Christian Werner, this rather thin and silent man, was not to be caught out so easily — he knew well enough what he could expect from his engine and above everything he knew he had to finish. Lautenschlager and Neubauer were already lying far back in the middle of the field.

On this last lap, almost within sight of the finish Ascari's engine seized up, presumably due to insufficient oil reaching one of the bearings. In despair the Italian driver and his mechanics tried everything to get it going again, even the spectators helped. Finally they tried to push the car as far as the finish, but in the meantime Christian Werner in the supercharged Mercedes and driving with the accuracy of clockwork had passed the finishing banner. When Ascari failed to appear the Italian public was speechless with disappointment, whereas in the Mercedes pits jubilation knew no bounds. At the side of Ferdinand Porsche, Christian Werner walked to the prize giving.

He had covered the 432km in a time of 6 hours 32.4 minutes, an average of 66.081kph (about 41.02mph) and this constituted a new record for the Targa Florio; Masetti was second in the Alfa in 6 hours 41 minutes 4.2 seconds, and third was another Italian, Bordino, in a Fiat in 6 hours 46 minutes 34 seconds. Lautenschlager was tenth and Neubauer fifteenth, proof of the toughness of the competition. As there was a separate 2-litre racing car class and as the Alfas and Fiats were over 2 litres in capacity, the Mercedes team finished one, two, three in that class.

Christian Werner won the Freiburg speed hill-climb for the three subsequent years with the 2-litre racing car and in 1925 and 1926 he even made the fastest time of day. (The times were not very rapid according to present notions: in 1926 he covered the course in 10 minutes 24.2 seconds, whereas even in 1960 we were managing less than 8 minutes with unsupercharged 1,500cc sports cars such as Porsche and Borgward.)

In 1927 Werner also won his class with a 2-litre car in the Eifel races on the Nurburgring, but in the sports car class one man was faster — Rudolf Caracciola driving the big 7.1 litre Mercedes SS, which had also come into being under the technical leadership of Ferdinand Porsche. Werner's average was 93.8kph as opposed to Caracciola's 96.5kph. During the Grand Prix of Germany a month later Werner was just beaten by his team mate Otto Merz in the big Mercedes at an average of 101kph and a year later, taking turns with Caracciola he shared the wheel of the winning car in the Grand Prix of Germany. In that event — they had to take turns because of the tremendous heat making it impossible to drive single-handed for five hours — they averaged 103.8kph and even the more agile and lighter 2.3 litre supercharged Bugattis driven by Count Brilli-Peri and Louis Chiron could not keep up.

Unfortunately Christian Werner died in the summer of 1932 at the age of only 40 after a long illness.

It took exactly 35 years for another German driver at the wheel of a German car to win the Targa Florio outright, although in 1955 Mercedes appeared once again in the list of winners, but then the 300 SLR was driven by Stirling Moss and Peter Collins. In 1956 surprisingly it was a 1,500cc Porsche Spyder RS upon which the winner's laurels were laid, this time driven by an Italian, Umberto Maglioli. In 1959 the two Germans, Edgar Barth and Wolfgang Seidel followed the tradition of Christian Werner in 1924 and won with a Porsche Spyder RSK.

In those years after the First World War not only the German industry but also the public were very enthusiastic about motor sport. Seldom had the town of Stuttgart given such a warm-hearted welcome to one of its citizens as the triumphal reception which awaited Christian Werner on his return from Sicily. An endless press of people covered the square in front of the town hall and the mayor made a special speech celebrating the Targa Florio victory. As responsible designer for the winning car, Porsche had to sign his name in the golden book of the town of Stuttgart.

Porsche was now very much at home at Daimler's and in the capital of Swabia; he was made an honorary doctor of the technical college of Stuttgart.

The reason for this honorary doctorate is noteworthy for it shows that even in academic circles motor sport was highly thought of in those days. The scroll stated: 'In recognition of his outstanding merit in the field of motor car construction and particularly as designer of the winning car in the Targa Florio 1924.'

8 At Daimler-Benz

FERDINAND PORSCHE worked for 5½ years as technical director at Daimler's — called Daimler-Benz after the two firms merged — and during that time a new series of touring and sports cars came into being.

To start with Porsche developed from the 2-litre 4-cylinder Targa Florio car a new 2-litre racing car with an 8-cylinder in-line engine; this had a supercharger in constant engagement fitted between the carburettor and engine. The first supercharged Mercedes types still had the supercharger feeding the carburettor.

With this 2-litre 8-cylinder Rudolf Caracciola won the first Grand Prix of Germany on 11th July 1926 at the Avus circuit in Berlin. The race distance was 392km (about 243 miles) and it was run in three classes: racing cars up to 1,500, 2,000 and 3,000cc. Caracciola came first after a very sensible and tactically correct drive and also made the fastest time of day at an average of 135.036kph (about 83.8mph); second fastest was Christian Riecken in a 3-litre NAG followed by an Alfa Romeo. This was Caracciola's first major victory and his name was tied to Mercedes racing history for a great many years to come. As from 1927 the 2-litre supercharged car was no longer used for major races as they considered that the big machines of 6.8 and 7.1 litres would be likely to have greater success. These bore the type indication of Mercedes S, SS, SSK and later SSKL and although they were to be found on all the racing circuits, they had originally not been developed as racing or sports cars but only as fast touring vehicles; in consequence, they were built to a great safety margin and even the two-seater SSK with its short chassis weighed just under 2 tons and considerable physical strength was needed to drive them.

The new range of 'blown' cars began with the 24/100/140hp, a tourer which was also available as a big six-seater limousine; at the same time a smaller capacity model the 15/70/100hp had been developed. These horse-power denominations were familiar to the public in those days; the first figure was the fiscal or tax horse-power, where 4hp equalled about a 1,000cc; in other words the 24/100/140 had a 6-litre engine. The second figure gave the horse-power without supercharger, whereas the third conveyed the power with the blower working. From the 24/100/140 the Mercedes K type arose. K did not mean 'Kompressor', but short chassis and the K was generally delivered as a four-seater open touring car; in this form it took part in a great many competitions. The K type was said to develop 145hp. The next step in this series was the Mercedes S, which had a cubic capacity of 6.8 litres and produced 160hp. S referred to sport and accordingly the body work was sporting in appearance, the standard model being an open four-seater with sweeping front mudguards. At the beginning of 1927 the S type was used by the works team consisting then of Rudolf Caracciola, Otto Merz, Willi Walb and Christian Werner.

From the S was developed the SS (super sport) for competition and barely a year later came the SSK (super sport, short chassis) which achieved legendary fame with its 7.1 litre engine, the power output of which rose from 185 to 235hp. The SSK Mercedes-Benz developed during Porsche's era remained from 1928 to 1931 the epitome of the internationally successful German sports and racing car; its main adversary was first of all the 2.3 litre supercharged Bugatti, a very much lighter and more manageable car but which had neither the same power nor the necessary reliability. The supercharged Alfa Romeo of 2.3 and 2.6 litres, the P2 and P3 types, appeared later. The 'blown' Mercedes was also very quickly modified from a sports car into a racing one by removing the headlamps and mudguards, the car being a two-seater in both instances. Otto Merz won with it on the Nurburgring in 1927 at an average of 63mph, then in 1928 as mentioned already it was Caracciola's and Werner's turn at 65mph and in 1938 Caracciola won at 66.5mph. The 1929 Grand Prix of Germany fell to Louis Chiron in a Bugatti and the quickest Mercedes driver in third position was August Momberger. In 1930 the Grand Prix did not take place. Caracciola's average in 1931 on the Avus was 111.5mph and he was followed in by Hans Joachim von Morgen in a Bugatti; this time the Mercedes bore the SSKL type indication which meant that it was a lighter edition.

Surprisingly, the big supercharged cars were also successful in the Freiburg hill-climb on the Schauinsland track, although in hill-climbs one would have thought the lighter Bugattis had more chance. In 1927 Caracciola won in the big sports car class there with a time of 10 minutes 23 seconds, although Rosenberger was 13 seconds faster in the racing class — we shall have occasion to refer to this gentleman at a later stage. In 1928 Caracciola and Chiron tied in the racing car class but in 1929 no Mercedes was placed fastest in the sports or racing car class. However, Caracciola came back in the sports car class the following year at 9 minutes 38.1 seconds, and in 1931 he beat von Morgen's Bugatti by two-tenths of a second.

Caracciola's most important victories with the SSK were beyond doubt his successes in the Tourist Trophy in Ireland in 1929 and the Mille Miglia of 1931 where he averaged 101.14kph and beat Campari in the Alfa by a good margin.

Hans Stuck also changed from the Austro-Daimler ADM-R to the Mercedes SSK; in 1931 the Stuttgart works signed him up and he won a whole series of hill-climbs in Europe and in 1932 also in Brazil.

The third driver who must be mentioned in this connection was Manfred von Brauchitsch, who bought an SSK in 1929 and won his class at his first appearance on the Gaisberg hill-climb near Salzburg. In 1931 he was third at the Eifel races and also at the Avus, still at the wheel of his privately owned SSK. It should be noted here that the SSK in racing and sports trim were normally available for purchase.

In 1931 they saw at Daimler-Benz that the SSK 'monsters' were no longer able to compete with the ever more powerful, smaller foreign racing machines and the works decided to cease competing officially and to wait for the new racing car formula which was due to come into operation in 1934; from 1931 to 1933 there had been no racing formula.

This was the reason why Daimler-Benz agreed that Caracciola should drive for Alfa Romeo in 1932 and 1933. Thus 'Caratsch', as they called him, appeared with a white-painted Alfa racing car at all important European events and also on the Avus in 1932. Also among the starters was Manfred von Brauchitsch with a Mercedes SSKL for which the aerodynamicist von Konig-Fachsenfeld had developed an exceedingly massive-looking streamlined body to suit the massive proportions of the SSKL, but which endowed the vehicle with a higher top speed than the Alfa Romeo. Although Caracciola could leave his braking later and corner more quickly on the two loops of the Avus, because of the Alfa's lightness and manageability, Brauchitsch made up the decisive seconds on the straights and won sensationally by 2½ seconds from Caracciola at an average speed of just over 120 miles an hour.

This was the last great international victory of the car, which under Porsche had been developed as a fast tourer.

The 'normal' series at Daimler-Benz which came into being during the 5½ years of the Porsche era consisted of the 8/38hp (side valve, 4-cylinder), and developed from it and called the 'Stuttgart' the 10/50hp, then came the 12/50hp which matured into the 14/70hp type 'Mannheim', with its offshoot the two-seater 'Mannheim-Sport', and finally the 18/80hp type 'Nurburg' which ultimately became the 20/100hp.

Porsche wanted originally to build the 8/38 with an overhead-valve engine but after the Daimler and Benz merger he was no longer able to decide which direction design was going to take, thus the 'normal' series was designed wholly with side-valve engines. Porsche realized his plans for an ohv 2-litre only after he changed over in 1929 to the Austrian Steyr works.

He had also designed a small car with a 1,000cc engine at Daimler-Benz and endeavoured to persuade the other directors and the board of the usefulness of such a project, but they were not very keen on such ideas because of a certain Mercedes-Benz style which somehow did not match up with any small car ideas. In any case Porsche had a very difficult task after the merger, because his ideas and plans were often criticized. Yet they did build thirty test samples of the 1,000cc car in the spring of 1928 and a few of these apparently were even sold later, but not one has survived. This small car was in no way similar to the Volkswagen, but was rather a miniature of the 8/38.

Within the framework of his constructive creation at Daimler-Benz he also busied himself with diesel engines for lorries. These diesel lorries were the first that could be usefully employed. Projects for a large aero engine in inverted V12 form were also on the drawing board and Porsche even studied the question of an air-cooled 2-cylinder motor cycle for which he designed the rear springing. Sometimes he ploughed his own furrow away from the beaten track of the normal production programme and his colleagues did not care for that. Just before leaving Daimler-Benz he sketched out a 3-litre 8-cylinder supercharged engine for a future racing car, with twin overhead camshafts. He had drawn the whole of the car, the gearbox of which was to be in unit with the differential, and swing axles were to be fitted at the back; this, when all racing cars had rigid axles, was a revolutionary idea.

9   Steyr–Founding of Design Office–Rosenberger

THE inner tensions in the Stuttgart works led to the suggestion that Porsche should undertake a longish study trip to the United States and after his return they wanted to keep him as an advisory designer to collaborate in all difficult problems; thus he could remain in Stuttgart and live in his villa.

But Dr. Porsche was never able to compromise and while looking round for a new position, the Steyr works of Austria suggested that he join them as chief engineer and member of the board. He started his new activity on 1st January 1929 and let the villa in Stuttgart to his successor at Daimler-Benz, Dr. Niebel. Porsche's return to Austria caused much enthusiasm. The Austrian motoring paper said: 'To know that an engineering genius like Dr. Porsche is back in Austria fills the Austrian motoring public with pride and it was a great deed of the Steyr works to ensure his collaboration. The composition Steyr-Porsche not only sounds well but should make fine music,' the paper stated somewhat emotionally. 'One of the greatest motor works in the world, and the greatest in Austria, has managed to capture the greatest car designer in the world.' At that time Steyr was in fact Austria's biggest automobile works. It had developed after the First World War into the largest competitor of Austro-Daimler. Steyr emerged from an armament works, J. and F. Werndl and Co. During the First World War they had an output of 3 million rifles and Steyr were considered to be one of the biggest gunsmiths in the world. When they discussed the question of starting production of aero engines with the government in 1916, the management conceived the idea that they might possibly also make motor cars.

In 1920 the first Steyr car was offered for sale, a robust, medium-powered 6-cylinder. In 1926 they made a smallish 6-cylinder which found great favour with the buying public, the Type XII of 1,560cc and 30bhp. Soon there came a bigger version, the Type XX of about 2,000cc capacity.

At Steyr they had the advantage that everything could be made under their own roof: there was a forge, rolling mill, and a foundry with large capacity output, a ball-bearing works belonging to them, a body shop in Vienna and the Steyr steel works in Judenburg were also part of the organization.

The types XII and XX, plus a larger car the series of which was running out (XVI) were in existence when Porsche took over as chief technician. He developed two new models based on the previous ones: firstly the Type XXX which had swing axles at the

37

rear (although Steyr had already tried this sytem before Porsche's time) and a capacity of 2,000cc. This was in fact the engine which Porsche could not get accepted at Daimler-Benz and the XXX remained for years the standard model of the Austrian company; it appeared in the first half of 1929.

Apart from this, he designed a large 5.3 litre 8-cylinder with overhead valves developing 100hp. This Steyr, called the type *Austria*, also had swing axles at the back and boasted over-drive, a thermostat and two plugs per cylinder. The *Austria* was just about ready for the Paris Salon in October and Dr. Porsche himself drove the elegant five-seater wire-wheeled cabriolet to Paris. The press referred to it glowingly at the show: 'the Austrian automobile industry has successfully and indisputably provided the show with one of the most modern models; the new creation of Dr. Ferdinand Porsche is much discussed and the stand is always crowded.'

The Paris Salon, the oldest motor show in the world, held for the first time in 1898, had always been a sort of magnet for Ferdinand Porsche and year after year he travelled to Paris, talked to the designers of other countries and often inspected the exhibited vehicles very closely.

The new Steyr models which he had brought into being in 1929 obviously seemed to attract the public and Porsche was content and in good spirits — until he returned to his hotel, picked up an evening paper and read something that really took him aback. In Vienna, so it said, a well known large bank had closed its doors, the 'Boden-Kredit-Anstalt' — of all things the bank with which Steyr worked closely, whereas their competitors, Austro-Daimler, worked with the other big bank in Vienna, the 'Creditanstalt am Hof'.

What the paper only hinted at he felt strongly straight away; the Austro-Daimler bank would obviously 'gobble' up the Steyr bank and in this way Steyr would undoubtedly get into the hands of Austro-Daimler, the very financial people with whom he had had such harsh arguments seven years before and who were his reason for leaving Austro-Daimler. He was filled with dark forebodings.

After the merger between the two companies his independence was considerably curtailed and the *Austria* even taken from the production programme; in the newly formed large company it was Austro-Daimler's job to produce large cars. The few *Austria* models that had been sold became very rare — like Mauritius stamps. In the late autumn of 1929 Porsche decided not to continue within the framework of the new company. He disliked intensely having his authority limited and soon developed a plan not to be employed by any car works at all but to found a design office of his own. He was quite sure that he could find a sufficient number of qualified engineers, but first of all he discussed this with his old collaborator, Karl Rabe, who agreed without hesitation to join the new design office as chief engineer. The only question that had to be resolved was where should this new office be?

Porsche decided during the initial discussions to establish the office in Stuttgart. The reasons were obvious: in Austria, as compared to Germany, there were only a few possible firms likely to place contracts and with such firms it was clearly necessary to keep in close contact. Stuttgart also seemed ideal because the most important German accessory works such as Bosch, Mahle and Hirth were situated there. When undertaking research and development work it was much simpler to have a personal conference with the specialists of the accessory industry rather than correspond with them lengthily. Another important reason was his villa which, although let, stood in Stuttgart.

Dr. Porsche was not a very commercially minded man and he knew that himself. It was therefore important to engage a sound commercial manager and he found him in the person of Adolf Rosenberger from Pforzheim, whose commercial ability was allied to his enthusiasm for the sport, witnessed by the fact that he had raced Mercedes cars between the years 1925 and 1928. During the Grand Prix of Germany 1929 he got into second place with his private SSK in the over 3-litre class behind Momberger. When Caracciola won the opening race on the Nurburgring in 1927 at the wheel of the Mercedes Type S Rosenberger again took second place, and in the same year he even managed to beat him at the Freiburg hill-climb and in the Klausenpass-climb he also won his class on one occasion.

Rosenberger did not have an easy time with Dr. Porsche and his devoted staff of engineers who had to be tamed commercially when over-enthusiastic design projects extended too far into the future. There were months when the engineers' salaries had to be paid in instalments, simply because there was not enough money. Rosenberger resigned on 30th January 1933 a few hours before Hitler came into power, which he must have foreseen together with all the consequences likely to arise; he went to America and changed his name.

A suitable office was found in the Kronenstrasse 14 in a building which was subsequently destroyed by bombing in the Second World War. This office, the official name of which was 'Dr. ing. h.c. Ferdinand Porsche GmbH., Konstruktionsburo fur Motoren- und Fahrzeugbau' (design office for engine and motor vehicle construction) was opened on 1st December 1930; it was entered into the company register at the beginning of 1931.

Nine designers formed the first 'team' at the Porsche works. All were Austrians; Rabe as chief engineer had his own room and in a second room were Messrs. Frohlich, Zahradnik, Kales (the latter later held a leading position at the Volkswagen works) and Porsche's son Ferry. Soon after the office had opened, Reimspiess, Mickl and Kommenda also joined. Reimspiess had been with Porsche since 1915 at Austro-Daimler and Mickl the aerodynamicist had been in touch with him since 1916. Kommenda was responsible for bodywork in those days and after the war he designed the external shape of the post-war Porsche 356. The entire team took part in the designs for the Volkswagen. Finally we must also mention Goldinger who was a sort of 'maid of all work' and, if we may say so, personal chauffeur to old Dr. Porsche, who had already engaged him in 1910 as a driver at Austro-Daimler. This closely knit staff of Porsche's collaborators always felt like a sort of family and this family atmosphere still exists today in the Porsche works.

Even before the Stuttgart office was officially opened, Porsche already had a big contract in his hands: the firm of Wanderer in Chemnitz wanted him to design a complete new medium-class car. In the Porsche office, they said amongst themselves: 'Let us number our designs consecutively and then we shall designate the types from these numbers, but let us not start with number one or people who give us jobs will think that we have only just begun!' For this reason the Wanderer car received the Porsche internal design number 7.

The car in question was the 2-litre Wanderer which soon went into series production and became quite popular. Its engine was an in-line 6-cylinder with wet liners in a light alloy block, having at first a cubic capacity of 1,860cc but soon bored out to 2 litres; apart from this they marketed a 1,700cc version. Both were equipped with a rigid front axle, but with a swing axle at the back and a leaf spring above it.

Obviously, not all design numbers became complete vehicles or even important parts. Sometimes, when the development of a certain type was in the offing numbers were left open, but occasionally this further development did not materialize. Yet the biggest part of these 'numbers' did become designs or completed projects.

Together with the contract for the 2-litre cars, Wanderer ordered the development of a bigger and more rapid vehicle. At first they wanted only one prototype, and an in-line 8-cylinder of 3,250cc came into being, the external shape of which was extremely attractive, the rear being designed on aerodynamic principles. (In those days the so-called streamlined cars normally had a straightforward vertical radiator, whereas only the rear came down in an elegant, unbroken line. Since, however, the front part is more important aerodynamically than the rear, which can only be given good airflow with difficulty, the streamlined cars of those days with the exception of the prototypes of Jaray, were not very fast in relation to their power output.)

For this 8-cylinder Porsche had foreseen a Roots-type supercharger which could be cut in and out at will. Yet this beautiful and impressive car remained as the sole prototype, for in the meantime in Saxony there had been negotiations about a merger between Horch, Audi, Wanderer and DKW; this subsequently became the Auto-Union and within the framework of this group it fell to Horch to construct large cars but not to Wanderer. Porsche retained type '8' as his own, and for the next few years it became his private touring car.

10 Zündapp Volksauto-the Russians-State Designer

IT IS with type '12' that we touch on a theme which is of the greatest importance to the history of the house of Porsche — the theme is the Volkswagen. In 1931 the Zundapp Works in Nurnberg decided to compensate for the recession in their motor-cycle business by the construction of a small car. Not having any designers with sufficient experience in the building of cars they approached Ferdinand Porsche. Their ideas struck an answering chord, for Porsche's ideas on a small car at Austro-Daimler had not got past the Sascha scheme, and at Mercedes-Benz not past the small pre-production series of the 1,000cc type, but now he had project sketches on the drawing board which he either wanted to offer or to realize himself.

Counsellor Neumeyer, who owned the Zundapp Works, had ideas as early as 1925 for the construction of a small car to be built alongside the motor-cycle production. At that time he had ordered a small car from England for design study and was in negotiation for new factory buildings near Munich where such a production could be realized. These plans, however, did not see the light of day and only the idea of a small car remained. Neumeyer at that time had thought up the word 'Volksauto' (people's car) to characterize this small vehicle, long before Hitler.

The first designs of the small car contracted by Zundapp were put on paper between the beginning of December 1931 and April 1932; they contained some important elements of the future Volkswagen, engine placed behind the rear axle, gearbox in front of axle, about 25hp from 1,000cc, central tube frame, streamlined two-door body, spare wheel in front. On one point, however, Porsche and Neumeyer kept having arguments. The latter insisted on a water-cooled 5-cylinder radial engine at the rear, whereas Dr. Porsche wanted to fit an air-cooled flat four or perhaps a 3-cylinder, but in any case an air-cooled engine.

Porsche at last agreed and the three prototypes built in the spring of 1932 had the 5-cylinder radial, though not in a vertical position to the longitudinal axis of the car but slightly inclined towards the front, to fit in better with the aerodynamic tail of the car. This arrangement became subject to a patent.

One of these Zundapp prototypes was fitted with a drop-head coupe and during 1932 the three cars were subjected to a great many trial runs which naturally showed up teething troubles — but that is, after all, the purpose of constructing prototypes.

Counsellor Neumeyer hesitated; the investment for building his own engines and bodies seemed too high. At that time he was pleased enough to pay the Porsche office the fees for the development and experimental work, amounting to some 85,000 marks. Then in 1933 the motor-cycle business revived and the suddenly intensified production occupied the works to such an extent that from the room point of view alone it was impossible to fit in the car project.

One of the prototypes of the type '12' was left and surely would have been in the Porsche museum today had it not been destroyed in 1944 during an aerial bombardment of Stuttgart. Soon, however, another people's-car type project came within the orbit of the Porsche office: this time the contract was from the firm of NSU in Neckarsulm, where Fritz von Falkenhayn had become managing director. But let us now interrupt the previous history of the Volkswagen project, for there nearly might not have been a Volkswagen or an Auto-Union racing car or a tractor, or indeed the Porsche 356 type. At the beginning of 1932 there was a strange telephone call to the office. A man with a strong Russian accent, but speaking in German, said that a Russian delegation of three engineers was in Germany and they would very much like to have discussions with the leading designers of the country and possibly place contracts. Would it be possible to have a meeting with Dr. Porsche?

Chief engineer Rabe thought a tractor was in question. Tractors were the slogan in Russia; agriculture needed to be motorized and, Rabe thought, for the Russians it would be enough to dig up a few design studies which had been started as early as the First World War.

The three Russians had obviously come straight from Moscow and the discussion took place in the corner of the Cafe Rosenstockle. It was soon apparent that they were excellent engineers and extremely well-informed about European conditions. As expected, they began by citing Stalin: 'We are at the eve of great changes in our country, the change from an agrarian to an industrial country.' One of the engineers went on to say that Stalin had stated that Russian history consisted of lost battles because they were always behind-hand technically. Now the day and the opportunity had come to catch up on the technical arrears with all the means available. After these introductory propaganda-like sentences, the conversation with the Russians got down to a sensible 'shop' one. All three spoke German and were polite and reserved; the next day they visited the office and studied the latest Porsche designs with great care. They were shown a few tractor designs but did not evince much interest in them.

Were there to be no orders then? Three weeks before Dr. Porsche had borrowed on his life insurance to pay the salaries of his engineers punctually, never mind his own future ... But if they were not interested in tractors, what did the Russians want? Their purpose remained obscure until the end.

Then suddenly they showed their hand and produced an official letter: 'We would like to show you that the period of reconstruction has begun in Russia. Technical progress, the motorizing and electrification of town and country, is being advanced by our new country's impetus. We would like you to judge for yourself the possibilities which exist in a country that has unlimited space and inexhaustible resources of wealth.'

Ferdinand Porsche was invited to Russia and three weeks later he went there by train. Incidentally, on one occasion the Russians had shown a flash of humour; one of them said, 'How nice, Cafe Rosenstockle (rose-bush), at home this would probably have been called the Cafe of the Bloody Sword.'

This was one of the strangest trips ever undertaken by a European of his own free will and quite probably the Russians never again permitted a foreigner to gain such an insight into their technical level, working methods or possibilities. Porsche went to Kiev, Kursk, Nijni-Novgorod and to Odessa. They took him down to the Caucasus and as far as the Krim. He saw motor-car works and foundries, turbines and tanks, tractors and aircraft, works and yet more engineering works.

In the evenings there were dinners and receptions. Vodka flowed in streams but Dr. Porsche would have preferred his Pilsner beer. As he always expressed his opinions quite openly he said that he was not very fond of vodka. The next evening he had Pilsner beer. Had they perhaps fetched it by aircraft? He was positively frightened by the civility with which he was treated and amazed by the things he was shown. The extent of the technical impressions captivated him. Naturally they had made him promise not to divulge what he had seen and it was obvious that he would keep his promise. He was even taken as far as the secret industrial centres behind the Ural.

But what did they want, these Russians? He remembered the big banner he saw in one of the foundries at Kursk. A few weeks previously Stalin had made a big speech about industry and this banner carried some extracts from this speech: 'The Bolsheviks must learn to master engineering, for engineering decides everything during the period of reconstruction. We lag behind by a hundred years, and now must catch up in ten years the advantage which the Western countries have. Either we achieve this or we go under ...'

Yes, in certain spheres engineering was indeed a long way behind Germany. Production methods in many of the plants seemed to be very primitive. Russian work was not on a technical level with European but it was possible to see a beginning, and there was certainly the endeavour. The Russians appeared to be still in the pioneering days of engineering.

But still he had not been told what they wanted. When they took him into the Ural he suddenly saw the light; they did not want his opinions or his patents, they wanted him, his personality and his ability. They wanted to persuade him that in Russia there was a multitude of interesting tasks awaiting him.

On his return to Moscow they submitted a contract. If he would sign it then all of Russia was before him. The motor vehicle industry, tank production, electrical works and the productive power of millions of Russians. From the day of his signature he would become 'State Designer of Russia'. A beautiful title, but there was more to come: he would find at the Bank of Moscow a blank cheque for any research work that he cared to name. Was not Europe, that poor continent, too small for his indefatigable spirit ... did he not always have disagreements with the big companies and their financiers who were not prepared to recognize his development work? Would the economic crisis in Western Europe not limit him?

This was an offer the like of which one gets only once in a lifetime, thought Dr. Porsche.

But there were clauses in the contract which limited his liberty, such as having to undertake not to cross the borders of Soviet Russia unless ordered to do so by the government. He could bring his family along and could have a luxurious villa in the Krim, but he had to remain within this enormous Russian territory. His contacts with Germany would be cut off, and there was something else he reflected on — three ideas were in his mind. They had almost become fixed ideas; his mind was set on them and he considered them as the crowning efforts of his life's work. He wanted to design three things. Firstly, a cheap and useful small car, a sort of people's car. Secondly, a racing and sports car with which he could demonstrate the limits of technical possibitity — he was, after all, exceedingly interested in the limits between Utopia and the real thing and he was aware of these without losing himself in them. Then he wanted one day to design a tractor, something like the Volkswagen but for the benefit of agriculture, something like a people's tractor, in fact.

Would he be able to achieve all this in Russia? Certainly not the people's car because to motorize the masses was still a very remote idea in Russia. The thought that every employee and every foreman should buy a little car, such an idea only fell on fertile ground in Europe and America. Russia needed other things: tanks, power stations, turbines, lorries, aircraft and engines. It did not need racing cars — motor sport was still a sort of foreign word. The Russians were not interested in technical limits but in a systematic building up; they wanted to overcome technical arrears.

That only left the tractors and they were certainly necessary in Russia. They would have to be bigger ones than in Western Europe, for there was more ground to cover. He thought of the seemingly unlimited space through which he had travelled in the express train — this had given him a conception of the enormous distances. All right then, with his tractors they would till the Russian soil. But what was this, this Russian soil? Did he have any relationship to it? Unwittingly he shook his head. The vast spaces of the Russian countryside were strange to him, and somehow sinister. He thought about it further. Odd, he said to himself, these are feelings which do not belong to a technician, for whom only the engine should be of interest.

But Dr. Porsche was a man who throughout the whole of his life was very close to his homeland. His family circle counted above everything; he had to have a quiet corner wherein he could feel safe, otherwise his world-shaking inventions could never have come to reality; he needed this levelling up and for the first time he became conscious that he also needed his home ground, Austria and Germany. The places he knew and where he understood the agricultural needs.

Tractors for the East? Why not, from the technical point of view that could be a very useful and interesting project, just as the tanks and the aircraft which the Russians needed, but his three big ideas were suited to German conditions. In Germany he could give them traction engines and tractors to till the soil. That was close to his heart — then the Volkswagen, the most important idea of the three, and the racing car — motor sport ever his secret love.

On the next day, Dr. Porsche returned to Stuttgart where he was urgently needed, where he had to try to get new contracts, do battle with financiers, with the suppliers, with delivery schedules ... There it was tougher to get on, but he stayed. And as if in recognition of this, the design office was full of new tasks in the following years, tasks that brought new lustre to his name the world over and at least provided him with the necessary financial security.

11 NSU-Type 32-Torsion-bar springing-Air cooling-VW 3 and 30

NO ONE tried to interfere in the design of the small NSU car, and because of this Porsche was at last able to bring his air cooling to the fore. The NSU design was larger and more roomy than the Zundapp one; it had a 1.4-litre engine planned on the classical Volkswagen system, with four opposed cylinders and overhead valves. It developed some 28 to 30hp and the prototypes had a maximum speed of about 70mph. The drawings were completed in the second half of 1933, the last ones being dated January 1934.

Just like the Zundapp, three prototypes of the Porsche type '32', as they called it, were built. Again, only three were built because the same situation arose at NSU as at Zundapp; suddenly the motor-cycle business boomed and there was no room to start producing cars. On the other hand, at the beginning of 1934, Porsche received an order to develop the 'real' Volkswagen.

The first two prototypes were bodied by Drauz of Heilbronn in the Weymann method, in other words they had wooden framework covered with artificial leather. One of them had a slightly curved windscreen which enabled an upward view — today one would probably call it a panoramic screen. It was Kommenda who was responsible for the body designs. The type '32' had a slightly longer wheel-base than the VW of today, it was a little roomier within and springing was by torsion bars. Shortly before this Ferdinand Porsche, the first designer in the world to do so, had perfected torsion-bar suspension; although some prior theoretical French patents from 1917 and 1919 existed, no one had actually built this type of springing. Someone once said about torsion bar springing that if Porsche had never invented anything else, this alone would suffice to imprint his name for ever in the pages of motor vehicle design history. Indeed, this system has become a form of construction favoured by the entire motor industry, and the Porsche cars of today are still so equipped.

One could even go further and state categorically that the invention of the torsion bar as a springing medium was the last of the basic inventions in automobile design; since then only details have been improved with no change in basic theory. The torsion bar brought agreeable financial advantages to the Porsche design office, for within a few months the system was being sold to the whole world and they designed torsion bar springing for Hanomag, Morris, Citroen, Standard, Volvo, Mathis, Austro-Fiat and Alfa Romeo. The years that followed also found the system used on racing and sports cars, as on the formula I Auto-Union racing car and also on the successful British ERA which caused such a furore in the 1,500cc class from 1935 onwards. The fact that the Porsche-designed Cisitalia formula I racing car after the war was so equipped is also hardly surprising. Now, of course, the patent period for all torsion bar systems has expired so that everyone can use them as springing media.

The third vehicle in the type '32' series was an all steel construction bodied by Reutter of Stuttgart. This firm, founded in 1906, has been closely allied to the house of Porsche since 1950 and built the bodies for the type 356. Reutter now belongs to Porsche. It is interesting that even then they had close contact with Porsche, Reutter having also constructed the bodywork for the first Wanderer cars which Porsche designed for the Chemnitz works. When the final Volkswagen project was ready, the 40 pre-production cars of 1938 to 1939 were also bodied by Reutter. The Drauz bodied prototype was distance-tested as early as the spring of 1934. Although Rosenberger no longer belonged to the Porsche team, he still worked with it in utilizing the Porsche patents abroad, and it was he who drove this car to Paris. There was no name plate on the car at all, neither Porsche nor NSU, and curious questions were simply parried. 'This is only a prototype.'

Air cooling had appeared before in Porsche designs. Indeed, the house of Porsche has ever been a protagonist of this sytem and remains so to this day. We mentioned that in 1912 there existed a 90hp air-cooled aero engine which Porsche designed while at Austro-Daimler. The motorized gun carriage of 1916 and 1917, then the most used Austrian traction vehicle, also had air cooling, being a 4-cylinder in-line engine of 66mm bore and 125mm stroke. This was most popular with the military because of its indifference to heat and cold. They even equipped shunting and narrow-gauge locomotives with air-cooled Austro-Daimler engines and in 1921 Porsche designed a 7hp engine for small traction machines on the same principle. Volkswagen air cooling was particularly successful in the desert version of that car, also in tractors and of course in the well-known Porsche 356 and the sports-racing cars of the type 550, better known as 'Spyder'.

The house of Porsche propagates air cooling, pointing out particularly that in transatlantic aircraft construction air cooling had completely won the day. It must be admitted, however, that what is true for aircraft engines running within a more or less constant revolution range, need not necessarily apply to car construction. Statistics tend to be impressive, however, especially those referring to the 24-hour race at Le Mans where Porsche had successfully represented air cooling in the 1,100cc, 1,500cc and 2-litre class; in the 750cc class the French Panhard did likewise and almost every year recently, a higher percentage of air-cooled entries have finished the race compared with water-cooled machines. There are exceptions to this of course, witness 1959 when not a single air-cooled Porsche car finished the race!

Those who oppose air cooling always argue at first that such engines are noisier than water-cooled ones. Let us not get involved in a technical discussion here, but it can be stated that Porsche with his staff had, during the last thirty years, materially contributed to the fact that air cooling became generally accepted in car design.

May we ask the reader's indulgence and go forward in time so as to close the chapter on the Volkswagen? The basic concept for the design and construction of the Volkswagen, referred to as the 'type 60' at Porsche's but outside as 'VW 38', was basically created during the winter of 1933 and 1934. Before the war only a few cars appeared, the golden age only starting ten years later under managing director Nordhoff's guidance. Two happenings accelerated the basic work.

Firstly, Dr. Porsche was asked to call at the Chancellery in Berlin through the intermediary of Werlin, a director of Daimler-Benz. During the conversation Hitler put forward his ideas on a people's car and his culminating demand was this: 'You ask at what price it should be sold, Dr. Porsche? — I will tell you; at any price under 1,000 marks.

Please submit your project!'

Dr. Porsche produced an expose dated 17th January 1934 which concerned the construction of a German people's car. 'I have thoroughly studied the question of a people's car and I cannot consider it as a mini-car which, by artificial scaling down of dimensions, output, weight, etc, continues along the well trodden paths of the traditional vehicle. It might be cheap to buy originally, but would never be cheap from the sociological point of view, as its value in use would be small due to reduced driving comfort and lasting ability. Especially in times of mounting traffic density, when safety is increasingly important, all measures reducing user value must be rigorously rejected.

'My interpretation of a people's car is a useful vehicle able to compete with any other car on the same level. If the traditional car is to be made into a people's car, then fundamentally new solutions will be necessary.'

He then gave the technical data for his project. It was to have an air-cooled 1,250cc flat-four engine fitted at the rear with a maximum output of 26hp peaking at 3,500rpm, a wheel base of 98.4in., a track of 47.2in., a dry weight of 1,433 lb, maximum speed of 62mph, maximum climbing ability in bottom gear of 30% and giving on average 36 miles per gallon. Independent suspension was to be used on all four wheels. In other words, these data agreed to a very large extent with the Volkswagen as it was designed and built at a later stage.

He added: 'Within the framework of my "neutral" design office in Stuttgart, I have a staff of selected collaborators who are in closest touch with my ideas ... My office can rightly be called "neutral" for it has no other interests except to plan and create and there are no ties with any branches of the automobile industry.'

Porsche had had his design costed and according to the wages and prices of materials of the day, the Volkswagen could certainly not be made for 1,000 marks. The price arrived at was 1,550 marks. In the Volkswagen design contract which he signed on 22nd June 1934 with the Society of German Automobile Manufacturers this sum was reduced drastically, even more drastically than had been demanded by Hitler: 'The calculations are to be based on a production cost figure of 900 marks per car, based on a series of 50,000 vehicles.'

The Society was to further the work with all means at its disposal to the benefit of the 'Reich', but before Porsche got going with the plan as he meant to, a number of discussions had to take place and a good deal of intrigue had to be scotched. To start with, the Porsche office was given 20,000 marks per month and with this the first experimental cars were supposed to be built within ten months. This was too short a time and far too small a sum with which to develop a vehicle ready for series production.

Most designers would probably not have even started under such conditions, but if Porsche had an idea in his mind he always wanted to realize it the same day if possible. Thus they began to build the first three experimental cars in the private garage of Porsche's villa where two lathes, a power drill and a milling machine had been installed and where twelve men were working. The first three prototypes were called the 'VW 3' series.

At the motor show in the spring of 1935 in Berlin, Hitler in his opening speech mentioned for the first time the name of Porsche and the Volkswagen concept in public. He said: 'I am pleased that, due to the capabilities of the brilliant designer Porsche and his staff, it has become possible to complete the first designs for the German Volkswagen and the first vehicles will be tested halfway through this year. It must be possible to provide the German people with a car that does not cost more than a medium sized motor-cycle and which is economical in fuel.'

To test the car during the middle of 1935 was of course out of the question, because of the slow manual work in Porsche's garage. In fact the tests did not take place for another year, due to lack of financial aid. In the meantime, plans had been drawn up to

47

build a further batch of prototypes, later to be called the 'VW 30' series, since it was a question of thoroughly testing thirty cars. The first press item about this appeared on 28th June 1935 in the journal *ADAC-Motorwelt:* 'Daimler-Benz takes part in the pre-production work on the Volkswagen, the experimental work of which has been financed by the Society of Motor Manufacturers, by making and supplying important parts and also the bodywork.'

The three cars of the VW 3 series were tried out in the second half of 1936 by Porsche engineers. Day and night, on two fixed routes, the cars were run first on an autobahn sector from Stuttgart via Karlsruhe, to Darmstadt, Frankfurt, Bad Nauheim and back and also on a route comprising many curves and mountains in the Black Forest: Stuttgart, Pforzheim, Baden-Baden, Offenburg, Kniebis, Freudenstadt and back to Stuttgart. Each car carried, apart from the Porsche engineer, an expert from the Society who constantly noted any faults and defects, what speeds were being used, and the weather conditions of the time. If any repairs had to be carried out this was always done in the garage of Porsche's villa.

Each of the three cars covered 30,000 miles and this test period was up just before Christmas of 1936. The experts then condensed their opinions in a report in which they admitted quite openly that a task had been undertaken which exceeded any hitherto achieved by the industry and which was thought to be beyond normal bounds. They admitted that the construction of the experimental cars had taken place under makeshift conditions without sufficient equipment and that certain defects could easily be remedied and were not of a fundamental nature. The performance and character were referred to as good, so good in fact that further development should be recommended.

In the following year, 1937, Daimler-Benz built the thirty experimental cars of the 'VW 30' series. These covered no less than *two million* experimental kilometres; they too were driven day and night and some cars exceeded 62,000 miles.

This time they were not driven by engineers, but by 200 men from the S.S. who, provided they were in possession of driving licences, had been called in at random from all parts of Germany just to test the Volkswagen. To maintain secrecy it was necessary to call in the services of the Security Police but at the same time the thirty experimental cars were to be tested under everyday conditions. The men who were ordered to drive were not experts, just ordinary drivers.

In the meantime, the government had taken a hand in the development of the Volkswagen. A further thirty vehicles were built, for demonstration and exhibition purposes only and a company was formed to prepare for the production of the Volkswagen; Messrs. Porsche, Werlin and Lafferentz were appointed as managers and directors. The next step was the building of the finalized type under the appellation 'VW 38' because this took place in 1938. The engines of the series VW 3 and VW 30 and finally of the VW 38 were of 996cc. The 1,134cc engine which powered the desert car was developed from it and proved itself not only in Africa but also in Russia; it had a higher ground clearance and a different rear-axle ratio.

The foundation stone for the Volkswagen works in Wolfsburg was laid on 26th May 1938. When they announced officially that the Volkswagen would be available to the 'KdF Savers' (KdF meant 'strength through joy'), a price of 990 marks was mentioned, a fuel consumption of 42mpg, with speeds of 12, 24, 40 and 62mph in the gears, tank contents of 5 gallons, tyre size 4.50 by 16, weight 1,430 lb, and a height of 61 in. At 3,000rpm (about 62mph) the engine was said to develop 23.5hp. There was no choice of colour. All were to be painted in a blue-grey tone.

Hitler stated at the foundation ceremony that the car was not to be called VW but KdF. In the first leaflet which appeared, the car was referred to by a title not surprising for the times 'The KdF car, as willed by the Fuhrer'. But the sentences that followed were certainly composed more by Porsche and his engineers than by the propaganda

Ferdinand Porsche, born 1875, the son of a tinsmith - died 1952. World famous
engineering designer

Porsche's first racing car. This machine set a new record for electric cars at Semmering in the autumn of 1900. Note wind-cheating front!

Porsche's electric racing car, 1900, developed for Mr. E.W. Hart of Luton. Four hub-mounted motors; the weight of the batteries was 4,000 lb

Lohner-Porsche, 'mixed-drive' racing car, winner of Exelberg hillclimb 1902, driven by F. Porsche

One of the first all-electric Porsche designed 'touring' cars. The Lohner-Porsche fwd by electric hub-motors!

1902 - the 'mixed drive' Lohner-Porsche on an outdoor dynamometer test!

The Austro-Daimler Taunus car photographed in London in 1907, driven by Otto Kaes, Porsche's brother-in-law. Said to have been driven also at Brooklands. 90hp - maximum speed 81 mph

53

The most successful pre-World War I design; the 'Prince Henry' Austro-Daimler, winning the 1910 Prince Henry Trial with Porsche at the wheel and Mrs. Porsche in the tonneau

A 1912 aero engine of four cylinders with ohv by exposed pushrods

A 1907 Lohner-Porsche fire appliance as used by the London Fire Brigade

An infantry 'train' used during World War I. The prime mover had a constant speed IC engine coupled to a dynamo which powered the individual hub-mounted motors of the trailers; they were self-steering to negotiate sharp bends

This 80hp tractor powered the 30.5cm mortar of the Austrian Imperial Army - it was a decisive factor in some of the 1914 battles

This model of the Austro-Daimler was very popular in 1912. The sole concessionaire in England was callled Francis Martin Luther

This 'Maya' Type Austro-Daimler was the prototype of the 'Prince Henry' car in 1909. Four cylinders, monobloc, side valves, 80 x 100mm bore and stroke. The Porsche 'tulip' shape is clearly seen

16-25 H.P. "ALPINE" model

THE AUSTRIAN DAIMLER MOTOR CO LTD.
112 Gt. Portland Street, London W

This tractor was used in World War I as a motorized gun carriage and called the 'Daimler-horse'. Later it was the first realization of Porsche's agrarian interests

Dr. Porsche personally tunes the engine of the Lohner 'Arrow' aeroplane, prior to a height test in 1912

A 1914 Austro-Daimler all-electric brougham, with hub-motors at rear. As late as 1923 it was used to take Ferry and Louise Porsche to school. Although there was of course a chauffeur, the children sometimes drove themselves

Lucky young Ferry Porsche; when he was only 11 years old, he had his own petrol-engined car - capable of about 35mph

The 1921-22 Austro-Daimler type 'Sascha' with an engine of 1,100cc, twin ohc, maximum speed 83mph. Alfred Neubauer is at the wheel

A beautifully finished show chassis of the 1929 Steyr 'Austria'

Hans Stuck, the 'King of the Mountains' with the sports Austro-Daimler ADM-R in a
'king sized' slide

The victorious Mercedes in the Targa Florio of 1924, as designed by Porsche (with cap)
photographed with Alfred Neubauer

A prototype designed for the Wanderer works of 3.3 litres with supercharger. It was never put into production but became Porsche's personal car

The 4-litre, 8-cylinder Steyr 'Austria' shown at the Paris Salon in 1929, of which only a few were built

The 1923 type 'M', 6-cylinder Austro-Daimler - a number of which were sold in England

In 1933 Porsche designed this 1,500cc car for NSU as a prototype. It had a flat-four engine at the back. The Volkswagen beginnings are clearly seen

office of the KdF: 'The weight distribution of about 44% in front and 56% at the rear can be called ideal and is on a par with the weight distribution of a racing car.' And further on it said: 'It seemed obvious to use independent suspension by swing axles in the design of the KdF; this has not only been used successfully in racing car construction, but also in tens of thousands of German private vehicles ... At the rear there is a stayed swing axle, a system which can be found in an almost identical application on the Auto-Union racing car.'

The connection between racing car construction and the series production car which had always been propagated by the house of Porsche was particularly obvious in this instance and it provides us with a lead-in to the theme of racing and sports cars. Before we discuss the Auto-Union racing car which Dr. Porsche designed for the racing formula of 1934 to 1937, it behoves us to mention that when the Volkswagen was designed he immediately considered a sporting version. One of the engines, for instance, was equipped experimentally with two carburettors to obtain increased performance and no sooner were the first 'VW 3' cars running than Ferdinand Porsche designed a VW sports car.

During the negotiations with the authorities the VW sports project reappeared time and again. Finally, however, it was turned down for the reason that a 'car for the people' was required and a sports car was not a car for the people. Thus, no sports car was built officially, but no one could prevent such a project from growing on the drawing board. Thus it was that Porsche had already foreseen a 1,500cc engine for his VW sports car.

When they planned the long-distance rally, Berlin-Rome, for September 1939, which would have been practically a road race, several firms began to develop aerodynamic bodies, for the first 400 miles were to be run on the Autobahn, Berlin-Munich. This meant that the gentlemen from the German workers front were no longer disinclined to revert to the sports car designs of Dr. Porsche. How about speed-tuning a Volkswagen for this event?

Porsche, who had in the meantime founded his own works to build prototypes in Stuttgart-Zuffenhausen, built three such Berlin-Rome Volkswagens. They had the normal VW chassis with a very streamlined, practically single-seater body; the engine was made to produce 40bhp and top speed was about 87mph. But the Berlin-Rome event did not take place, for the war broke out in September 1939 and these three cars remained at the Porsche works. One of them has simply vanished, being probably destroyed by bombs, but another was used by the invading Americans at Zell am See in Austria and they very much enjoyed driving it. As they got too warm in it, they simply cut off the roof and they drove it as long as there was oil in the sump; then it was broken up for spares. The third car still exists today and since 1948 has been in the ownership of the well-known Innsbruck driver, Otto Mathe, who, as late as 1950 and 1951, used it for racing and rallies in Austria with considerable success; now it is in the little Porsche works museum.

12 Auto-Union racing car

WE must now switch back to the year 1932, the year in which Dr. Porsche decided to build a racing car. This vehicle, later to become famous as the Auto-Union racing car, arose from Ferdinand Porsche's own initiative. No one had given him an order for it. All he had to go on was the new racing formula which had been decided in October 1932 by the International Sports Commission in Paris. This is what was decreed: 750 kilos maximum weight without oil, water and tyres but within the framework of this maximum weight any engine size with or without supercharger was permitted. This formula was to apply to the years 1934 to 1936 but was eventually extended until the end of 1937.

This type of formula was very close to the ideas of Ferdinand Porsche. At a later date he often said that a maximum weight limit with an entirely free choice of engine tended to leave the designer with the broadest latitude possible and therefore would be the most interesting one. Within the framework of such a formula, the development of a high power-to-weight ratio would be fostered.

In fact, his technical mind was excited by it and on 15th November 1932 a calculation sheet came into being, handwritten by Rabe, based on facts discussed by Dr. Porsche, Kales, Rosenberger and Rabe. This sheet forecast quite accurate technical data for the future Auto-Union racing car: a V-16 engine, with cylinders set at an included angle of 45 degrees; maximum rpm at first 4,500 (to be increased later to 6,000), maximum speed 182mph, bore 68, stroke 75mm, cubic capacity 4,358cc, 7:1 compression ratio.

To enable Porsche to build this racing car a new company was registered under the name of Hochleistungsfahrzeugbau GmbH (High Performance Vehicle Construction Co. Ltd.), independent of Porsche's design office. It was even foreseen that this company should later enter the car in races, showing clearly the sporting enthusiasm of Porsche and his staff; even Rosenberger, who was the 'minister of finance' in those days, was enthusiastic about this plan. His successor in the year 1933, although commercially very critical and exact, was just as much of an enthusiast for motor racing.

Apart from the formula car, a sports car also took shape on the drawing board, designed as a three-seater aerodynamic coupe powered by the self-same V-16 4.4-litre engine at the back, equipped with a supercharger but detuned to give 200bhp. Steering was to be in the middle and the two passengers would sit on either side and slightly aft of the driver, on very comfortable seats. It was to weigh about 2,860 lb, equal to about 14.5 lb per horse-power. At that time this was a power/weight ratio that no sports car could even approach. The 5-speed gearbox was so arranged that bottom should give 47mph, second 60mph, third 75mph, fourth 95mph and fifth 125mph. This, a dream car for all sporting motorists, was unfortunately never built.

In the meantime, the directors of the newly established Auto-Union company had visited Porsche, for this new group was not opposed to motoring sport. DKW motor-cycles had had considerable success all over the world, Wanderer cars were often seen in reliability trials and rallies, Audi had a good name from the days of the first Alpine trials and so it was decided to take an interest in the new racing formula. The right man for the design of such a racing car would obviously be Porsche. Would he be interested?

'Design such a car?' Porsche asked and smiled at the two directors of Auto-Union: 'I've got it already here in my pocket.'

Thus the racing car design passed from the company owning it into the hands of Auto-Union. In the first year of its appearance it was still called the Auto-Union-P to show appreciation to the designer. For Porsche it became more than just the design with the number '22' and he was present at the first trials in the winter of 1933-1934 in Monza and also on one of the Italian autostrade. He witnessed the original record attempts in March 1933 on the Avus when Hans Stuck demonstrated the car for the first time to the German public and achieved the absolute hour's record of 134.9mph. During the first years of the new formula he was present at almost every race, not only to check lap speeds with two stop-watches but also to film his car and driver and to supervise the whole organization from the technical point of view.

Those who were there will never forget when Dr. Porsche, shortly before the start of a race at the Nurburgring, seeing that the radiator of one of the Auto-Unions was leaking, lent a hand himself to help stop up the leak temporarily. Usually also Dr. Porsche decided whether the carburettors were to be tuned with a weaker or richer mixture after studying the 'picture' provided by the sparking plugs.

The first Auto-Union racing cars developed 295bhp in the year 1934; the last ones, at the end of the formula, gave up to 545. The size of engine which could be used within the framework of the 750 kilo formula was amazing — the last model had a cubic capacity of 6,330cc. Yet no case had ever come to light, neither at Daimler-Benz nor at Auto-Union, when faulty material had brought about an accident. This shows clearly that the designers had worked with great care and tremendous conscientiousness, since the weight in relation to the engine size was so very low. The following table shows the development of the Auto-Union racing engines during the currency of the 750 kilo formula.

16—Cylinder Auto-Union Racing Engines during the Currency of the 750-kilo Formula

	1934	1935	1936	1937
Cubic capacity (cc)	4,360	4,950	6,010	6,330
Stroke/bore (mm)	75/68	75/72.5	85/75	85/77
Supercharger boost: atmospheres ...	0.60	0.75	0.95	0.94
Compression ratio	7.0 : 1	8.95 : 1	9.2 : 1	9.2 : 1
Output (bhp)	295	375	520	545
At rpm	4,500	4,800	5,000	5,000
Torque (lb/ft)	380	477	627	650
Output per litre (bhp/litre)	67.5	76.0	86.5	86.0
Piston speed (ft/min)	2,226	2,364	2,777	2,777

Auto-Union racing car

During the first year's racing, Auto-Union cars appeared a little sooner on the circuits than those of Daimler-Benz, which were not quite ready. At the first major event on the Avus, only the Auto-Union team was present. Their first racing manager was a former driver for Mercedes, Willi Walb, later he was superseded by Dr. Feuereissen. The racing manager in the Auto-Union Grand Prix team did not have such a sovereign position as Alfred Neubauer of Daimler-Benz, this being due to the fact that Dr. Porsche always had his way from the technical point of view; often he gave valuable advice and help.

At the Grand Prix of Germany in 1934 for instance, there had been a lap by lap battle between the then top Auto-Union driver Hans Stuck and the Mercedes ace, Rudolf Caracciola. Towards the end Caracciola had retired and Stuck was leading, but with four laps to go, whilst passing the pits he pointed at his radiator. His thermometer had been showing 100º centigrade and he was worrying lest the radiator contents would boil, thus losing water and overheating the engine. At the Auto-Union pits they thought of signalling him to stop, but Dr. Porsche explained that after eighteen laps the radiator water could not suddenly be getting too hot! Probably the thermometer has packed up, and Stuck should be left to get on with it, he opined. Stuck himself was extremely worried but he passed the finishing banner and the car held together ... It had in fact been the thermometer that was at fault.

This was the first Auto-Union victory in a race of international calibre, Hans Stuck's first start at the Avus having ended in his retirement and Momberger finishing in third position. Young Guy Moll of France won in an Alfa Romeo whereas at the Eifel races Daimler-Benz won with Manfred von Brauchitsch.

In 1934 the official team of Auto-Union consisted of Hans Stuck, August Momberger and Prince zu Leiningen. Stuck won not only the Grand Prix of Germany and Switzerland but also the Masaryk circuit in Czechoslovakia. Furthermore, he was first in four international hill climbs, in Germany at Schauinsland, Kesselberg, Feldberg, and in France in the Mont Ventoux event.

The Swiss Grand Prix had even witnessed a double victory by Auto-Union, for Momberger occupied second position after Stuck, whereas the Frenchman Rene Dreyfus in a Bugatti was third. In the Italian Grand Prix in September 1934 Stuck and his relief, Prince zu Leiningen, finished second behind the Caracciola/Fagioli team.

The two German firms who had commenced building racing cars when the new formula came into force, were outstandingly successful in the first year on practically all racing circuits except in the French Grand Prix, contested that year on the road circuit of Montlhery where the winners were three Alfa Romeos driven by Chiron, Varzi and Moll.

Stuck also achieved seven world records in the year 1934 and eight international ones in the 3-5 litres class. In the autumn of 1934 the Auto-Union racing car had been fitted with a partially enclosed body, with a little coupe top and shrouded wheels. This was not a fully streamlined car as we know it, but Stuck reached a top speed over the flying-start kilometre of 203.2mph. The grand prix car without enclosed wheels when fitted with the Avus back-axle ratio did at that time reach the projected speed of about 183mph. On the Avus on 20th October 1934 Stuck managed an average speed of 151.6mph for the hundred kilometres from a standing start, although at that time the fast, almost vertical, curve had not yet been built. The world's record over the standing kilometre was taken at 101.3mph.

When we compare these figures with today's great averages and lap speeds, it becomes very clear that the chassis design of that time was not comparable with today's. When Stuck won the German Grand Prix in 1934 he achieved an overall average of just under 76mph, corresponding to a lap time of 11 minutes 0.8 seconds. Of course the races of those days necessitated one, if not two, tyre changes and refuelling stops; the fuel consumption of the supercharged engines in the days of the 750-kilo formula was in the region of 3 to 4 miles per gallon. Most of the lap speeds on the Ring were just under 11 minutes, albeit with vehicles which, with high axle ratios, developed top speeds on a par with the best racing cars of the 2.5-litre formula of 1954 to 1960. The power/weight ratio in the year 1934 must have been in the region of 5.5 to 5.7 lb/bhp and therefore not up to the standards of the grand prix values of the 2.5-litre formula. On the other hand, an engine with over 4-litres and a supercharger is bound to have a very much better torque curve than a normally aspirated one of 2.5-litres.

Yet in 1954 with the unsupercharged 1,500cc Porsche-Spyder, the horse-power of which at that time was around 110 to 115bhp, race averages were just as high as those of the 1934 formula cars. This comparison clearly shows technical development over the preceding twenty years.

Nineteen-thirty-five brought four Auto-Union victories in important international events (Hans Stuck won the Grand Prix of Italy at Monza and Achille Varzi the Grand Prix of Tunis) and Hans Stuck also won two hill climbs. Despite this, Daimler-Benz were the more successful in that racing season. The Stuttgart works had a wider choice of fast drivers. Momberger and Prince zu Leiningen had shown themselves in the 1934 season to be good and reliable drivers but they could not be considered top-class for the 750-kilo formula cars. Therefore, Auto-Union kept a look out for new drivers and at the Eifel races of 1935 Bernd Rosemeyer was entered for the first time. Until then he had been successful on NSU and DKW motor-cycles.

Rosemeyer's name was closely linked with the history of the Grand Prix Auto-Union. He was very much encouraged by Dr. Porsche right from the beginning of his career and he would always turn to the older man for advice.

The Auto-Union tended to have a lot of oversteer and a number of drivers who tried it could not get on with this characteristic. Rosemeyer, on the other hand, mastered the car in a manner which hardly any other driver could approach. It was particularly remarkable that he only just lost to Caracciola over the last two kilometres on the Nurburgring (which was his first race) during the Eifel race of 1935 and then only because the Auto-Union was no longer running evenly on all its cylinders.

In the Swiss Grand Prix of 1935 Rosemeyer was already the best man in the Auto-Union team and was placed third behind the Mercedes drivers Caracciola and Fagioli; he obtained the same position at Monza where he was co-driver with Paul Pietsch, the latter having been engaged as reserve driver for a few races. At the Masaryk event at the end of the season he achieved his first victory in an international grand prix. Whilst the 1935 season was sometimes referred to as a Mercedes one, the 1936 season was definitely for Auto-Union. The cars were very much improved that year and their engines gave 520bhp. As a result Bernd Rosemeyer pulled off some outstanding victories such as the German, Swiss and Italian Grands Prix, in fact a series which could only be likened to Fangio's successes with Mercedes in 1955. Auto-Union were also successful in Tripoli where Achille Varzi won at an average speed of 128.9mph.

This is the time to mention Hans Stuck again, who was second at Tripoli by a mere four seconds. On the Berne circuit he was third after Rosemeyer and Varzi, thus completing the Auto-Union hat-trick for this race. Let us also not forget Ernst von Delius who was then part of the Auto-Union team, having previously driven 750cc racing cars. In 1936 he was third at Monza, but crashed fatally in 1937.

It was Rosemeyer who, in 1936 on the Nurburgring, was the first to get below a time that was in those days likened to the 4-minute mile. The point was to better 10 minutes for the lap. In the third lap of the German Grand Prix he reached 9 minutes 56.4 seconds. At that time he used to call Dr. Porsche 'dear Uncle Doctor'.

13 America-Crossing by Queen Mary

IN 1937 Ferdinand Porsche was so busy with other matters that he could no longer devote much time to motor racing and it was in that year that he undertook his second trip to America. He had been there previously in 1936 for a short space of time without any publicity and was only accompanied by his secretary, G.H. Kaes. The Americans already considered him a very eminent man and at the car plants he was shown all the latest ideas. At Packard's he made a quick decision, bought the latest 8-cylinder model and drove it through America.

When about to return from America an interesting episode occurred. Porsche had booked a passage on the *Bremen* but heard during the last days of his stay in the States that the *Queen Mary* was due to leave two days before the *Bremen*. The *Queen Mary* was then the biggest liner in the world and had only just been taken into commission.

'I want to cross on the *Queen Mary*,' Porsche said to his secretary, 'Please see to it that I get a cabin.' He just had to travel on the biggest liner in the world and see its engines. There was no reason, after all, why ships should not stimulate his engineering thoughts. Apart from this, Porsche was very obstinate, ideas occurred to him *en passant* and he simply had to have them carried out, no matter what.

But Germans, and naturally also Dr. Porsche, were at that time subjected to very strict currency regulations and trips on foreign ships cost foreign currency. Therefore Porsche had booked his return trip in March on the *Bremen* and, of course, his dollar allowance for the U.S.A. had long since been used up.

The office of the North-German Lloyd was asked whether they would take back the ticket and pay back the money in dollars. They lifted their hands in horror — quite impossible! That would constitute an offence against the currency regulations. Then the secretary suggested that they should telephone Berlin to increase the permitted amount of currency by the sum needed for the *Queen Mary*. After all, Porsche was an important personality in Germany. All right then, they would ask Berlin. The cable reply was clear. No extra currency! There were to be no exceptions and the authorities in Berlin were obviously very displeased by the fact that Porsche particularly wanted to travel on a British ship.

The secretary informed Porsche of all this. 'But I want to cross on the *Queen Mary*,' was his reply. What was to be done? The secretary, after a moment's thought, went to the office of the British shipping company. When he explained the circumstances he was introduced to someone in authority to whom he made known who Dr. Porsche was and how he had made up his mind to travel on the *Queen Mary*. It was an *idee fixe* of his because he was tremendously interested in the technical arrangements of this great ship. But the problem was money, or to be more exact, foreign currency which for obvious reasons could not be obtained. The Britisher then asked to be excused a moment and went to see one of his directors. The secretary sat there and thought to himself: 'They will think I am crazy and probably will want to lock me up.' No sooner had these thoughts passed through his mind than the Britisher returned and said briefly: 'And which cabin would Dr. Porsche want?' By this time the secretary was master of the situation and replied audaciously: 'The best one!'

Thus it came about that Dr. Ferdinand Porsche, without a penny in his pockets, travelled on the *Queen Mary* in a luxury suite which had in fact been used by the real Queen Mary during the first crossing of the ship, and on top of that he was given a few pounds spending money. The Commodore was delighted to have another world-famous guest aboard, apart from Douglas Fairbanks and his wife the former Lady Ashley, the film actress Merle Oberon and violinist Fritz Kreisler.

The Commodore had not reckoned on Porsche's curiosity. When he was asked whether his stateroom was comfortable he said yes, indeed it was, but could he also see the engine room. They passed him on to the chief engineer, and Porsche's secretary again told the tale about the German professor who particularly wanted to see the engine room and the engines, because he had a sort of technical spleen. The chief engineer said he was sorry but there was a particular regulation which made it impossible for foreigners to see the engine room. 'Yes,' agreed the secretary, 'but surely in this case there were special circumstances ...' In special circumstances, they said, permission could be granted on the basis of written application to the company's headquarters in London. Couldn't they possibly ask for this permission by radio? So they duly cabled to enquire whether a certain Dr. Porsche could be permitted to inspect the engines ... And permission was granted. He asked the leading engineers all the things he wanted to know and they gave him the requested information without any trouble.

Then there was a storm, a storm the like of which was seldom seen even in the Atlantic, with a wind force between 10 and 11. Yet Porsche kept to his habitual walk round the ship once a day for relaxation. In the very middle of this storm he asked one of the engineers: 'Tell me exactly, what is the angle up to which the *Queen Mary* can roll on to her side? At which angle does she keel over and cannot straighten up again?' The engineer looked nonplussed at the man with the slide-rule who wanted to know everything. 'According to calculations, the bridge would be touching the water, sir,' he said, 'but I would not like to be on the bridge when this happens.' 'Excellent,' said Porsche, and got his camera ready to get a picture of the angle of inclination which the world's largest liner would assume during wind force 10. Even that he had to know accurately. When the *Queen Mary* docked in Southampton, a newspaper reporter asked if anyone had taken pictures during the storm. They told him to go to Dr. Porsche — and the Porsche photographs duly appeared in the London daily press.

Porsche stayed a few days in England to have a look at the Austin works, following a personal invitation by Lord Austin.

The second trip to America in 1937 was not such a private affair, for he was accompanied by Werlin, Dieckhoff and Lafferentz and his 27-year-old son Ferry was also in the party.

This time Ferdinand Porsche and his party were personally received by Henry Ford and they had long discussions about the Volkswagen question. Ford was given a detailed idea by Ferdinand Porsche and his son just how they pictured the small car of the future in Europe. Old Henry Ford listened carefully yet sceptically to what was being said, for

European ideas could not be applied to America. Apart from this, Ford's manufacturing programme ran on very conservative lines. Whilst he was alive, independent suspension was unknown in the Ford works and the step from mechanical to hydraulic brakes had been a very tough battle. Henry Ford still mourned the universal success of his legendary Model T.

Finally, Dr. Porsche asked him whether he would not come to Europe. He would gladly act as his guide to the German industry. But Henry Ford shook his head. He could not see any possibilities of that for the moment, for there was bound to be war in Europe ere long.

War? Porsche and his party looked at one another with surprise. Porsche believed just as the others, that they were about to start on an epoch of peaceful economic progress and the very thought of war was remote. Political questions interested him very little, all he really wanted were interesting constructional tasks so that he, together with his collaborators, could solve technical problems to enable him to live well and to extend his own works. Those were the things that spurred him on and provided new ideas. Politics bored him and he never did enter into political discussions.

The third Reich gave him the title of professor, and together with the aircraft designers Heinkel and Messerschmitt, he was presented with a German National prize. Hitler personally received these prizewinners, talked pleasantly to them and praised them. But even that did not interest Porsche. Designing was his world, not the receiving of prizes. He completely shook the minions surrounding the Fuhrer by calling him 'Herr Hitler'. Yet the latter did not seem to mind this, Porsche was simply regarded as an eccentric.

14 Racing–Records–DB versus Auto-Union

AFTER inspecting the Ford works Ferdinand Porsche went on to the Vanderbilt Cup races. Nasty tongues wagged that he had specially fixed his American trip to coincide with the race date to enable him to follow the Vanderbilt Cup race from the Auto-Union pits. Bernd Rosemeyer won the race, but in later years America never again attempted to run events according to a formula current in Europe. At Indianapolis there has always been a special formula, even after the war, which was as different from the European racing formula as the track itself. Indianapolis is a track whereas in Europe racing is generally on road circuits.

In 1937 Bernd Rosemeyer put up a number of records with the Auto-Union racing car in the 5- to 8-litre and 3- to 5-litre class. He was the first man to exceed 250mph on a normal road — on the Autobahn between Frankfurt and Darmstadt. This happened on 26 October 1937 when he attempted the flying start 5 kilometres which he covered at an average of 251.2mph.

For these attempts they used the last development of the Auto-Union racing car within the 750-kilo formula, having a 6.3 litre engine of 545bhp and a fully aerodynamic body. The two world's records for the standing start kilometre and mile Rosemeyer put up on the same day, but used the standard form of grand prix monoposto without streamlining, because this was lighter and had better acceleration. These two absolute world records stood for more than twenty years; the standing kilometre at 19.08 seconds equalling 116.81mph and the mile at 25.96 seconds equalling 128.5mph. Only at the end of 1958 did an American driver, with a so-called 'dragster,' manage to improve on the kilometre record, using a car specially built for this record attempt.

Rosemeyer put up fastest lap on the Nurburgring with a 750-kilo formula car in 1937; apart from him Auto-Union also fielded Ernst von Delius, H.P. Muler (the latter had made a name for himself as a motor-cycle racer) and Hasse who had been a rally driver — all of them good drivers but not quick enough against men of the calibre of Caracciola, Brauchitsch and Hermann Lang. The lap times by Hasse, Muller and Delius were between 10 minutes 10 seconds and 10 minutes 15 seconds; Nuvolari, with the 12-cylinder Alfa, managed 10 minutes 8 seconds, Caracciola 10 minutes 4 seconds, Brauchitsch 9 minutes 55.1 seconds and Hermann Lang, a new driver for Daimler-Benz who had started on motor-cycles, got down as low as 9 minutes 52.2 seconds, an incredibly fast time for 1937. Then Rosemeyer stated boldy, 'I'll go faster still' and promptly managed 9 minutes 46.2 seconds. This was not an official Nurburgring record because practice times could not qualify as such, but in the 1937 Grand Prix it was Rosemeyer again who put up fastest lap at 9 minutes 53 seconds. A British motoring writer started his report like this: 'It was clear that there would be a pitched battle between Mercedes-Benz and Rosemeyer.'

This was a strange way of putting it, for he should have said 'between Mercedes-Benz and Auto-Union' as after all, five Auto-Union racing cars stood on the starting grid. But Rosemeyer was at that time head and shoulders above the rest of them, so that all the interest was centred on him.

For the records run in the autumn of 1937 Rosemeyer had a car which was differently streamlined from the one which was finished in January 1938 and with which he was eventually to kill himself on the Autobahn near Frankfurt. It may be that the body-shape was the last secret of his death drive.

The autumn record attempts by Daimler-Benz were not as successful as they had hoped in Stuttgart and Auto-Union had, so to speak, scooped the cream. Corps commander Huhnlein had ordered that record attempts would take place only once a year during a so-called record week. In January 1938 Daimler-Benz entreated Huhnlein to grant special permission for yet another record attempt, the reason being that whereas they had not been entirely ready in the autumn, they now were, and had a new car which was very much quicker and which might improve on the Auto-Union records by at least 20mph. In view of the impending motor show this would be of extreme importance to the prestige of German sport.

Permission was duly granted, but naturally Auto-Union heard about this Mercedes plan and said that they also could go faster. If Mercedes were to be given special permission, surely Auto-Union ought also to be permitted to participate in these further attempts. It came about that Caracciola was successful in his record attempt and put the flying-start kilometre record up to 270.4mph with the 5.6-litre Mercedes having a fully aerodynamic body, a speed that has never been exceeded on a road up to this day. It was achieved in the very early hours of 28th January 1938, but Auto-Union had also arrived from Frankfurt and wanted to attempt an attack on the new record.

In the autumn of 1937 Auto-Union had developed a body shape in which the wheels were not enclosed separately, but from the front enclosure to the rear a straight, horizontal line had been achieved which meant that the vehicle was considerably higher along both sides than the old aerodynamic car and a better frontal area factor had also been developed by wind-tunnel tests. Dr. Porsche knew of both types of bodywork, but advised against the faster one with the higher sides because he thought that its side-stability would be less and therefore any cross-winds would have very much more influence on straight running.

When they heard, at Auto-Union, that Mercedes would be at the start with a car which could run up to at least 265mph they decided, unbeknown to Ferdinand Porsche, who had other problems to deal with at that time, to hand Rosemeyer the car with the smaller frontal area.

In fact, this was a car capable of developing a top speed of some 275mph and it is probable that Rosemeyer could have bettered Caracciola's record by a few miles an hour. The kilometre and mile with flying start were the quest and Rosemeyer first drove up the course to warm up; on his return he was satisfied with the power developed. He then started on the actual record attempt but just after a bridge across the Autobahn he was caught by a gust of side-wind against which he was powerless. The machine was positively swept off the Autobahn and entirely demolished. Rosemeyer died instantly.

Ferdinand Porsche was not present during this record attempt; for the first time he had not been personally responsible for a record attempt with 'his' car. His first comment when he heard of Rosemeyer's death was: 'I am sure I would not have let him start had I known it was windy, especially since the car was so sensitive to side-winds.' Nothing was further from Dr. Porsche's mind than to reproach anyone, but Bernd Rosemeyer's fate touched him very deeply.

In this connection let us again mention Hans Stuck who, for almost all his racing life, handled only Dr. Porsche's designs. First, the almost legendary Austro-Daimler ADM-R, then the Mercedes SSK and SSKL; from 1934 to 1937 the Auto-Union racing car and on a few occasions after the war the Porsche Spyder.

Undoubtedly, Stuck was not as fast as Rosemeyer from 1936 onwards and Nuvolari, who joined Auto-Union in 1938 when the new formula came into being (3-litre supercharged or 4½-litre without supercharger) was also undoubtedly quicker. Because of that, people often used to say that Stuck was only second best, so to speak, and only really outstanding in hill climbs. Yet this is not true, for in 1937, the last year of the 750-kilo formula, Stuck showed on several occasions that he was first class. It must be said here that vehicles with a power/weight ratio of 3.3 lb per hp (the most favourable ratio ever possessed by a racing car) were certainly not easy to drive. On the Auto-Union of 1937 it was possible to spin the wheels on a straight dry road when accelerating hard from 86mph. The accurate grading of the throttle was even more difficult on those grand prix cars than it is on today's machines.

The fact that today's times are considerably more rapid is not only due to improved road-holding and brakes, but that today's grand prix car can be given full throttle coming out of bends far more easily than the cars of those days. There is only one racing circuit in Europe on which the pre-war records have not been lowered, the Bremgarten at Berne, where the Swiss Grand Prix used to be held every year; but even this statement must be qualified because in the last few years this race has not taken place. The last grand prix event there was in 1954, and more's the pity that this rapid, difficult and real driver's course has not seen another big race; this is entirely the decision of the Swiss authorities and not the Swiss Automobile Club. Fangio won there in 1954 in a Mercedes and made fastest lap with a time of 2 minutes 39.7 seconds, which is 101.8mph. Thus, he was faster than Ascari with a 2-litre Ferrari the year before and also faster than the times achieved in 1950 and 1951 with the 1.5-litre supercharged Alfettas. Yet the time put up by Fangio is considerably above the values achieved in 1937 with a 750-kilo formula car. In practice for the Swiss Grand Prix of 1937 Caracciola got down to 2 minutes 32 seconds, Brauchitsch 2 minutes 36 seconds, and Lang 2 minutes 37 seconds. Naturally, Rosemeyer was fastest for Auto-Union with 2 minutes 33 seconds. Hans Stuck was just a second behind that at 2 minutes 34 seconds and this is proof enough that he could not be considered 'second best' especially as the Berne circuit is all fast curves which certainly separate the sheep from the goats. During the race Stuck was behind Caracciola, Lang and Brauchitsch, but although in fourth position he was still best of the Auto-Union drivers.

The Freiburg hill climb in 1937 was the scene of a bitter battle for the saving of fractions of seconds, but here also when Stuck handled the 'P-Wagen' for the last time, he was well able to beat the others; Hermann Lang's time was 8 minutes 29 seconds, Caracciola's 8 minutes 17 seconds, Rosemeyer 8 minutes 12 seconds, but the 'Bergmeister' won at 8 minutes 11 seconds. The practice times were better by more than 30 seconds, for during the race itself the weather was below par and the lower reaches of the hill were still damp after rain.

The Auto-Union racing car of 1938 and 1939 was built on the same system, i.e. rear engine with the Porsche-designed springing and the man responsible for it was Professor Eberan von Eberhorst. He taught at the Technical University in Dresden and was a great friend of Dr. Porsche. In the two years before the war Hans Stuck appeared almost solely in hill climbs, always at the wheel of the 3-litre Auto-Union; in 1938 he became German mountain champion again and even road racing champion. Dick Seaman won the Grand Prix of Germany on the Nurburgring in 1938 with a Mercedes, second place also went to Mercedes, the car being shared by Hermann Lang and Caracciola; Stuck was third which was sufficient to give him the maximum number of points counting towards the championship. Altogether Stuck can look back on 78 racing victories whilst driving Ferdinand Porsche's designs, and a large number of second, third and fourth placings, and nine championships. Furthermore, he accounted for thirteen records.

15 Land-speed record car

EVEN when Ferdinand Porsche was no longer responsible for the design of the Auto-Union racing car and fully engaged with the Volkswagen and the design of tractors, the motor sport theme once more reared its head in rather a strange manner.

Ever since the first motor races there has been the wish to know the absolute maximum speed of which a vehicle is capable over a relatively short distance. Even before the First World War special machines had been built not for competing in long-distance events, but for the sole purpose of achieving the absolute maximum speed over the distance of one kilometre (after a fair-sized run-in) on a road as flat and as wide as possible. After this kilometre they had to be gently braked, brought to a standstill and turned around, then this so-called 'flying kilometre' had to be run again in the opposite direction to allow for possible influence by the wind, weather or the road surface. It was quite possible that after the short total distance of some 7 to 14 miles the engines and tyres would be quite finished, yet this did not matter. The main thing was the reaching of the absolute maximum, albeit briefly. Before the First World War the so-called 'Blitzen-Benz' was the most famous among these record breakers; it reached over 131mph and later even 142mph. In 1927 Major (later Sir Henry) de Hane Segrave reached 188mph for the first time, at the wheel of a very special Sunbeam record car. Since then it became a tradition that wealthy Englishmen held this absolute world record with special cars, in which were usually fitted aircraft engines. After Segrave came Malcolm Campbell, later Sir Malcolm Campbell, who reached 275 and finally in 1935 309mph. Captain George Eyston reached 359.3mph in 1938, and in 1939 John Cobb put the record up to 369.7mph. This then was the situation before the Second World War.

When one hears that Cobb's tyres alone cost over 13,000 pounds, one can imagine how expensive the building of such a record car is, not only was the question of tyres a problem but also the track, for since the days of Segrave it was no longer possible to attempt the world's record on ordinary roads.

First they tried the hard packed sand of Daytona Beach and then they discovered the dried out salt lake in Utah in the United States where there was practically unlimited space with a reasonable surface in August and September when the ground is firm enough. It seems unnecessary to mention that a middling size pebble can cause a car to jump 15 or 20 yards into the air during a record attempt, spelling immediate death to the driver. This apart, the people concerned with the record are glad if the tyres last 14 odd miles. With these monsters some 2,500 to 4,500bhp must be transferred from the engine to the road wheels.

Opinions are divided as to whether land speed records are of any value. One thing, however is sure; they are not so useful in the development of the series-produced car as are the great races, where it is always a question of finding out how long this or that part lasts; yet a record car creates its own far-reaching problems and its construction is certainly not without value. On the other hand, the amount of money spent to achieve the extremely high speeds of today bears little relationship to the value obtained.

National prestige is, however, closely bound up with such records, far more so than class records and it was this very question of prestige which became of paramount importance to the third Reich. Germany was undoubtedly one of the leading countries as far as series-produced cars were concerned and certainly the most successful constructor of racing cars, therefore the only thing that was missing was the absolute land speed record. Porsche had designed such a super machine for this attempt before an official order had even been given. He was not interested in prestige, but only stimulated by the thought of the ultimate limits. This is comprehensible for there has always been a certain fascination in the absolute maximum of which a man and a machine are capable. Man wishes to show in this way how far his talent, abilities and power extend and this, somehow, is the desire to grow beyond the limits of his existence, a limit man knows only too well.

National prestige and Porsche's dreams to reach the limits of the possible were joined by the high-class craftsmanship of Daimler-Benz. On 23rd July 1937 the first discussions took place, the Stuttgart works having again established an advisory contract with Porsche for the years 1937 to 1940.

Originally they wanted to try this car also on the Utah salt lake but when the government heard about the projected land speed record contender, Corps Commander Huhnlein ordered that a German record car would have to be driven on German soil. To this Porsche replied straight away that this would not be possible, for there was not a broad enough stretch available in Germany. This was countered by Huhnlein with 'then we shall build one.' Thus the record stretch at Dessau came into being, about 6 miles long, built of concrete, without a centre strip. But in Porsche's opinion even this was not sufficient. The width was about 60ft but on the salt lake there were 300 to 600ft that could be used if they were needed. Then came the question of the length. Porsche had worked out the following theoretical graph: to achieve about 375mph it would be necessary to have a run-in of 3.7 miles, then the measured kilometre would start and then about 1.4 miles would be needed for careful braking unless the additional air brakes shortened that distance. This meant at least 6 miles for the flying kilometre and another half-mile or so for the flying mile, but only 6 or so miles were available before a slight curve started.

Porsche was not going to take the responsibility for this, apart from which he hoped to achieve 400 to 405 miles. Under exceptionally favourable circumstances and by using maximum revolutions it might have been even possible to reach a limit of some 430mph. But the government remained deaf to the entreaties that the salt lake, being at an altitude of 3,600ft and creating better aerodynamic conditions than the low-lying Dessau, was more suitable. In 1940 they wanted to organize a Dessau record week and during that period the absolute world record was to have been established. There is no need for us to go to the United States, they said, and perhaps it was a good thing that the attempt never took place for it is very foolish to let chauvinism overrule sense when it is a question of world records.

The Porsche-Daimler super record car had three axles, the two rear ones being driven. The driver was in front, and the engine behind him, being a V-12 aircraft unit made famous in fighters as the type DB 601 and able to develop 2,500bhp and as much as 3,030bhp for short periods. Its cubic capacity was 44-litres. The entire car weighed 2.8 tons and was almost 29ft long. There were short, side-mounted, wing-like fins with negative curvature to increase pressure on the wheels. The hydraulic foot brake acted on all six wheels. The Continental Tyre Company developed special tyres, size 7.00 by 32, to withstand 435mph. There was no gearbox, it was push- or tow-started and then the engine would be connected by means of the clutch. The duralumin sheets of the removable bodywork were only 0.3 to 1mm thick.

The tail fin design of the record car was covered by a German patent in 1939 which had been applied for by Porsche together with his chief theoretician, Mickl. In the patent application the shape of the record car was only vaguely indicated, for work on it went on entirely in secret.

Ferdinand Porsche wanted Hans Stuck to establish this record by way of terminating his career as a racing driver and he took Stuck into his confidence about the car. In a book that appeared in 1939 in Berlin and in which Stuck described his career as a racing driver he mentioned the record car in a chapter devoted to Dr. Porsche.

This was the only public mention of the record car in those days. The war interrupted its final development and it stayed at Daimler-Benz and since then has become the most prized exhibit of the Daimler-Benz Museum in Unterturkheim.

16 Volkswagen planning – Tractors – Tanks

NOT only the design of the Volkswagen on the drawing board but also its actual series-production and the creation of the works were close to Porsche's heart. Not for nothing had he been to America twice, particularly to learn the latest production methods of the new world.

On the outskirts of Wolfsburg, the 'Volkswagen town,' there is still today a small, brown-painted house surrounded by a garden and fruit trees, from which there is a pleasant view of the entire town. It could be a summer cottage or a comfortable hunting lodge. It was put up in 1938 and Ferdinand Porsche had it built so that he should have his own place when travelling from Stuttgart to the newly constructed Volkswagen works, for he went there often.

During the war his son-in-law, Dr. Piech, lived there; he had married Louise Porsche in 1927 and was a Viennese lawyer who became commercial director and general manager of the Volkswagen works, working in close liaison with Ferdinand Porsche. This single storey wooden house was called the 'Hut' by Porsche and his collaborators and at first consisted of a large living room, two small bedrooms and a kitchen, but it was later extended.

The large living room was dominated by a big tiled stove and the place was furnished with antique furniture. Many were the conferences that took place in the 'Hut,' but also some pleasant parties were held there, with many guests, when the first Volkswagens were produced. When the cook asked what Dr. Porsche wanted to eat in the evening, Ferdinand Porsche used to order goulash with much paprika and with this he drank a glass of Munich beer. Old Porsche was a man who lived simply, and it is not only an anecdote when they said of him that he always carried a dry roll or a piece of bread in his pocket which he liked to chew if a technical problem or a conference kept him from a meal.

There was splendid shooting around the cottage before the war and from time to time he used to go hunting but never shot at any animals. He preferred to look for mushrooms and to explain that the others should do the shooting, he felt sorry for the deer.

In the autumn of 1937, after the end of 'his' last Auto-Union racing season, a new chapter started, not only in Dr. Porsche's life but also in the history of the works. The idea of building tractors had long been with him and his note-book, which he always carried, had the following notes for November 1937: 'Tractor must be cheap to buy, cheap to run, through excellent design -- universally useful in all agriculture, but low price must not influence all-round usefulness even in difficult terrain. Must be strong and robust and foolproof.'

Thus far the notes in his book -- and it must be admitted that Porsche kept very closely to these concepts when the tractors were finally built. The first inter-office memorandum about the design of a Porsche tractor was dated 24th November 1927. Even then it proposed to use an air-cooled engine of 12bhp at 2,000rpm. Its speed in difficult terrain was to be about 2mph, 4mph on easy work, and 10mph when driven on the road. According to the usual system at Porsche's the tractor was given a design number and was called 'Type 110.'

Six months passed, during which detailed drawings and calculations were made. The Porsche engineers at that time studied with very great care all the tractor designs which existed in Germany; the Porsche tractor was to become a 'people's tractor,' that was the idea from the very beginning.

Such a device would only sell if the farmer could dispense with all beasts of burden. In other words the tractor would have to be able to do all the work previously done by the beasts. About 70% of all work on a German farm consists of hauling, only a third being actual work in the field. The type 110 had an hydraulic clutch; only this system enabled a tractor to pull smoothly without jerking, just like the oxen. The Porsche engineers were suddenly involved in agriculture.

The type 110, just as the Volkswagen, had a rear engine and the driver sat in front. Front and rear units of the tractor were separated, it was a matter of a single-axle vehicle to which a front portion could be coupled up. However this solution was abandoned and the people's tractor was designed on four-wheel lines and only in that way did it prove fully useful.

On 2nd June 1938, a week after the foundation stone of the Volkswagen works had been laid, chief engineer Rabe passed a memorandum to the works. 'According to Dr. Porsche's orders, three complete agricultural tractors of the type 110 are to be built. Delivery of the first is due on 3rd September of this year, two further models to follow ten days later. The engines are to be ready in time to enable two weeks of brake testing to be carried out. A works schedule has been established to obtain material, the working thereof and for assembly.'

Then came a very revealing sentence: 'It will appear from this schedule that the period of works holidays has been considered as bridged by having parts made in other works. As far as the engine assembly is concerned which also falls due during this time, special measures will have to be taken....'

It seemed that the construction of the tractor was considered at the time of such importance that postponement of works holidays was considered for the sake of assembling the first engines for the three prototypes. The engine was in fact one of the major problems, because the government attached a lot of importance to the use of generator-gas.

No less than twenty-five different types of agricultural tractors were available on the German market at the time which, from the point of view of spare parts and simplification, was most unsatisfactory. Only three of these had diesel engines and therefore people were surprised when Porsche provided for such an engine during the development of his tractor. On the basis of the experience with the type 110, a new improved model, the '111,' was designed. Three engines were foreseen for this and the first item of the technical description mentioned a diesel engine of 12bhp, but a petrol and generator-gas engine were also designed. In 1939 an elaborate experimental programme was prepared. This contained reaping of corn and grass, ploughing with attachments, potato planting, hedging and ditching, binding, transport of wood, reaping of beet in muddy ground, driving a threshing machine, pumping, harrowing and sowing. The experimental engineers were constantly on the go and close collaboration with the agriculture college at Hohenheim was established.

When the war began Porsche naturally received orders for a number of important but entirely military designs. But he did insist that the work on the tractors should continue and a slightly more powerful version was in preparation, the type '112,' which now had 15 instead of 12bhp.

Again Porsche kept tenaciously to the question of further development of diesel engines, although the generator-gas problem became more and more acute.

The experiments continued. Dr. Porsche had in the meantime been nominated an honorary professor and his son Ferry took over the particular care of the tractor development whilst his father was held up by conferences in Berlin or was called to the general headquarters to lecture. From the test reports in 1940 it is quite clear that every detail was subjected to the utmost care — the major constructional outline having been fixed already and the test runs of the engines being satisfactory. 'Cylinder-head nuts must be more accessible,' it said in the report, 'reaper drive with short shaft on the right should be checked for wear by Professor Fischer in Hohenheim.' These notes showed clearly that the Porsche engineers worked very systematically on the problems of the tractor.

Plans for the making of a people's tractor out of the Porsche design did not only ripen from the engineering but also from the organisation point of view. One morning the citizens of Waldbrol in the Rhine country saw big proclamations on their notice boards to the effect that the Fuhrer had just signed the following decree: 'As the people's tractor is of decisive importance to the development of our agriculture I hereby order that the building of the necessary factories in Waldbrol in the district of Cologne-Aachen is to be commenced immediately so that the production of the tractor invented by Dr. Porsche can begin. For the enlargement of the town which this project requires, I extend the executive powers of Building Inspector Speer, for the new buildings and extensions of the town of Waldbrol.' On that day the townspeople put out their flags, for in their minds' eye they already saw Waldbrol flourish. It would become another Wolfsburg, but bigger still and even more important; during the war obviously only preliminary work could be carried out, but surely hostilities would be over soon since France had been conquered!

Secrets leaked out regarding the plans for the ultimate proportions of the production sheds. They were going to be of vast size, four in number, one of 50,000 square metres and three of about 35,000. The greatest tractor works in the world in fact.

The engineers at Porsche's continued working on the tractors running at Hohenheim. The Russian campaign had started and Professor Porsche was tied up more and more in the inescapable maelstrom of war production. He designed the 'Ostradschlepper,' a traction engine which was a further development of the artillery one designed in the First World War. This, however, never reached the production stage for the Russian campaign was getting into ever worsening straits when the big traction engine was due to be tried. Porsche designed tanks and two of his models became famous within the framework of the German army: the Porsche 'Tiger' and the 'Ferdinand.'

A third tank design was the so-called 'Mouse.' This only existed in two prototypes and was therefore barely known. It was the biggest tank that had ever been built in the world — a colossus of 180 tons due to be used in the battlefield in the manner of a battleship and almost invulnerable with its armour plating of 250mm and the tremendous fire power of an 18cm gun. Since, however, there was hardly a bridge able to carry 180 tons, Porsche made the 'Mouse' waterproof so that it could 'wade' across rivers of up to 40ft in depth. In such a case however, two tanks were necessary with a cable to join them, for they were powered by electric motors.

All Porsche's tanks were powered by the same system he had invented in the far-off days when he worked for Lohner: the 'mixed drive' where a petrol or diesel engine drove an electric dynamo which in turn provided electric power for the hub-mounted motors which ensured a gearless, resilient drive. The 'Tiger' tanks of Porsche also had twin air-cooled engines, air cooling being a well-known speciality of Porsche's. Whether a supertank like the 'Mouse' had any technical value is easily answered. It had none. But it was not Professor Porsche's job to worry about this — he received the order to build such a colossus and although hardly any responsible person believed in the possibilities of realizing such an idea, Porsche did achieve the feat that this 180 ton tank actually ran and was manoeuvreable. To order the development of such a monster in the year 1944 in view of the war situation and the shortage of materials was unforgivably stupid.

In the meantime the Volkswagen proved to be very successful in its double guise, as an amphibious and a cross-country vehicle. It was successful on all fronts both in the — 40°F. cold of Russia or the 104°F. ground heat in Africa. The troops were happy with this unpretentious and many-sided vehicle. The cross-country VW became an accepted part of the infantryman's equipment. The Porsche engineers developed the VW engine also into a very useful stationary engine.

The last but one tractor development during the war was the type '113;' like the type '112' it had a 15bhp engine and with the aid of additional fittings had an even greater number of uses than before; its two cylinders were no longer in V-form but in-line, and air cooling by means of a ducted fan was retained.

But what happened to Waldbrol? As late as the beginning of 1944 production figures were set for the enormous factories which, however, only existed on paper and in model form. The first step was to produce 100,000 tractors per year by working two 8-hour shifts per day. The second step was a production of 200,000 and the third as much as 300,000 per annum; the latter figure meant 1,000 a day — such figures were even then discussed. But the war situation in 1944 made these plans collapse like a house of cards and the Waldbrol project quietly disappeared from the planning conferences. It was a Utopian project, like so many other things during that time. Never did Waldbrol see a factory, nor was a tractor ever made there.

A last project came into being in the summer of 1944. The Porsche type '293,' a tracked vehicle with a pulling power of 1 ton and seats for transporting people. At first, fifty of these were to be built, but because of the constant bombardment of Stuttgart it was no longer possible to produce them undisturbed and most of the parts of this tracked vehicle (which was also available in wheeled form) were made in Italy.

Then Professor Porsche received the order to transfer his works from Stuttgart to Carinthia. He was reluctant to comply with this, not only because conditions in the little Carinthian town of Gmund, south of the Katschberg, were very primitive, but also because to him Stuttgart had in the meantime become his second home and he simply did not want to leave it. Old Porsche had a very pronounced attachment to his native soil and also for the place in which he lived. Even the world of engineering could never get him away from this.

17 Gmünd–Porsche arrested

THEN came the debacle, and for Professor Porsche — now 70 years of age — and for his collaborators a hard and bitter time began. Rabe and his engineers were in Gmund and not even the railway ran as far as there; the design office was in a disused barracks beside which the cows grazed. The old professor and his son were on their estate near Zell am See, but between there and Gmund was the frontier between the zones and as Professor Porsche was now of German nationality he was not allowed to cross it.

In June 1945 the Americans took him to Hessen where, in an old castle, an interrogation centre for people of prominence had been set up. The old gentleman was treated with respect and given a little freedom. Speer said of him that it was stupid to lock him up, for he had never had the least thing to do with politics. A few weeks later he was given orders to return to Zell. On the return journey with his old chauffeur, he passed through Stuttgart and it seemed obvious to have a look at his former works at Zuffenhausen. It was still standing but had obviously been taken over by the occupational forces. The old professor asked to see the commanding officer to enquire if he would at least be allowed to walk through what had once been his works. They told Porsche that the commanding officer did not even wish to receive him and he, whose world of technical creation was entirely above the world of politics, just shook his head uncomprehendingly.

Rabe had in the meantime maintained the position in Gmund but how was he to earn money in this remote place in those days when there was no connection across the zone frontiers? One thing came about entirely by itself: in Austria, a great many Volkswagen cross-country and amphibious vehicles were in the hands of the Allies and those who followed them. These ex-German 'Wehrmacht' vehicles were partially in very poor condition. There were few workshops about and even those were not quite competent to deal with a Volkswagen and so they used to say: 'Why don't you go to Gmund, there you will find the people who designed this thing. They will be able to help you.'

So they started to repair old Volkswagens in Gmund, but that was not sufficient to provide a living. It was necessary to find work for the designers. Design cars? No longer of interest, there was nowhere to build them. Only one thing simply had to go on in those turbulent times: agriculture. As the Porsche engineers were familiar with the needs of farmers through the construction of tractors, the obvious thing to do then was to build agricultural equipment.

By using left-over tank track wheels they built two-wheeled carts. For the farmers they rebuilt reapers and made spares for other agricultural machines. The house of Porsche in Gmund collaborated closely with the agricultural co-operative in Klagenfurt and once again they designed tractors.

On 27th October 1945 there were already in existence exact blueprints for a new type suited to the requirements of the post-war period. It was called 'Diesel Tractor 313' and equipped with a four-stroke diesel engine, 2 cylinders in-line, air cooling by ducted fan, 1,400cc, and produced 17bhp at 2,000rpm. The front wheels were shod with 5.00in by 16in tyres and at the rear with 8.00in by 20in. Various extras and additional equipment were foreseen, such as a power take-off and couplings for agricultural equipment, a reaping attachment, trailer attachments and many others. All were hydraulically controlled. A grab and a hydraulic lifting device were also planned. But Professor Porsche was not allowed to witness the first triumph of the new tractor, he was only informed about it at a later stage for in the meantime he, with his son and his son-in-law Dr. Piech, were taken to Baden-Baden. The French were planning the construction of a people's car and Porsche was to design it. The negotiations started auspiciously, but the political tendencies in France changed quickly from one extreme to the other and suddenly Porsche was arrested and imprisoned without ever being told the reason. A few weeks later he was taken to Paris and there given quarters in the porter's lodge of Renault's villa. The first experimental cars of the '4 CV' had just been finished, but did not satisfy their engineers. Porsche's opinion was sought and he made a number of suggestions for improvement which were gratefully accepted by Renault.

Tough and wearying were the days of imprisonment for Porsche and his closest collaborators. Louise Piech, the professor's daughter, was anxious for her husband and father, whilst together with Rabe and Mickl she tried to keep the firm going. Ferry Porsche returned from imprisonment a little sooner than his father and thus was able to assist energetically on the current projects.

Two French friends and one Italian did, however prove themselves very helpful during those dark days; Raymond Sommer, the well-known French grand prix driver, Charles Faroux, the doyen of French motoring journalists, and Piero Dusio, an Italian industrialist who had in the meantime approached the Porsche office in Gmund with a number of enquiries.

18 Cisitalia project – Dusio

IN November 1946 Commendatore Piero Dusio, managing director and part owner of the Cisitalia works in Turin decided to build grand prix cars in his works, the design of which was to be entrusted to the Porsche office.

During the 'thirties Dusio had been a racing driver himself and in those days there were two types of championships in Italy, one for works drivers and the other for amateurs, private owners or call them what you will. In 1934 Piero Dusio, driving a blown 2.6-litre Alfa Romeo, became Italian champion of the latter category. In the championship list of the day other well-known names are inscribed: Count Lurani, Carlo Pintacuda, Moretti and Count Castelbarco. In the Mille Miglia of 1934 Dusio managed seventh place in the general classification — quite a feat, and in the Targa Abruzzo he battled long and hard with Guy Moll for the lead. The Italian paper *Gazetta dello Sport* wrote: 'Piero Dusio is not new to racing. His activity extends a few years back and he shows the qualities of a safe and reliable driver, fully deserving the championship.'

After the war he built sporting vehicles in his works and his idea of building grand prix cars arose from launching the successful little 1,100cc Cisitalia which in sports and racing form had scored a number of successes all over Europe, not only in its own class, but sometimes also in the general classification.

Between the years 1946 and 1949 almost all the famous racing drivers had tried the little Cisitalia: Ascari, Taruffi, Stuck, Bonetto, Nuvolari, and Lurani were all seen at the wheel; later these cars were bored out to 1,200cc. Let us recall the Mille Miglia of 1947 when Nuvolari very nearly won the general classification in a Cisitalia sports car and was finally only beaten by Biondetti with his 2.9-litre supercharged Alfa Romeo. Then there was Taruffi's second place in the overall classification of the Giro Sicilia in 1948 and the memorable 1,100cc race before the Grand Prix of Switzerland in Berne in 1948 where Taruffi won before Stuck and Bonetto. Cisitalia then managed to beat the entire phalanx of Simca-Gordini.

Piero Dusio had high ambitions and the little 1,100cc racer was not enough. To gain world acclaim it was necessary to race a grand prix car and one had to have the most brilliant designers, especially if one wished to have it running in the shortest possible time. Since Germany had lost the war, the Porsche people in Austria were not too well off, which meant that a lot of wonderful brains were lying fallow there, ready to be made use of. Dusio had also further ambitions apart from building the grand prix car; a 1,500cc sports car was to be constructed and were not the Porsche engineers able to design tractors? And what about turbines?

The first negotiations with the executives of Porsche took place during early December of 1946 in Zell am See. These resulted in four orders which the Cisitalia company placed with the Porsche office: a grand prix car which was given the design number 'type 360,' a 1,500cc sports-racing car (Porsche 'type 370'), an 11hp small tractor (Porsche 'type 323'), and a water turbine (Porsche 'type 385'). All this was to be designed by Porsche for Cisitalia and production would be realized under the name of Cisitalia.

We know however that during this time Professor Porsche was not at home but, together with his son-in-law Dr. Piech, in prison in Dijon. Ferry Porsche had returned from prison but the man officially in charge at the house of Porsche and who signed the contracts with Dusio was chief engineer Rabe.

Two further men who had important roles during these first negotiations with Cisitalia were Messrs. Hruschka and Abarth who received authority on the 10th December 1946 to negotiate on behalf of Porsche and look after their interests. Hruschka, an engineer, had already worked as liaison for Porsche at the end of the war in Italy and was supposed to direct the planned Porsche tractor production at the O.M. factory. Abarth used to race on the dirt track in Austria and was personally known to several of the people at Porsche's, but was not a member of the firm. Hruschka later became a director of Alfa Romeo, and Abarth achieved renown later through his special exhaust manifolds and expansion chambers and in the last few years through his Fiat-based sports and granturismo cars.

Of the four projects Dusio designated the grand prix car as the most important. On 6th December 1946 it was decided that the first basic drawings should reach Cisitalia in three months and Dusio affirmed that the Turin industry would give him every support with the manufacture of parts and supply of accessories, but he expected the designs to be advanced to such a degree by September 1947 that the first car could be assembled; he had gone to Porsche's especially because there his plans would be translated most quickly into reality.

Ferry Porsche went immediately to Vienna to get the necessary official permits, especially the one concerning money transfers. We seem hardly to remember today how difficult such international orders were, especially during the days of strict Allied control.

Dusio appeared very worried about his project. As late as December 1946 he demanded a statement from Porsche's office to the following effect. Was it likely, he asked, that due to the absence of Professor Porsche the car would be delayed or perhaps would not win a race later? Were they *au fait* in Gmund with everything that Professor Porsche was doing in France, and what would happen if he were to design a similar racing car there? Finally, Dusio wanted to know whether perhaps Porsche had designed a 1,500cc Auto-Union racing car at the beginning of the war and was this likely to turn up somewhere one day?

This particular rumour floated through the technical press for a long time and it was even said that the Cisitalia project was nothing but an extension of the 1,500cc Auto-Union racing car which had been planned a long time ago. This, however, was not correct, for the Cisitalia was an entirely new design without direct antecedents. The fee, which was to be paid by Dusio to Ferry Porsche and his office, served to a degree to provide the exceptionally high sum which France required to release Professor Porsche from Dijon. The old gentleman arrived on 5th August 1947 in Kitzbuhl where the French kept him first of all at the Hotel Klausner. He was not allowed to travel to Gmund or to his estate at Zell. Two days later there was a discussion between Professor Porsche, his son Ferry and chief engineer Rabe, when the general layout of the Cisitalia grand prix car was submitted to him for the first time. Porsche studied the drawings for a long time in silence and said at last: 'If I had designed it I would not have done it any differently.'

87

Now to the technical details of the Cisitalia. During a discussion on 20th December 1946 at Porsche's it was decided to have a flat 12-cylinder engine of 55.5mm stroke and 56mm bore amounting to 1,492.6cc. The stroke/bore relationship therefore was over-square in the ratio of 0.902 : 1, in other words even more so than the BRM. The first design was reckoned to run up to 10,000rpm with an average piston speed of 3,315ft/min. The power output was conservatively suggested as 300bhp at 8,500rpm and a maximum torque of approximately 195 lb/ft at 6,000rpm. The 12-cylinder flat opposed engine had 4 shaft-driven overhead camshafts, 2 to each block of 6 cylinders. One 18mm sparking plug per cylinder was foreseen and two valves; there was to be a Hirth crankshaft and dry-sump lubrication. The supercharging was going to be by means of two Centric blowers, although in the very first project three Roots-type superchargers were suggested. The superchargers were geared at 10 : 17, in other words 8,500rpm of the engine corresponded to 5,000rpm for the blowers. A maximum boost of 3 atmospheres was arranged and two Weber twin-choke carburettors were to supply the superchargers with mixture.

The valves were designed at an included angle of 90 degrees, but the sparking plug was not fitted vertically into the head but curiously offset not only from the vertical, but also from the cylinder axis.

From the first the vehicle was to have four-wheel drive which could be engaged or disconnected by means of a lever underneath the steering wheel. Thus they hoped to increase the adhesion of the wheels during acceleration, which, with a power/weight ratio in the region of 3½ to 4½ lb per horsepower and the resulting wheel-spin tendency, could be very important. Four-wheel drive seldom appears in racing car design because this arrangement means increased weight, which in itself nullifies a part of the extra accelera-tion. Also there is a likelihood of increased mechanical trouble due to the additional drive of the front wheels.

The last Porsche-designed racing car, the Auto-Union of 1934, had a rear engine and, provided that first class drivers were available, the results obtained with this system were quite satisfactory, therefore the Cisitalia racing car was also so arranged. Contrary to the Auto-Union and later to the Porsche Spyder, the Cisitalia not only had the engine and clutch but also had the gearbox in front of the rear axle so that the rear wheels really became the rearmost part of the car.

The 5-speed gearbox of the Cisitalia was the first of the ring-synchronized gearboxes, but with the difference that not all pinions were equipped with a synchronizing ring. For the five speeds, only two rings operated — one for changing up and one for changing down. The gear wheels were in constant mesh and gear changing was on the motor-cycle system which meant either pushing or pulling the gear lever forward or backward. To push it forward meant changing up, and pulling back, changing down. The first designs also considered the possibility of alternative hand and foot changing. We have said that the gear wheels were in constant mesh, which meant of course that the bottom gear pair would have to withstand terrific revolutions if, in fifth gear, one had reached 10,000rpm; in fact, they would rise to 30,000rpm if a gear ratio of 3 : 1 in relation to the 1 : 1 fifth gear is taken into consideration. No gear wheels could have withstood this for any length of time and therefore a step-down bevel box was fitted before the gearbox to reduce the revolutions to the ratio of 10 :4.8.

This step-down gear was so arranged that the shaft leading to the front drive was placed as low as possible. In front, the drive was stepped up by means of another bevel box so as to be level with the front differential and three universal joints were incorp-orated in the drive shaft; a limited-slip differential was fitted to the rear axle only. Based on an axle ratio for a fast circuit and presupposing a fully-aerodynamic body, Rabe conservatively assumed a power output of 300bhp with a torque of 155 lb/ft, enabling the following speeds to be obtained: first gear 80mph, second 102mph, third 127mph, fourth 157mph and fifth 210mph.

Springing was on the traditional Porsche system of torsion bars front and rear and the rear wheels were also located laterally by long suspension arms; hydraulic shock absorbers were planned for front and rear. Two-leading-shoe brakes were to be fitted in the normal manner, brake-drum diameter being 340mm and the width of the brake shoes 55mm, and extra large air scoops for the drums were provided. The centre-lock wire wheels had 5.50in by 17in or 5.00in by 18in tyres as necessary. Track was identical in front and rear at 130cm, and wheelbase 260cm. The long wheelbase arose, of course, out of the rear engine layout, and the overall length was just over 13ft. The bodywork had a long and low bonnet, the air intake to the engine being placed very low. The Cisitalia engine was liquid-cooled with a radiator containing some 5 gallons and the cooling medium was to be glycol.

The chassis was a space frame in chrome-molybdenum steel. The fuel filler was directly in front of the driver's seat, the tank was not over the front suspension, but ran alongside the chassis on both sides of the driver's seat. Each side contained about 21 gallons. Since in those days alcohol-based fuel was permitted, the compression ratio was 15 : 1.

Dry weight of the car (without fuel and oil) amounted to 718 kilos and 344 of those were on the front axle and 374 on the rear. The weight distribution therefore had the relationship of 47.9 to 52.1, which hardly changed when the tanks were full, for they were disposed around the centre of gravity of the car.

Naturally the car would have been a little lighter if only rear wheel drive had been used, but the Porsche people thought that the additional weight of four-wheel drive was more than justified. Professor Eberan von Eberhorst had made some very thorough calculations concerning this question. As a matter of fact he had been called in to help in the development of the Cisitalia car but only appeared on the scene after the principal layout had been fixed. Let us be more specific. On 21st February 1947 chief engineer Rabe sent to Eberan on orders from Ferry Porsche, a handwritten list of questions which was referred to as highly confidential. Since they had no data in Gmund regarding the details of the Auto-Union racing car, yet wanted to draw on the experience obtained with it, they asked Professor Eberan such questions as 'What was the thermal value of the racing fuel in the Auto-Union days? What was the material from which the connecting rods were made? How was frothing of engine oil overcome? What were the oil temperatures used? What was the influence of fuel vaporizing on the working of the supercharger? What was the overall efficiency of the Roots blower?' Professor Eberan went to Gmund in the spring of 1947 and worked there in an advisory capacity without being employed by Porsche's. As far as the calculations for four-wheel drive were concerned he worked out an interesting comparative set of figures in June 1947 in respect of the type 360. The rear-drive only car was assumed to weigh 650 kilos and the four-wheel drive one 720; engine output was the conservatively estimated figure of 300bhp, and an air resistance factor of Cw = 0.288, which was below the factual value, was assumed. The calculation was based on one kilometre from a standing start. Assuming a frictional value of the road surface of 0.9 the car with rear-wheel drive would have covered the standing kilometre at 174.8kph and the four-wheel drive one at 188.0kph; had the friction coefficient been 1.0 the figures would have been 181.1 and 191.0 respectively (the Auto-Union car with which Rosemeyer put up the world records in 1937 weighed, inclusive of driver, 960 kilos. It had a 4-speed gearbox and a Cw factor of 0.621). Eberan pointed out in particular that the advantage of four-wheel drive would tend to increase the more slippery the road surface became.

None of the engineers from Porsche's offices were permanently at Cisitalia's in Turin; they all worked in Gmund, but Hruschka and Abarth, who were in Italy anyway, were both employed by Cisitalia.

To try out the engine design, a single-cylinder test rig was built which had the same

89

capacities, same supercharger pressures and revolutions as the planned engine. With this rig Cisitalia made extensive tests and on the basis of these a number of improvements in detail were incorporated which increased the estimated power of the planned engine to 450bhp at 10,500rpm, a most satisfactory result.

But Cisitalia did not possess a sufficiently large and high revving dynamometer and when the first engine was getting towards its finishing stage they bought a used installation from Fiat and rebuilt it. The completed engine was, however, never brake-tested in Italy to the extent where the maximum power output at those very high revolutions was established. The engine was certainly put on to the dynamometer to run it in and to test it on part load. The 450bhp (i.e. 305bhp/litre), although an exact estimate from the engineers' point of view and based on experiments with the single-cylinder rig, was never realized on the engine itself.

Dusio had great hopes that the Cisitalia grand prix car would be on its wheels in the spring of 1948 although in all probability he had overestimated his own financial means and underestimated the material and labour involved in the construction of a grand prix car. It was quite obvious that a vehicle bristling with so many new design features could not be made into a runner in a little over a year, but it shows Dusio's serious intentions when it became apparent that he had ordered spares for a total of six grand prix cars or started manufacturing them himself, for, according to him and Porsche, six cars were necessary to set up a complete grand prix stable.

Auto Italiana published a note on 15th November 1948 according to which the design development work on the Cisitalia grand prix car was almost completed. Apparently, they went on to say, the car, which was giving about 400bhp, would soon be tested at Monza. A lot of people pricked up their ears on seeing this paragraph; not only the sporting enthusiasts but also the financial experts, for during the late summer of 1948 Dusio's works were in a doubtful financial position occasioned by the heavy expenditure on the planned construction of six grand prix cars.

At that time Commendatore Dusio had started negotiating with the Argentine and the first press commentary about this appeared on 11th November 1948 in an Italian paper. The headline stated: 'Italo-Argentinian contract concerning large industrial undertakings.' The article mentioned that the Argentine government, in the person of General Peron, was in the process of forming a company called 'Autoar' which was to undertake the construction of touring and sports cars, also commercial vehicles and tractors. Autoar was a shortening of the complete title: Auto Motores Argentinos. The press went on to say that the chairman and managing director of the Argentinian company was to be Piero Dusio and technical collaboration from Porsche and leading Italian engineers had been ensured.

The Autoar plan meant the beginning of the transfer of the Cisitalia project to the Argentine and, to be truthful, not before time, for in February 1949 the Cisitalia works were in such financial difficulties that the creditors — mostly accessory manufacturers — got a preliminary judgement at the Turin law courts, for the debts at the time amounted to 240 million lire. At the same time 400 workmen at Cisitalia went to court in respect of wage arrears amounting to 25 million lire, but the management of the Cisitalia works appealed against the judicial sequestration and, for the time being work continued.

The news item in *Auto Italiana* in the autumn of 1948 was premature and on 30th March 1949 Gmund was advised that the preliminary tests had not been concluded and that the gearbox and rear axle would still have to be checked and therefore there was no question as yet of testing the completed car. They did, however, invite Nuvolari to inspect the car and he was also photographed at the wheel of it in company with Dusio, but obviously these pictures were made for propaganda purposes. Nuvolari never did drive the car and indeed, it never ran in Italy. It must be said, however, that the first of the planned six cars was completely built in Italy.

To reduce the negotiations with the Argentine to their simplest denominator, it can be said that in the summer of 1949 Peron was prepared to cover Dusio's debts, provided he and his engineers plus the entire Cisitalia project with the completed car and the finished parts would come over to the Argentine. Anyway, Porsche's received a telegram in Gmund on 12th May 1949 from Dusio in Buenos Aires in which he said that he was happy to announce that all basic arrangements with the president's office and the ministries concerned had been concluded.

At this point 420 workers and employees at Cisitalia were given notice, with the result that no further work was carried out on the grand prix car. Dusio's wife sold her palazzo in Turin to satisfy some of the creditors.

In South America matters financial do not progress very quickly unless palms are extensively 'greased.' thus it took about a year before the Cisitalia grand prix car was shipped from Turin to the Argentine. At that time the Porsche office had other worries and the engineers were preparing the move from Gmund to Stuttgart; this happened on 14th March 1950, on which day an inventory was taken at the Cisitalia works in Turin to know exactly what could be taken to the Argentine.

During this inventory it became apparent that a complete grand pix car existed and so did the largest part of a second car, but not entirely assembled. The second car was short of the distributors, magnetos, fuel pumps, valves, oil tanks, brake master cylinders and other small parts. As far as cars numbered 3 to 6 were concerned only a few parts were available which could not remotely be built into complete vehicles.

Negotiations in the Argentine took a long time and only in the autumn of 1950 was there any consolidation of Autoar; at the beginning of September Peron officially visited the firm. Suddenly the German papers brought sensational news: 'The turning point of racing — Fangio will drive a Porsche design,' thus proclaimed the banner headlines. Named Cisitalia, but under the Argentinian flag with Peron's protection and handled by Argentinian top-class drivers, Fangio and Gonzales, this Porsche, the most modern grand prix car, would be seen in action during the first races of the 1951 season: 'Peron has now decided to use the Cisitalia-Porsches and three experimental racing cars with all spares and equipment have been shipped to the Argentine....'

Yes, those were the news items, but the truth was different: there was no question of three cars, for not even the first was ready to race. (Ferry Porsche said: 'Argentina is far away and so the umbilical cord to the car has been cut off if we no longer look after it.') Fangio drove for Alfa Romeo in 1951 and Gonzales for Ferrari. Pomeroy of *The Motor* said: 'With a dry weight of about 720 kilos, a small frontal area and an engine giving about 380 to 450bhp, together with four-wheel drive, the Cisitalia is potentially the most fantastic racing car that has ever been seen in the world and it is very regrettable that the financial difficulties in Turin prevented the Porsche 360, which bristles with ingenious ideas, from being seen on the racing circuits of Europe.'

During 1951 and 1952 little was heard of the car and Porsche's in Stuttgart were no longer comprehensively informed what was happening to it; apart from that they had almost forgotten it for the Formula 1 of those days (1,500cc supercharged) was still theoretically current until 1953 but practically it had died at the end of 1951, for at that time Alfa Romeo had renounced participation in motor racing, Ferrari had developed a 2-litre car and so had Maserati. Thus almost all races in 1952 and 1953 were according to Formula 1 which laid down a cubic capacity of 2-litres without supercharger. At the same time the new Formula 1 of 2½-litres unsupercharged was on the horizon and this was due to come into operation in 1954. Corrado Millanta in his 'Italian Diary' which at that time he used to write for the Stuttgart paper *Auto, Motor und Sport* said on 25th October 1952 that Cisitalia was waking up again and that father and son Dusio were about to get their works in Italy to function again. He said that they were progressing by small steps. Next to the motor works was a large shed in which 300 women with sewing machines

91

were producing uniforms in large quantities and the considerable amount of money thus coming in was benefitting the motor works in which the type '303', a sporting 1,100cc cheaper than the previous car but as attractive, was being made. Another model built incorporated a 2,500cc 4-cylinder BPM (motor-boat) engine.

They did try once at Cisitalia to get into motor car production by making touring cars with sporting tendencies, but these products had nothing in common with the Porsche designs of 1946 and 1947. However, this experiment also ended in difficulties and the newly started production stopped again.

Millanta continued in October 1952: 'There is yet another sensational news item. Dusio intends to develop the famous Cisitalia racing car further. He told us that he would go and see Porsche to find out exactly if and how it would be possible to fit a 2 or 2.5 normally aspirated engine into the 1,500cc chassis. Apparently only one car was taken to the Argentine and parts for three or four other cars were still at Cisitalia.' (But Millanta was not correctly informed. Although there were certain parts available, they were neither sufficient nor finished to the degree necessary to produce a complete vehicle). He continued: 'From an entirely personal point of view we would be pleased if this racing car could become reality, for we were very close to it when it was "born" in 1946-47.' However, reality was very far removed from Millanta's hopes. Not even the first steps were undertaken to fit an engine of the new formula into the Cisitalia chassis. The basic idea probably came from the Italian grand prix driver Bonetto, yet Millanta was absolutely right when he said that he was present at the birth of the Cisitalia grand prix car for he was the go-between for Porsche and Dusio and he furthered and interpreted the project.

In this late autumn of 1952 plans came into being in the Argentine to infuse new life into the Cisitalia racing car. Two reports exist about that period; one by the Italian Gianni Rogliatti which appeared in the Italian technical paper *Velocita* in 1957 and the other report was from the pen of the Argentinian motoring correspondents Hansen and Kirbus in the London paper *Autosport* on 16th November 1956.

Rogliatti starts his report with a melancholy sentence:

'All stories concerning something that did not achieve its object are sad, yet this is more than a sad story, it is an interesting romance which deals with the end of a car that should have been the most extraordinary racing car of its time.

'One fine day in December 1951, the height of summer in the southern hemisphere, I went with a friend to the Autoar works near Buenos Aires and there in the stores under a dust sheet was "the vehicle." Even today I can remember the tremendous impact its sight made upon me. In the days of the Alfetta, the Maserati 4 CLT and the Talbot, the Porsche seemed smaller, lighter, more compact and very low. The constructional details were extraordinary.'

Rogliatti says, quite rightly, that use of this vehicle would have been problematical since cars designed by Germans tended always to be more complicated than others. The specialized personnel was missing, and those who directed Autoar did not seem very enthusiastic. In the meantime the car was painted in the Argentine colours, yellow and blue, and the name was changed from Cisitalia to Autoar. After a few months and within sight of the 1953 season they decided to try and put the car into operation.

The basic idea was to let the Autoar-Cisitalia start at the end of January 1953 in the Buenos Aires Grand Prix being run under *formula libre* rules which meant that even a Formula 1. 1.5-litre supercharged car could be entered.

But could was the operative word, for the car was a non-starter because there was not enough time to prepare it. Kirbus and Hansen wrote: 'A few days before, 275-280bhp had been attained at 8,000rpm and the car was hurriedly tested on the Friday before the race, on a straight in San Isidro, near Buenos Aires, where it was discovered that the ground clearance of slightly over 3½ inches was insufficient in view of the soft suspension. Just in time for final practising and classification trials on the Saturday, the car appeared suddenly at Buenos Aires Autodrome, where the ever helpful Felice Bonetto offered to try a couple of laps with it. It should be noted that it had been found that the final drive ratios in the front and rear drives were different, a discrepancy which it was attempted to eliminate by the use of differently sized tyres.'

Bonetto was not happy with the machine and after the first lap he stopped at the pits with the car enveloped in a tremendous cloud of smoke. This was only due to a leaking oil line dripping onto the hot exhaust, and was easily put right, but the car could only be run with rear wheel drive. Clemar Bucci, an Argentinian racing driver, drove the car for two slow laps and found that the gears could not be properly engaged and several times he accidentally selected neutral which was present between each gear. Under these conditions it was realized that the car could not start in the race and Autoar duly withdrew the entry.

They said that Bonetto had put up a lap of 2 minutes 32 seconds, which was a very good first lap if compared with the lap record of the time by Ascari in 2 minutes 20 seconds. As far as the road holding and brakes were concerned both Bonetto and Bucci were extremely satisfied, for they came up to the best grand prix standard; however, the engine seemed nowhere near ready. It was taken away again and partially dismantled. According to Rogliatti however, the Argentinian directors became more and more impatient and even the chief engineer Rossi who had come from Fiat got fed up with this and left.

In the early summer of 1953 the engine was once more put on to the dynamometer and Rogliatti stated that tests produced 385bhp at 9,000rpm, whereas Hansen and Kirbus wrote that 365bhp had been reached at 10,500rpm.

Encouraged by these results Bucci was asked to undertake record attempts in July 1953, for until that time the South American record for the flying kilometre stood at 140mph. This had been established by an unknown driver from Chile and could have been lowered by any racing car of the period, but, like so many local records, it had been forgotten. Now they had the idea at Autoar to push the record up to about 187mph.

'At last and during the Argentinian winter, with midday temperatures of near freezing and a strong wind, they managed to get the engine going, but due to the unsuitable fuel mixture it did not get warm enough and the plugs sooted up. Eventually Bucci started and managed 146.6mph at 7,000rpm in one direction. During the attempt in the opposite direction an oil pipe broke, a piston was holed and the engine stopped just after Bucci reached 142.2mph. The resulting average of 144.7 was of course ridiculous for this type of car, but the political result was worse, for further attempts were stopped and the car was pushed aside.'

Let us reproduce Rogliatti's final sentence in his report: 'And so ended, forgotten, one of the most interesting cars of all times, a vehicle that demonstrated the intelligence of the person who had designed it....a mechanical jewel fit to occupy the place of honour in a museum.'

Whilst Rogliatti wrote this, the car was gathering rust and dust in a small garage in Buenos Aires. That it should be in a place of honour in a museum was certainly a justified comment and Ferry Porsche was also of this opinion. Thus, in the spring of 1959, they brought this 'mechanical jewel' back to Germany, to the Porsche Museum in Stuttgart that was opened in the autumn of 1959. And so there has been a consoling end to the sad story of the Cisitalia which now stands on view in the Museum.

19 Ferry Porsche

IT is now time to include a more personal chapter which should be entitled: Ferry, the son. For it was Ferry Porsche together with chief designer Rabe who settled on the most important fundamentals of the Cisitalia grand prix car and although the British had put in Rabe as 'official custodian' it was Ferry Porsche who took over the management of the Austrian business whilst his father was in prison.

Ferry Porsche was born on 19th September 1909 on a day when his father was at the Semmering where a race was in progress. When he returned home that night they told him: You have a son! Ferry grew up in the paternal villa close to the works in Wiener-Neustadt, in a large park in which there was a market garden, stables, two cows, geese and chickens. Close by was a tennis court — in other words a veritable boy's paradise. In 1913 he had his first pedal driven car which was built for his father at Austro-Daimler exactly in the shape of the Prince Henry Trial car. The next one was a tricycle with pneumatic tyres and then a bicycle from Puch; naturally the latter was not an ordinary one but a racing one weighing only 14½ pounds.

For Christmas 1919, when he was only 10, he was given his first 'real' car. It had a 2-cylinder air-cooled engine as used on the little Austro-Daimler narrow gauge loco-motive, two speeds forward, a leather lined cone clutch, rear wheel drive without differential and the front axle was similar to the one fitted to the Ford model T.

Father Porsche wanted to explain to his son how to drive, but before father could say a word, the boy drove round the park, managing the clutch very neatly. When father furiously asked him who had taught him to drive Ferry admitted in a small voice to having started to drive six months ago and having used the various vehicles around the works, some of these being ancient Daimlers with chain drive and external gear change. His feet were not strong enough to use the clutch whilst sitting, so that when he changed gear he had to operate the clutch standing up.

Dr. Porsche was understanding and even the police in Wiener-Neustadt knew of the little car driven by Ferry Porsche. Obviously his father had strictly forbidden him to drive it on the public roads for it had no registration number, but this did not disturb young Ferry very much. He simply trusted to luck and hoped that the son of the managing director of the largest motor-car works in Austria would not get into trouble. The police grinned, closed both eyes, and Ferry motored around the entire district even as far as 14 miles away.

The little car, producing about 3½bhp, was also driven around in winter and due to its narrow track, good ground clearance, and absence of a differential it would sometimes get through where other vehicles had long become stuck. When the lad drove it fast he had to be careful lest the front tyres left the rims when cornering.

The simpler servicing, such as adjusting brakes and clutch, he did himself in the paternal garage. Only one thing was definitely forbidden and he kept to it: he was not allowed to drive his little car to school. In Wiener-Neustadt Ferry Porsche first of all went to the elementary school, then to the first two forms of secondary school, later after the family moved to Stuttgart, Ferry went to the next higher grades of secondary school.

Father Porsche viewed the driving attempts of his son with critical eyes and on the whole was satisfied with him. When he was barely 13 Ferry was permitted to drive a Sascha sports car within the confines of the works. When Goldinger the chauffeur was not present, Ferry drove the family cars from the garage to the villa. At the beginning of 1923 he planned to assemble a car himself, having acquired a number of reject parts from the Sascha production.

The authorities were more severe in Stuttgart, but he rode a light motor-cycle at the age of 14 and they gave him a special permit for this. At 16, in the autumn of 1925, they let him pass the car driving test. From now on he was present at every experimental or test run which his father undertook provided there was enough time, and old Porsche often let him drive and sat by his side. He trusted his 16-year-old son implicitly.

He was hardly 17 when he drove an experimental Mercedes back to Stuttgart from the family's summer holiday place on the Worther See. Although the roads of the period did not have very good surfaces one could still achieve relatively high averages because the traffic density compared with today was minimal. Ferry particularly liked driving the 15/17/100hp Mercedes and also the K type, both of which were used experimentally by the family for a certain period. Even during the time in Wiener-Neustadt Ferry used to spend odd evenings or Sunday in the design office purely from curiosity and some of the designs from those days have remained in his memory. He asked his father childishly naive questions to get to the bottom of things but old Porsche never explained technical drawings unless his son specifically asked for it and whilst Ferdinand Porsche was at Daimler young Ferry often came 'visiting' in the design office. Around Easter 1928 his father sent him to Bosch for a year's thorough apprenticeship. His sister Louise passed her driving test at 18 and drove a lot and very well. Like all youngsters Ferry naturally also wanted to ride a motor-cycle and once he had a 500 BMW, but father took that away later, motor-cycling being too dangerous for the boy. After his time at Bosch, Ferry followed his father to Steyr where he received systematic instruction in mechanics, mathematics and technical drawing.

After the Porsche design office in Stuttgart was founded, Ferry was engaged quite officially as a draughtsman. Apart from this, his father used him as a test driver, especially on the 2-litre Wanderer which had just been built. He was given certain sectors of work such as shock-absorber tests, carburation problems and collaboration with the electrical engineers at Bosch.

When NSU commissioned the type '32,' the predecessor to the Volkswagen, Ferry was delegated to NSU as liaison for Porsche and later he also collaborated on the designs of the Auto-Union racing car. He first competed in a minor event in 1926, a club rally of the Automobile Club of Wurttemberg. The year 1934 saw him compete in a three-day Harz Rally which in those days was a classic event in Germany. He drove the 2-litre Wanderer and finished in his class as the only unpenalized competitor. Auto-Union sent an official Wanderer team for the 2,000 kilometre Baden-Baden rally; the cars were two-seaters with closed aerodynamic bodywork. Ferry Porsche was 24 then and one of the team — so was a certain Bernd Rosemeyer. Ferry was quite talented and in the first section through the Black Forest, a road well known to him from test runs, he was even faster than

Ferry Porsche

Rosemeyer, his co-driver being good old Goldinger.

The first road-trials of the Auto-Union racing car saw Ferry at the wheel, but in the following years his father would not let him drive in competitions, for in the elder Porsche's words, 'He might get to like this sort of thing and want to become a racing driver, but his job is to design.' He was then charged with interesting detail work concerning the supercharger and the crankshaft of the Auto-Union racing car.

Ferry was married in 1935 and had four sons: Ferdinand, Gerhard, Peter and Wolfgang. In 1937 he went to the United States with his father and this trip provided him with very valuable impressions. In 1939 he was assistant works manager of the Zuffenhausen works; during the war he escaped call-up and in 1944 arranged the move of the works from Stuttgart to Carinthia and very cleverly circumvented the government's plan to transfer the firm into a district that today is in Czechoslovakia. On 29th July 1946 he got back to the family estate at Zell am See after having been released from French imprisonment. This estate has since become his second home within the close circle of the family.

Somebody is bound to ask what his hobbies are. He started ski-ing at the age of 7 and is good at it, as is his sister. When he is on the Worthersee he likes sailing and has participated in regattas. He also likes to hunt occasionally. He is a great dog lover, preferring airedales and fox terriers. Although devoted to engineering and sport he cannot be said to be a man of closely circumscribed interests. There is hardly a problem which one cannot discuss with him; as opposed to others, he is modest, sometimes even too much so and tends towards shyness: an introspective engineer, whose horizons are world-wide.

20 Ferry Porsche–The 356

IT was Ferry Porsche who, in the winter of 1947-48, gave the impetus to develop further a car which had taken shape on the drawing boards under the type number '356' at the time when the first Cisitalia orders were received. The 356 project was not all that new, for as we have seen, the house of Porsche had ideas concerning a VW sports car with a 1,500cc engine before the war. In those days the German workers front had dismissed the sports car idea, but now there was no one to forbid it.

The main problem consisted in the obtaining of parts, and for the first 356 sports prototype most of the electrical equipment was purchased in Switzerland, the Bosch plugs on the other hand being obtained from Germany by one of the employees filling his trouser pockets full of plugs prior to crossing the frontier. There was probably a personal reason why the sports car had to be built, for the Porsche engineers repaired old army Volkswagens and the main transport consisted of such cars, but these were not to Ferry's taste.

Naturally, they investigated in several countries whether there would be a likely market for such a sports car, for Austria was far too small to absorb a series of such vehicles but to create interest it was first necessary to build prototypes.

In the spring of 1948 the chassis was ready. They were not quite courageous enough to build a fixed-head coupe, but wanted to produce an open two-seater at first. A frame was designed, the engine was placed in front of the rear axle and the gearbox aft of this, but there was as yet not enough luggage room, for the fuel tank was in front with the spare wheel. An 1,131cc Volkswagen engine was fitted; springing front and rear, steering and gearbox were original VW parts. At first the engine had a single downdraught carburettor, but later two were fitted. Compression was put up to 7 : 1 which was a risk because of the very poor petrol then available in Austria. Considerable modifications to the cylinder head had taken place and the result was near enough 40bhp.

This first Porsche, bodied as an open two-seater, weighed about 1,340 lb and thus had a power/weight ratio of 33 lbs per hp; with the result that it was a lively vehicle. The chassis had run for the first time in March and the completed car in the last days of May 1948. Professor Eberan von Eberhorst had also tested the car; quite close to Gmund is the Katschberg, which at that time had a 1 in 3½ gradient on the northern side (nowadays it has been flattened out to a mere 1 in 6). This was an ideal testing ground. Not far from

Gmund was also the Grossglockner and the pass road across it had been finished before the war. Incidentally, in 1938 before the Grossglockner race was held, Dr. Porsche demonstrated his first Volkswagen there and proved that the car had a useful performance even in the high mountains.

On this road shortly after Heiligenblut, Ferry Porsche broke down whilst testing the 356 prototype in company with the engineer Rupilius, who later went to the Argentine. A suspension arm broke on the rear axle, but fortunately a highway maintenance depot was not far away. It was evening, around 7 o'clock, but the sun was still shining. Ferry Porsche went into the building and found the people there very co-operative, especially as they had an old VW desert car for official use. Porsche and Rupilius found in the material store a couple of pieces of U-section steel which fitted near enough. In a very primitive manner they drilled holes into one of these and in just over two hours the car was running again.

The car was sold at the beginning of September 1948 for 7,000 francs to Switzerland; such amounts of foreign currency were then exceedingly necessary for Porsche to be able to finance the purchase of spare parts which came from Switzerland. This was scarcely a legal transaction, but how else were they to exist or to build cars? The prototype stayed in Switzerland for years, passing through several hands in the meantime. In 1954 a young Swiss driver managed to get second place in the Kandersteg hill climb in the sports car class with this prototype, into which a 1,500cc super engine had then been fitted; the car was very light, of course.

Porsche bought it back in 1958 for the museum and when one looks at it very closely today, one can see that the U-sectioned piece from the road menders is there still.

It had been planned from the very beginning to fit the type 356 with a fixed head coupe, the open two-seater being only a provisional prototype. The first report in the technical press about the 356 appeared in a prominent position in the Berne technical paper *Automobil-Revue* dated 17th July 1948, and its title was 'The youngest scion of a great name'. The tester in the *Automobil-Revue* wrote: 'It will not be necessary in the future for enthusiastic owners of Volkswagens to tune their cars for extra performance, for the man really able to do this is seeing to it that a special vehicle will soon be available: it is Professor Porsche himself. Not long ago the Porsche design company, now operating from Gmund in Carinthia, in the British zone of Austria, began road tests with the prototype of a newly created sports car, the type 356, and the results are now completed with such success that it will soon be possible to think about series production. This car, which is derived from the Volkswagen, has incorporated in it the extensive experience of Porsche and his staff, experience gained during the design and conception of the Auto-Union racing car. Apart from small differences, the engine, transmission and suspension are like those used on the Volkswagen. Entirely new, however, is the chassis, which is exceptionally stiff in torsion and which is of box-section with a rigid floor. To suit this it is fitted with an aerodynamic body in the shape of a two-seater coupe.'

Thus the Porsche 356 was presented for the first time internationally and the tester continued: 'Porsche built first of all a two-seater open sports car as an experimental vehicle and the purchaser of this, Mr. R. von Senger from Zurich kindly lent it to us last week for a short test drive. During the practice period of the impending grand prix we batted this vehicle round the Bremgarten circuit and became very confident with it in a very short time. This is how we imagine modern road motoring to be, where the advantages of modern springing and the resultant driving comfort are combined with the adhesion of an equally modern, low and handy sports car.'

The house of Porsche could be well satisfied with such a test report and in the following weeks and months orders began to come in from every country. Twenty cars were wanted in Sweden, fifty in Holland, twenty of the latter immediately if possible.

From Portugal there was an order for fifteen cars with the remark that if there were problems regarding import and export licences then they would be prepared to offer compensating business with Austria, supplying sardines in return for Porsche cars!

In the year 1948 the problem of import licences was a tremendous one. Soon there came a telegram from Holland stating that at the moment there would be no import licences for sports cars from Austria. On the other hand, Porsche's at Gmund would not have been able to cope with such large orders in so short a time for there was a shortage of material and skilled workers. One must also remember that this little town in Carinthia was not even connected to the railway line — how then was one to produce a reasonable series of motor cars under such conditions? The first coupe was finished at the end of August 1948 so that in the photograph showing it together with the prototype, both have Carinthian registration numbers. In the winter of 1948-49 small scale production started and five cars per month were built. All bodywork in those days was executed by hand over wooden formers by a panel beater whom Porsche had known personally from the days at Austro-Daimler. This man, who was undoubtedly an artist in his field, was the be-all and end-all of the entire production for a period of six months. When he did not work, the production stopped so to speak, and this happened frequently, for he was somewhat fond of a drink. If artists have such weaknesses then they have to be respected, for on the other hand when delivery schedules became too much behindhand, he did work through the night on numerous occasions.

Altogether, Porsche's in Gmund then employed about 300 people, including the design technicians who, then as now, had a number of orders from abroad to cope with.

On 17th September 1948 a new contract with the Volkswagen works was signed. According to this, Porsche's were not allowed to design a car for another company if it was likely to become competitive with the current Volkswagen type. The Volkswagen works were entitled to use for its designs any of the Porsche patents, free of charge, but had to pay Porsche a royalty for each Volkswagen leaving the works at Wolfsburg. Naturally the Volkswagen works agreed that Porsche should use Volkswagen parts in the development of a sporting vehicle and also make use of the Volkswagen service chain — this incidentally is a very important point; for one of the main problems of sports car manufacturers is the absence of a well set up service all over the world. On the other hand, the Porsche engineers had to be available to the Volkswagen works in an advisory capacity.

In the late summer of 1948 the first brochures for the type 356 appeared and these were printed in Vienna in German, English and French. They were simple two-page, two-colour leaflets on which the car was only shown as a drawing. Under cubic capacity they stated '1,131cc', but shortly afterwards the car was standardized with a bore of 73.5mm and a stroke of 64mm, providing 1,086cc.

This first leaflet also mentioned a drop-head coupe and thanks to the ties they had with Switzerland it was agreed with the Beutler body works in Thun to build there the first drop-head coupe bodies for the 356. Both the open car and the coupe were made of light alloy in the first series with the result that the weight was relatively low. The leaflet mentioned 1,550 lb. The light alloy coupes had swivelling quarter lights which, however, were not continued in production later in Zuffenhausen when the steel body was built. Many years were to elapse before they were again used in the series production car. The light alloy car also had two-leading-shoe brakes in front — Porsche's were in contact with Lockheed in England — whereas the first series from Zuffenhausen were only fitted with the normal Volkswagen brakes.

The bumper bars in the light alloy series were attached to the body and the windscreen was V-shaped. Some cars were fitted with individual front seats and some had the bench type. The first leaflet was a little naive in its statements: 'At maximum cruising speed 43mpg can be attained.' This and similar sentences propagated the new car which was stated to have a maximum speed of 86mph. It did in fact manage this timed speed, and actually some of the light alloy cars even exceeded it.

Wheel base, front and rear track, height and width which appeared in the catalogue were still current for the Porsche coupe 12 years later, and this continuity of such important characteristics must really be called a phenomenon in these days where types are altered continuously in accordance with changing public taste.

In the spring of 1949 the Porsche 356 was shown for the first time at an international motor show: Geneva. At that time it was being exported to many countries and one of the first cars was sent to Prince Abd el Moneim, a cousin of King Farouk; later he sent very proudly a photograph of the car to Porsche's showing the 356 coupe in front of the Sphinx and the pyramids. Prince Abd el Moneim who, after Farouk was deposed, was chief regent and whose Porsche car simply carried the number 44 without any other letters, arrived in 1950 with this vehicle in Zuffenhausen to have it inspected. The Prince was fairly fat and, so as not to rub against the lower edge of the steering wheel, he always spread a large silk handkerchief on which the royal Egyptian monogram was embroidered. This handkerchief was spread out between his shirt and the steering wheel and as a matter of fact he was quite a good driver.

The light alloy series made in Gmund consisted of exactly fifty cars, four of which remained at the works, later to make sporting history.

21 Back to Stuttgart

IT became clear to the Porsche management in the early summer of 1948 that in the circumstances prevailing in Gmund it would be impossible to arrive at a sensible rate of production. As the old works were in Stuttgart it seemed obvious to start negotiating for a return of the works and to transfer the entire production to Stuttgart. Dr. Klett, the mayor of the town of Stuttgart, was approached in July 1949 and showed himself well disposed to the idea.

The mayor passed the suggestion on to the office of military government in Wurttemberg-Baden with his recommendation. On 13th August he received the first official reply to the effect that the bipartite affairs advisor, Mr. Brunton, would undertake the necessary steps. A tough struggle developed for the old works. On 15th September 1949 the Porsche company received the first direct advice from the military government to the effect that for the time being the works were fully employed by the army and that this would continue until about 1st July 1950, although around that time the unit using the property would be transferred elsewhere.

This was at least a ray of hope and as a result, a small staff from Porsche's arrived towards the end of 1949 in Stuttgart to prepare all that was necessary for a move. This endeavour was greatly accelerated towards the end of February and the management in Stuttgart sent a memorandum to Professor Porsche in Zell am See on 24th February 1950 which said in effect: 'Yesterday Mayor Dr. Klett spoke to General Funk at our request, the latter being the commanding general of the United States Forces in Wurttemberg-Baden. The general told Dr. Klett that after the Motorpool's scheduled removal into the barracks at Cannstadt, the Porsche works would be given up by occupation forces. They would clear the premises not later than 1st September 1950.'

At a later stage this story was told rather well by Professor Albert Prinzing, an economist and former official of the German Foreign Office and a friend of Ferry Porsche's during his school days. He had in the meantime joined the Porsche company in a managerial position and conducted the whole negotiations with the military government. The building of the Porsche car and its production in Stuttgart were, in the words of Prinzing, firstly an economic problem and only secondly a technical one.

When asked by Ferry to do what he could in Stuttgart in view of the Porsche fortune being under trusteeship of the purchasing manager, Mr. Kern, due to the family being abroad, Prinzing found that an additional complication arose in that the licence fees from the Volkswagen works plus the rent for the old works occupied by the American occupation forces, started coming in.

'As I am an economist and know the tax laws well, it was my duty to advise Professor Porsche and his son that something would have to be manufactured very soon ... Thus we started planning towards the end of 1949 and I will never forget this so-called heroic epoch when we looked for and found a place in which to work. I said to the old professor that it would bring us luck to start in the spot where a fortune had at one time had its foundation.'

Prinzing went on with his fascinating tale: 'We found a spot not sufficiently well-known in Germany — the garage of the Porsche Villa on the Feuerbacher Weg! In this garage the first ever VW was built and there the production of the new Porsche also originated, but with the addition of the room of Amalia, the cook. I had to battle against six defendants and against the housing office to get the cook's room. It was, as we called it afterwards, our 18-square-metre works. I was new to it in those days, but I remember that if we were four we had to hold our conversation in the courtyard.'

After mature reflection Porsche decided not to build the car bodies and a number of coach-builders were asked to submit quotations. Among them were Reutter, who were chosen, but not because it was practical from the location point of view (the Reutter works at Zuffenhausen were only a few steps from the Porsche works). The old professor was the one who finally decided: 'You have this offer and you have that offer. Here or there the prices are a bit more advantageous and so on, but I'll tell you what, go to Reutter. Never mind the money; you see, Reutter has the best foremen.'

22 Beginning again

WHEN the Porsche Company started manufacturing, the military government's reply was still before them; the move would take place at the latest on 1st September 1950. They came to an agreement with Reutter that they should use a part of one of their workshops as a temporary measure and so started producing cars in a space of exactly 500 square metres, laying down a monthly schedule of eight to ten cars. Later these 500 square metres yielded no less than eighty cars per month!

The move did not take place because the Korea crisis appeared on the horizon and on account of this the negotiations with the Americans extended over a period of several years. The entire commercial management and the design office were working in a wooden, single-storey prefab about 100 yards from the old works. The exterior was indeed primitive, but perhaps it was not a bad omen that they should restart in a pioneering sort of way.

In the spring of 1950 Professor Prinzing undertook a trip through Germany to make contact with the VW organization, the future distributors, and with any private customers who might be persuaded to buy the new Porsche car with its steel body. Six weeks before the production in Zuffenhausen actually started he had sold on a firm basis thirty-seven cars and everyone was very proud of this. In those days the Company were of the opinion that it would be impossible to sell more than 500 cars of this type in the world, or certainly not more than 500 cars in the first two years.

But it soon became apparent that the Porsche 356 appealed to far more buyers than was originally thought. During the first months they only used the 1,100cc engine of 40bhp, and although the car did have a maximum of about 84, it was only equipped with ordinary Volkswagen brakes. Not until the end of 1950 was the 1,300cc engine available which gave 44bhp and a maximum of just over 90mph; the first improvement on the chassis consisted of two-leading-shoe brakes in front and subsequently cooling ribs were fitted to the brake drums. The gearbox remained the same, unsynchronized, necessitating a certain amount of feeling when changing gear.

From the first few months stories grew up around the Company. It was said, for instance, that the mechanics at Porsche's, those few who were the nucleus, apparently *tested* a customer who might come to the works, to find out if he was a good enough driver to change gear without making a noise. If he was unable to do this the mechanics used to say: 'We shan't sell him one, he doesn't deserve it.'

The individual fitters at Porsche's were certainly more than just average mechanics in a 'normal' car works with series production. An individual fitter used to assemble the engine and, having finished it after about 25 hours work, he would stencil the crankcase with his initials. If a customer later came with a claim or a repair, then the mechanic responsible for the engine was called to account. Was this not truly pioneering?

Famous names soon appeared in the list of customers. The Duke of Harrar, Count Metternich, Prince zu Wied, the two Princes of Hannover, Prince zu Furstenberg and his brother Fritz, Mohamed Taher Pascha, Prince Thurn und Taxis, the writer Knittel, film actresses and even the Krupp family drove Porsches. This sort of thing was talked about abroad and from 1951 onwards exports soared prodigiously.

In 1950 the works did not participate in sporting events, but a few private owners managed to get the name of Porsche into the sporting columns for the first time. In June 1950 Porsche cars were first seen in a big international rally. Prince Joachim zu Furstenberg shared with Count Konstantin Berckheim a 1,100cc coupe, and Prince Fritzi Furstenberg together with Count Hardenberg, driving a drophead 1,100cc, competed in the Swedish rally of the Midnight Sun in which Countess Cecilia Koskull also drove a light alloy Porsche coupe made in 1949. The Furstenberg-Breckheim team won the 1,100cc class and Cecilia Koskull the Ladies Cup — the first international victories of Porsche cars.

Shortly afterwards, on 24th and 25th July 1950, the Innsbruck driver Otto Mathe won the 1,100cc sports car class in the international Austrian alpine event with a car from the old series. Mathe, who before the war had been a dirt-track rider and had lost one arm after an accident, won the Alpine Cup, the Edelweiss and Gold Medal, the hill climb section on the Katschberg and Prebichl and the speed test at Zeltweg.

The third success was booked to the account of the German drivers Rudolph Sauerwein and Count von der Muhle-Eckart who competed in the Interlaken International rally with a new 1,100cc coupe. They won their class and got into second place in the general classification. Incidentally, the overall winner was Walter Ringgenberg in an M.G. Later he drove Porsches and became Swiss champion.

Just to interrupt this chronicle of sporting successes, here is an account of the continuation in tractor design. Porsche's got into touch with the Allgaier company in Uhingen who, as early as 1949, built under licence the AP17, the first Allgaier tractor on the Porsche system. This was followed by the type AP22 also a 2-cylinder diesel, which had 22bhp. Almost 25,000 Allgaier Porsche tractors were built before the association between the two companies was changed and Porsche-Mannesmann came into being, since when tractors have been produced in Friedrichshafen and are called only Porsche. But we shall come back to this.

On 3rd September 1950 Professor Porsche celebrated his 75th birthday in Stuttgart and on that day Porsche owners from all over Germany assembled to show their allegiance to the famous designer. The drivers and cars were lined up in front of castle Solitude near Stuttgart and to them came Professor Porsche, much moved by this homage. He went from car to car, shook hands with all the drivers and said a few words to them. This, you might say, was the first of the Porsche rallies and in the following years this meeting of Porsche drivers has become part of a strange feeling of togetherness which at first was based on the fact that this was such an unusually-shaped motor-car. To flash headlamps when Porsche meets Porsche dates back to 1950; in those days the owners would even stop to talk shop. In the autumn of 1951 Professor Porsche suffered a stroke; weakened by his two years of imprisonment he was not able to get over this and died on 30th January 1952. An immense number of people turned up for the memorial service on 3rd February and Father Johannes of the Benedictine order spoke the funeral oration. The Minister of Transport, Seebohm, said in his speech: 'We are not only standing at the bier of the great designer, but we are burying with him the heroic epoch of the motor-car. Ferdinand Porsche was the last of the great designers whose name was famous all over the world. He belonged to the likes of Daimler, Benz, Bugatti and Lancia whose names denote the make of a motor-car. Today's designers remain anonymous, their names being only known to their colleagues in the same line. The public today knows much better the names of the organizers and financial bosses of the companies — he who rests before us here was blessed by a kind fate which handed the motor-car to his inventive genius and on which his creative ability could find complete fulfilment.'

Henceforth design responsibility lay in the hands of Ferry Porsche.

23 Works Team–Le Mans –Records

IT was in 1951 that Porsche, for the first time, entered a 'works' team in a great international sporting event. It was no accident that the classical 24-hour race of Le Mans was chosen to demonstrate the quality of the machine. The great Charles Faroux was clerk of the course at Le Mans, the very same Faroux who knew Professor Porsche well and was roughly the same age, and through whose negotiation it had been possible to put up the large sum needed to secure Porsche's release from prison. When Ferdinand Porsche was in Paris for the last time in 1950, Faroux asked him to nominate two cars for the 24-hour race and this Porsche had promised to do.

This was to be the first appearance of a post-war German car at Le Mans and the works were a little anxious, not through lack of confidence in the car but on account of public opinion in France and in particular in the region of Le Mans where the Resistance had been very active. Quite obviously feelings were not likely to be exactly pro-German. Charles Faroux, however, guaranteed that there would be no friction and he was proved right.

At this Le Mans in 1951 only a single Porsche was at the start. A silver-grey light alloy coupe (one of the left-overs from the series built in Gmund) which had been fitted with a slightly tuned 1,100cc engine. Power was only just 44bhp and the front and rear wheels were fully enclosed; using a high axle ratio, about 100mph was available.

The car was driven by the two Frenchmen Veuillet and Mouche and they won the 1,100cc class without trouble despite the fact that the other competitors drove 'real' sports cars, whereas the Porsche was an entirely series-produced coupe, in fact in today's parlance a 'gran turismo' vehicle. Veuillet was the Porsche concessionaire of France in Paris and just like Mouche he was experienced in long-distance events, having driven 3-litre Delages.

The success of 1951 was won the hard way and its previous history is of interest. The Porsche Company had asked Paul von Guilleaume to be team manager at Le Mans (later he became sports president of the ADAC). Occasionally he even drove himself and before the war had competed in the Adler team at Le Mans and won his class there. They sent him to Le Mans with one of the later competition cars to find out the state of the circuit, what sort of axle ratio would be suitable and where the team should have its headquarters.

Whilst checking the course at high speed he collided with a cyclist who thoughtlessly crossed the circuit. Guilleaume tried to miss him, but in so doing the Porsche was extensively damaged.

A few weeks later one of the mechanics of the racing department returned on the Autobahn from Frankfurt to Stuttgart also at the wheel of one of the Le Mans cars. Suddenly, and for no reason, a car on the other side of the road travelling in the opposite direction got across the dividing strip and rammed the Le Mans car almost head on. Thanks to an adroit manoeuvre at the last moment the racing mechanic avoided the worst and only suffered slight injuries, but the car was a total write-off.

Before the race they cannibalized accidents number 1 and 2 into one complete car so that they could appear with two vehicles as had been promised to Faroux. The second car was entrusted to a German/French team. Since Rudolph Sauerwein had driven successfully at Le Mans before the war he was engaged by Ferry Porsche as the only German for the 1951 event; during practice and in the rain Sauerwein made a mistake on the centre line at White House just as he was being overtaken by a faster car. There was a bad accident and Sauerwein suffered for years from the leg injury he sustained. The car was almost entirely destroyed and there was no question of rebuilding it by the time the race was due to start.

Thus only one car started in this, their first Le Mans. But there was another important international event in 1951 for which Ferry Porsche nominated two cars: The Liege-Rome-Liege rally and again the light alloy coupes were used for this. One of the cars, fitted with an 1,100cc engine, was entrusted to Huschke von Hanstein (in those days he was not working for Porsche) together with Petermax Muller and the other fitted with a 1,500cc engine was driven by Paul von Guilleaume and Count von der Muhle. Both cars finished extremely well placed; the Hanstein-Muller team was second in the 1,100cc class, whereas Guilleaume won the 1,500cc class and was third in the overall classification. This, despite the fact that over the last 200 miles they had gearbox trouble which meant the car running only in third gear; fortunately on these last sectors there were no more mountain passes to cross.

In this Rally event of August 1951 the 1,500cc engine ran for the first time, although this fact had not been publicised. In fact they said that the car in the 1,500cc class had a 1,300cc engine although it must have been quite clear from its performance on the mountain passes that it could not have been a 1,300cc. The 1,500cc engine was finally announced in the late autumn of 1951.

This was a further systematical development of the previous engine and constructional principles had been adhered to exactly. The only change was in the stroke and bore. This 1,500cc engine as used in series production developed 60bhp and the 'super' and standard did not then exist.

There was yet a third instance when Porsche made the sports headlines. In the last days of September, shortly before the Paris Motor Show was due to open its doors, a team of five drivers consisting of Petermax Muller, Walter Glockler, Huschke von Hanstein, Hermann Ramelow and Richard von Frankenberg appeared with a light alloy coupe to try and set up records at the Montlhery track near Paris.

Three vehicles went with the party: a 1,100cc coupe, a 1,500cc coupe, and an open sports-racing two-seater which Walter Glockler had built himself. It was at first intended to attack the medium length distance records of the 1,100cc class — no simple matter for a series-built car, for the record for 500 miles, 1,000 kilometres and six hours stood at the speed of 98.16mph. These three distances were improved to 100.03mph, 101.4mph, 101.1mph on the night of 29th September 1951. The night following, the five drivers attempted records with a 1,500cc car.

This attempt had as its goal an attack on the absolute world's record of 72 hours with a 1,500cc engine. It was not known beforehand whether the car would stand up to this but the argument was that if they could achieve a number of class records, they would be satisfied. The 72 hour record in those days had been established at an average of 80.71mph by a 3-litre Citroen as long ago as 1935.

The Porsche lapped the autodrome at a steady 103 to 105mph. This, when taking into consideration the necessary stops for refuelling, oil checks, tyre and driver changes, gave an average around 99mph, which was maintained for more than 48 hours. Thus the old class records were improved by a considerable margin. There was just one dramatic moment: precisely as usual, the car stopped for refuelling and driver change in front of the small pit; the engineer held the fuel hose in his hand, the tank closure snapped open (to save time during refuelling the tank filler was fitted on the outside of the bonnet), they turned on the valve but not a drop of petrol came out!

All the people around, mechanics of Porsche, engineers of the German accessory industry, the French officials, everybody stood and gaped like hypnotized rabbits, seemingly incapable of action. Suddenly a wild yell for the chap on the tank truck. He jumped out of the lorry cabin, climbed on top of the tank, fiddled with the valves, turned all stopcocks — but still not a drop came out of this quick fuelling tank wagon that had been specially built for this record attempt. Again they yelled: 'Is the tank empty?'

'No,' he bellowed from the top, 'it's still half full with 400 gallons.'

At least 30 seconds had elapsed, and 30 seconds is a long time when a record attempt is being staged, because every stop at the pits is deducted from the overall time and so the average drops. Suddenly one man had an idea: he was not from the works, but a Porsche owner from Germany who was there out of sheer enthusiasm as a spectator. He had heard on the radio of the record attempts and drove over from Germany to Montlhery to watch the Porsche record attempts; in his privately owned car was a 4½ gallon canister, only 30 yards away. He sprinted back with it, the fuel went into the tank and the aluminium coupe rushed on.

Thus the record attempt was saved for the next hour and during that time they found the trouble in the tanker. One of the valves was not opening and did not release the petrol, but this was soon put right. The Porsche people were beside themselves with pleasure that a private person, a Porsche customer, had actually been master of that situation.

A few hours later came less pleasant news. It was night, a little after 2 a.m.; Petermax Muller was driving, having taken over the car according to programme and done his stint of the 'night shift.' The sound of the engine was even, but suddenly a roar was heard and then silence. Petermax arrived at the pits coasting with a dead engine. The pits woke up quickly enough and whilst braking he yelled out of the window 'Gearbox gone!'

Right in the middle of the banked curve a gear had jumped out and had caused the engine to speed up and roar. The driver had vainly tried to get back into fourth but no gear could be engaged. When long-distance records are attempted, any number of mechanics are allowed to work on a car, but they are only allowed to use those spares which are actually carried aboard. The items that may have to be changed must, from the beginning of the record attempt, be carried on the car and sealed by the officials observing the run. This applies to any object, even a nut or a pair of pliers. Only oil, fuel and tyres may be supplied from the pits.

Porsche's racing mechanics took down the gear selector rods. Was it perhaps a mechanical fault in the remote control or was the trouble in the box itself? If that were so then it would have been all up with the record, for tools to work on the gearbox were not carried on board, apart from which such a repair would take far too long.

Five minutes passed, seven, eight — relentlessly the clocks ticked on. By now all the drivers stood around the car, even those who were off duty. This is a curious thing — as long as the engine growls its contented way one can sleep by the circuit as deeply as at home, but when the engine suddenly stops beyond its scheduled place one wakes up abruptly, just like the people who live on the edge of a volcano, for when the bubbling suddenly stops they know it is about to erupt. The French official watched the mechanics like a hawk to ensure that they should only use those tools that were actually carried on the car; a single smuggled-in screwdriver and all records would be annulled.

By now the car had stopped for ten minutes. Suddenly one of the mechanics managed to get it into third gear, but none other. Then it became obvious: something in the gearbox — the old unsynchronized gearbox which used to transmit 25bhp and now had to cope with full throttle of a 70bhp car — had probably seized up, perhaps a pinion, perhaps a bearing, nobody knew for certain. One thing they did know however, that the third gear was now in and the only one that could still be used. Whatever happened they must not touch the gear lever, for any movement would probably ruin the box for good. So, drive on third gear only.

But was there any point in this? It meant running at very much increased revs and even then it would not be possible to maintain the speed at which they had been running until now. On the other hand, the high ratio rear axle enabled about 100mph to be obtained in this third gear. The engineers took their slide rules: if they wanted to capture the 72-hour record it meant driving at an average of 86-90mph, otherwise the overall average would sink below 93. Tension increased — the car was running again — but would the engine stand this and would third gear remain engaged?

After the refuelling stops and driver changes — every two hours — it meant starting up in third gear. For that the car was pushed 20 yards behind the start line. At the start line, which must not be crossed with the car being pushed, one of the drivers stood and yelled 'Let go!' Then all the 'pushers' had to let go at once. Even if only one had touched it beyond the starting line, all the efforts of the past hours would have been nullified!

Thus they achieved the 72-hour record, and the world records in all classes were increased from 145.5 to 152.3kph, equal to a distance of 10,978 kilometres in these 72 hours. This was the third world record in the tables for Germany. The other two were still those held by Bernd Rosemeyer for the standing kilometre and mile dating from autumn 1937 and, since the Auto-Union racing car of those days was a Porsche design, it meant that the three present world records could be booked to the account of Porsche designs. (One year later the 72-hour record was broken by a 3.4 litre Jaguar and pushed up to 106mph).

Dirty and oily as it was, the car was subsequently taken to the Porsche stand at the Paris show. At that time the works at Zuffenhausen had just built the thousandth car, so there was a double reason for celebration. The Glockler car, the open sports/racing two-seater, had also put up three short-distance records in the 1,500cc class at Montlhery, these having previously belonged to Bugatti. Below is given the exact list of all the records in 1951 which proclaimed the name of Porsche all over the world.

1,100cc Class, Porsche Coupe

						Old Record	New Record
500 miles	...	...	...	...	...	...	158.00 kph	161.8 kph
6 hours	...	...	...	...	...	...	159.4	162.8
1,000 kilometres	...	...	...	...	...	159.7	162.71

1,500cc Class, Porsche Coupe

						Old Record	New Record
3,000 kilometres	...	...	...	...	...	153.33 kph	158.96 kph
2,000 miles	...	...	...	...	...	...	153.7	159.04
24 hours	...	...	...	...	...	...	152.00	159.00

Works Team — Le Mans — Records

1,500cc Class, Porsche Coupe

						Old Record	New Record
4,000 kilometres	...	...	...	...	...	152.00	159.13
3,000 miles	...	...	...	...	...	147.67	159.25
5,000 kilometres	...	...	...	...	...	147.23	159.19
4,000 miles	...	...	...	...	...	147.29	158.00
48 hours	...	...	...	...	...	147.94	156.66
5,000 miles	...	...	...	...	...	144.36	156.49
10,000 kilometres	...	...	...	...	...	127.8	154.29
72 hours	...	...	...	...	...	145.5	152.34

The 72-hour record is reckoned as a world record apart from the class record. Total distance 10,978 kilometres.

1,500cc Class, Glockler-Porsche Open Two-seater

						Old Record	New Record
500 kilometres	...	...	...	...	...	185.3 kph	188.10 kph
1,000 kilometres	...	...	...	...	...	182.4	186.18
6 hours ...	....	...	...	...	...	181.8	184.66

Fastest lap 195.184 kph. Total distance 1,107 kilometres.

In the summer of 1951 Porsche also competed in another international event which however was not so well-known, and two works cars were nominated. This was the Baden-Baden rally and the regulations stipulated that the crew reporting at the biggest number of controls within 33 hours would be the winners. Not mincing words it meant that this event was in fact a road race on the public highway. The Travemunde Rally also was based on similar regulations. Neither ministry nor police protested against this in those far-off days, for Germany's traffic density was not a fraction as thick as it is today. One can hardly imagine this now.

In the Baden-Baden rally there was one check point in Stuttgart, or to be more exact, on the Autobahn exit at Stuttgart-Echterdingen and another one in Munich. Also it was not forbidden to drive back and forth all the time between just two controls and it therefore seemed ideal (so as to reach the highest average) simply to stay on the Autobahn and drive back and forth between Stuttgart and Munich as often as possible.

There was only one snag to this and that was the American speed limit: on the Autobahn maximum speed was 50mph, and in built-up areas 24mph. Naturally, one could still try to travel at 90mph, but one had to avoid being caught by the police cars operated by the American military police. Porsche were particularly interested in this competition because it enabled a high speed test on the Autobahn to be carried out, ie. 30 hours' full throttle work with a 1,300cc car, and this was bound to show up any weak points as far as the chassis and engine were concerned.

The Porsche Company had special plates which were inscribed 'Test Car'. Any car with these was not likely to be checked by the American military police and these plates conveyed a sort of maximum speed permit and the imposed 50mph could be exceeded. Therefore, as the whole was a large-scale test for the works, both works cars in the rally carried these plates, the crews being Prince zu Leiningen, the former Auto-Union racing driver, with Count Berckheim and the other Count Orssich with R. von Frankenberg, both cars being clearly marked 'Test Cars'. The fastest time from Stuttgart to Munich which was then achieved and including the stamping of the road book in Munich and a small diversion due to repairs of one of the Autobahn bridges, amounted to 2 hours 59 minutes and this with a car which had a top speed of only just 93mph. In today's traffic conditions even a car with a maximum of 115mph is unlikely to approach these times despite the bridge now having been repaired, simply because it would not be safe in view of present traffic conditions.

This rally provided an important lesson for Porsches. After exactly 16 hours of flat-out driving, the treads of the standard tyres flew off on both cars. Porsche's had sent works mechanics to the control post Stuttgart-Echterdingen, and subsequently during this 'Autobahn rally' the cars were fitted with special racing tyres. This test showed, however, that the normal tyres of those days (a number of different makes were used and none lasted longer) were at the limit of their capacity if vehicles were operated on the Autobahn at speeds around 93mph. This provided the impetus for the German tyre industry to develop new tyres suitable for sustained high speeds. Maxima of 92-95mph today are rather tame values even for series-produced touring cars of the middle and large classes, but for a time the 1,300cc Porsche was the fastest production car available in Germany.

The contemporary motoring journalists who tested the car were very delighted with the new sort of driver-feeling which the Porsche conveyed. Instead of just test reports they tended to write poetical eulogies which showed that the Porsche car penetrated into a new motoring limbo, for no other cars were so low and possessed such astonishing road holding.

Ernst Hornickel, in the *Neue Zeitung* said: 'This is the dream car of old Ferdinand Porsche which now carries his name. All the knowledge of motor engineering that this fortunate man acquired during his life are epitomized in it. The Porsche driver has a new sensation unknown to the ordinary driver, and whoever manages to experience it thoroughly will recognize and remember it. With playful ease he reaches 80-95mph, a speed-range not normally used. A strange yet strong force keeps him on the ground yet he seems to glide along soundlessly as in a sail plane. The man who manages to unleash the power of this beautiful mechanical animal suddenly becomes embued with a happy feeling whilst realizing that here a genius has brought about a new motoring conception and the vehicle itself has entered into a new era.'

H.U. Wieselmann was a little more restrained in his appreciation in *Auto, Motor und Sport,* but he also said: 'The fact is that the Porsche, all other considerations apart, is the most beautiful series-built car in the world today, and this fact makes it difficult to convey the extent of one's impressions in mere sober sentences.'

24 Mille Miglia

THE 'beautiful mechanical animal' started its victory procession all over the world and as the 500-square-metre production shop at Reutters was quite insufficient (a so-called 'racing shop' was attached to this which could just about house two cars and four mechanics) and as, on the other hand, there was no telling when the Americans would finally return the old works, it was decided in 1952 to build a new works in Stuttgart-Zuffenhausen, a few hundred yards from the old place.

On the sporting side the works entered one car in the spring of 1952 for the Mille Miglia; a light alloy coupe with a 1,500cc engine producing about 70bhp. It was handed to the Italian Count Lurani and he, together with Count Berckheim, competed in the 'gran turismo' class of the Mille Miglia. The few cars which were kept at the works from the Gmund days were entered again and again for sporting events for they weighed about 220 lb less then than the steel-bodied production ones.

Count Berckheim had an interesting experience near Stuttgart whilst testing the car on the Autobahn: he was just passing the Stuttgart-Echterdingen exit at maximum speed, about 112mph, when he saw one of the white road patrol cars of the American military police which supervised the 50mph limit. It was too late to brake so Berckheim decided to get away from them. The Americans tried at first vainly to follow him, but Berckheim had forgotten that the patrol cars were fitted with radio. The Americans therefore turned round, rejoined their post and called the next control post to say: 'White car of unknown make, low built, proceeding towards Ulm at far too high a speed. Stop driver and arrest him.'

The next control post, consisting of two American policemen and a German one, was exactly 20 miles further on the Autobahn. Berckheim approached it at just over 112mph because the road was slightly downhill. From far away he saw the red lantern that was being swung so he braked the Porsche to a standstill and innocently inquired from the window 'And what can I do for you, officer?' The latter looked at his watch, having had the message only 11 minutes ago. He held a whispered conference with his American colleagues; it was quite impossible that a car should cover 20 miles in 11 minutes; there was no such thing, such speeds belonged to aircraft. The Americans agreed and the German policeman said: 'Excuse us please for stopping you, but we are looking for a car that must be following you and that has broken the traffic rules. You can carry on.' With

The 1934 Porsche designed Auto-Union record car. Maximum speed was in the region of 200mph

The 750 kilo Formula (1934-37) Auto-Union 16-cylinder racing car, with torsion-bar suspension

The V3 (first series) Volkswagen built in the garage of Porsche's villa in Stuttgart in 1935

The chassis of the above

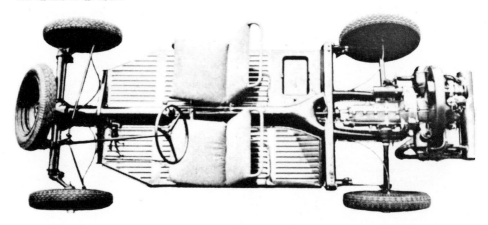

114

Hans Stuck with the 1934 record car

The very first Porsche-like car, built on a 1939 VW chassis for the Berlin-Rome trial,
which did not take place owing to the war. It produced 40bhp with a maximum speed
of over 88mph. Now owned by the well-known, one-armed Innsbruck driver, Otto Mathe

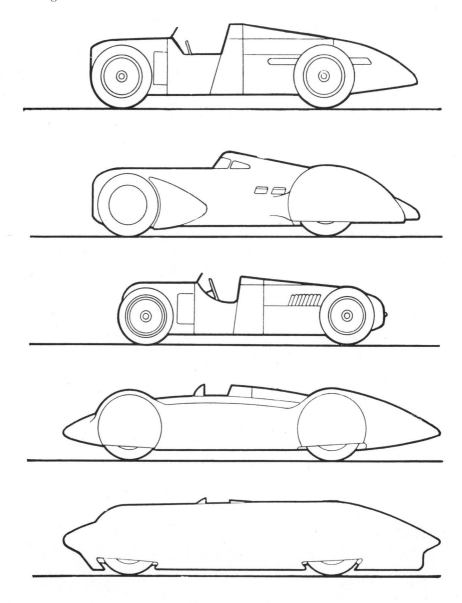

(Top) Auto Union profile as raced at Avus
(Second) Partially enclosed for record attempt
(Third) The 6.1 litre model driven by Rosemeyer who won the German GP in 1936
(Fourth) Fully streamlined for records - achieved a speed of about 250mph
(Fifth) Rosemeyer was killed in this car in January 1938; slab-sided body due to enclosed front and rear wheels with maximum possible speed of approximately 270mph

The 1938 car designed by Porsche for Daimler-Benz to attack the Land Speed Record; it never ran, however, and is now in the museum at the works in Stuttgart

The first Porsche tractors were tested during World War II, of which some were partially powered by gas generators

117

Ferry Porsche here photographed at Le Mans

Kommenda the body designer, the Professor and Ferry Porsche in Gmünd, Austria, with the prototype Porsche in 1948

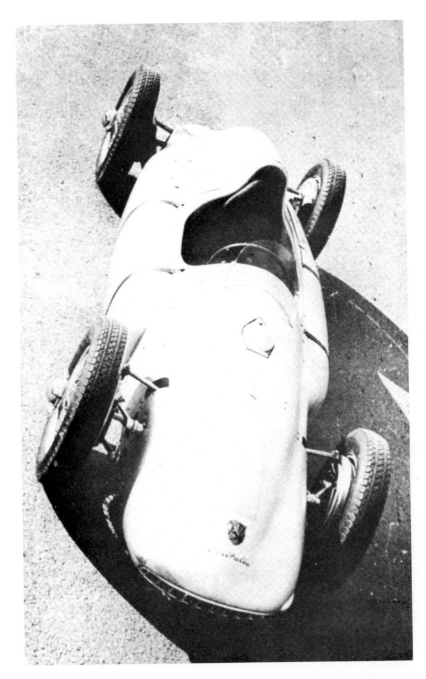

The ill-fated Cisitalia, flat 12

The so-called 'racing department' in 1950 where there was hardly room to turn around. Here the Liège-Rome-Liège cars are being prepared

The Walter Glockler Porsche-Special at Schauinsland in 1951. The car led to the design of the Spyder

121

The 4-camshaft Spyder during practice for the sportscar
GP of Germany

The 1953 Le Mans car with coupé top and 1,500cc 'Super' (78bhp) engine. Herrarte
from Guatemala won the 1,500cc class of the Carrera Pan-americana with this car

In 1955 a cross-country vehicle appeared - known as the 'hunting car'

The 1956 prototype with the shortened wheelbase. Here Richard von Frankenberg drives it at Solitude

The 'finned' car in the 1956 Le Mans. It was the prototype for RSK and had an improved chassis and 5-speed gearbox

The 550 Spyder in its final form in the 1954 Mille Miglia, winning the 1500 sportscar class with Hans Herrmann driving

The Formula II car appeared in 1959 at Rheims and Monte Carlo driven by Joakim Bonnier

The 'new look' Porsche in 1959

The Jean Behra-built Formula II Porsche here driven by Hans Herrmann

The late Jean Behra with Huschke von Hanstein, Porsche's racing manager and GT driver

The late Count Wolfgang von Trips on his winning way as European Mountain Champion in 1958; here seen with the RSK at the Gaisberg hillclimb near Salzburg

The Porsche tractors have similar type-names to the Porsche cars. This is the 'Super' at work.
All of them have air-cooled diesels

this vehicle Lurani and Berckheim won their class in the Mille Miglia. It was a particularly important Mille Miglia for Germany, as it marked the return of Mercedes to motoring sport and three 300 SL cars had been entered by the works. Kling, a new man in the Mercedes team, achieved second position behind Bracco in a 3-litre Ferrari, and Caracciola got into fourth place with his 300 SL.

Lurani and Berckheim did not have an easy job. On the last but one sector between Florence and Bologna where the Futa and Raticosa pass have to be crossed, they had the old gearbox trouble: suddenly there was only third gear left and the last 200 odd miles from Bologna via Piacenza and Mantua to Brescia had to be covered in this third gear, which meant 6,000rpm at about 90mph.

In Bologna they were leading by 7 minutes on time allowance from their closest rival, Musitelli in a Cisitalia coupe although behind in actual distance. It was touch and go whether it would be possible to hold this advantage, for Musitelli had a good information service *en route* — he was told that he was close behind the Porsche and so he endeavoured to close the gap on the flat section after Bologna. However, this resulted in his having to retire with engine trouble when only 90 miles from the finish.

The Italians were clever and immediately stood in front of the racing number on the car so that the other competitors should not know it had retired. But Lurani knew the Cisitalia of Musitelli very well and having seen that it had stopped, realized that there was now no longer any difficulty in winning despite the handicap of third gear only.

Apart from the light alloy coupe three privately owned Porsches (one of 1,500cc and two of 1,100cc) were running in the class of series production sports cars (the splitting up of the classes was not quite so clearly defined in the FIA regulations as it is today). For the 1,100cc engine a new camshaft was available which imparted considerably more speed, and the drivers called it the Fuhrmann camshaft having heard that it had been designed by Dr. Fuhrmann at Porsche's. With this the car managed about 93mph and developed around 46 to 48bhp, but only one of the three privately owned cars finished in the 1952 Mille Miglia: that driven by Count Metternich and Count Einsiedel who thus won the 1,100cc class.

The other 1,100cc was handled by Richard von Frankenberg and H.U. Wieselmann, Editor-in-Chief of *Auto, Motor und Sport,* who wanted to have direct impressions of this, the major European road race. This car was fitted with an additional oil cooler underneath the engine and whilst crossing a very bumpy level crossing the drain plug of this cooler contacted the road, the oil escaped and a big-end bearing seized up. So ended a somewhat stormy drive, shortly after Pescara.

Helmut Polensky was at the wheel of the 1,500cc coupe and he had arranged for an Italian co-driver. In the Mille Miglia all co-drivers have an extremely important job: during practice they must note particularly dangerous places and all the most important curves and corners. From these notes which are known as the 'bible' the co-driver must read off the right warning at the right time during the race. Perhaps in this manner: '200 yards after the signboard "Motta" right-hand bend, can be taken flat.' But Polensky's Italian was poor and the Italian could not speak German. Both, on the other hand, spoke reasonable French and because of this the Italian read out the instructions in French. In one spot during the night the Italian mixed up the words 'gauche' and 'droite' in a language which, after all, was unfamiliar, so that Polensky did not place himself correctly for the curve which suddenly turned left instead of the expected right. The car got into a bad slide broadside, touched the kerb, and turned over.

Fortunately nothing happened to either of them, but the roof was so pushed in that it was impossible to sit up straight in the car. The windscreen was broken but that would not have mattered so much, for both carried goggles just in case ... But to try and compete in the Mille Miglia without being able to sit upright was impossible. This particular curve was at the entry of a small village and all at once the entire population

129

crowded round; in any case Italians tend to line both sides of the road during the Mille Miglia to watch the cars go by.

Polensky's Italian co-driver yelled for a hammer to beat out the roof and immediately some people ran off to try and get one, when from the large crowd of people a great colossus of a man came over, the local butcher. 'Nonsense,' he growled, 'never mind the hammer, let me get into the car.' Respectfully, they all gave him room. The giant inserted himself into the car with his back to the crumpled roof. Then he drew a deep breath, tightened his muscles and with a plop the roof resumed very nearly its old shape!

On the sector to Rome, Polensky endeavoured to make up for the lost time, but this caused engine trouble, necessitating their retirement.

In 1952 the works again sent the light alloy coupe to Le Mans and to the Liege-Rome-Liege rally. Three Porsches started this time at Le Mans. Two of the cars had 1,100cc engines and although Huschke von Hanstein and Petermax Muller had to give up whilst leading their class, it was won by Veuillet/Mouche for the second time. The 1,500cc car was driven by two French drivers and occupied a good position, but the officials disqualified it because during a short stop at the pits the drivers omitted to stop the engine, which is clearly directed in the regulations. It was a decision which caused a lot of dispute, as it was only a question of seconds and in all probability the driver had switched off, but the engine had run on for a moment, but Porsche had to give in.

This race was a double victory for Mercedes, for Lang/Riess and Helfrich/Niedermayr were first and second respectively after the Frenchman Levegh in a 4½-litre Talbot had to give up one hour before the end with oil pipe trouble. Levegh had at that time a very considerable lead and had driven single-handed for 23 hours.

Liege-Rome-Liege was a triumph for Porsche, of a kind never again to be seen by a single make of car in this competition. Polensky/Schluter won the overall classification with a 1,500cc light alloy coupe, the Belgian Stasse and Hans Herrmann were third and von Guilleaume/Scheube fourth. Ninth position in the overall classification was held by the German private entrants Werner Engel and Hansleo von Hosch, and in tenth place was again a works car with von Hanstein and Petermax Muller. Incidentally, these two were running in fourth position in this event of 91 hours duration and covering 3,200 miles but they were rammed by another car and so arrived 22 minutes late at the next control; apart from which they had to drive through the night with only one headlamp.

Thus, amongst the first ten in the overall classification in the Liege-Rome-Liege there were five 1,500cc Porsches, and Germany won the club team prize, the marque team prize and the national prize. Polensky and Schluter were rally champions the following year.

When we talk about the 1952 season we must also mention a small event which brought about a new era in German motor sport. On 6th April 1952 there was a motorcycle race called the 'Dieburg Triangle Race'. During this there was also a heat for series production sports cars up to 1,100cc. The race organizers of Dieburg were to be congratulated in that they, at that time, were the first to undertake this seemingly risky step when the 'gran turismo' concept did not exist. Yet there was quite a number of sporting motorists who wanted to participate in a race with their 1,100cc Porsche cars, and not only in rallies. At the time they obviously did not have much of a chance with their series-built cars in a sports-car race in which every sort of tuning and any type of special body was permitted. They needed their own, strictly series production class, in Germany.

But such a class constituted a risk for the organizers, for the sports cars and motorcycles which made up most of the programme not only impress the public with their speed but also with the noise from their unsilenced engines. Thus a race for series-production 1,100cc cars all of one type and in comparative silence was likely to be a dull affair, except perhaps for the gay variety of their body colours.

But the experiment was a success — the 1,100cc Porsches were almost all of the same speed so that very exciting battles ensued in which the skill of the better drivers was quickly evident.

Although drivers and technical journalists were exceedingly impressed with the road holding of the car of the period, it could not compare with the standard set five years later. The Porsches of these early days were extreme oversteerers, tending to 'come round' very quickly, yet the vehicle could be well controlled and, when one got used to this characteristic, it was a very safe car as it 'warned' the driver of its intentions. For the public lining a racecourse it was very effective to see the Porsches tail-sliding through corners yet staying firmly on the road.

Even drivers of considerable experience have often spun a Porsche. Count Metternich described this very amusingly in his report of the 1952 Mille Miglia and as this characterizes the Porsche road holding of the day we may as well reproduce his words:

'The road was very winding and coming from the Adriatic we were most of the time in third gear. Suddenly there was a long straight in front of me — at last an opportunity to get into top. I chased the good old 1,100 up to 5,900rpm, got into fourth and was going just over 90 at the end of the straight. There the road goes downhill a little and into a gentle right-hand bend. I was just thinking about taking this in third; but never mind, we've been in third long enough! It had just started to rain and I entered the bend from the left-hand side of the road when suddenly I felt an old "friend" on my left moving forward: the 1,100cc engine! "He" got to be quicker and quicker, I tried to change down but it was too late, "he" had overtaken me. And now we started our pirouette. We spun several times so that we saw the trees sometimes through the left- and sometimes through the right-hand window. Wittigo Einsiedel held on tight to his seat, as hard as he could, without a word. I twiddled the steering to left or right without choosing, just like driving a dodgem at the village fair. Suddenly we hit something at the rear which put us into the correct direction — Florence. Once more Providence was with us and all we had to do was change a rear tyre which had burst on contacting a small kerbstone.'

The series-production car races found imitators and were even arranged on the Nurburgring, but here they were limited to 1,500cc, so that the 1,500 Porsches (only lightly tuned 60bhp cars — the Super did not exist then) had a good chance. The first Nurburgring race in the series-production class was won in 1952 by Max Nathan in front of Rolf Goetze. Ferry Porsche himself was at the Nurburgring and when the cups were handed over he also stood on the dais, an indication of his enthusiasm for this type of sport.

During practice for this race a driver from Stuttgart, of whom no one had heard and who was not taken very seriously, achieved fastest lap, although he soon retired from the race with gearbox trouble: a certain chap called Hans Herrmann. This series-production race, which was to become more closely circumscribed by the FIA two years later, brought about a new epoch in Germany for private entrants and it gave them the chance to compete on famous circuits with approximately equal vehicles, vehicles which constituted a very sound step up to the faster sports and racing cars. Hans Herrmann's career is a good example of this. There is no German driver of note, even in the works racing teams, who, having started his career within the last few years, did not do so in a privately owned Porsche.

25 Porsche Super-Spyder-550-Formula 2

THE 1,500cc Porsche gave 60bhp at that time, and for the autumn a 'Super' engine was planned with 70 horses. At the same time the works were then to supply a less high revving, lower compression, standard edition of 55bhp. It was no longer compatible with safety to transmit 70bhp via the old gearbox or to equip a car which was capable of 105mph with brakes which, in diameter and shoe width, still conformed to the VW dimensions. At the autumn motor shows of 1952 two most important innovations appeared on the Porsches.

The first was the fitting of the big brakes; these were now of 280mm diameter instead of 240mm and had cooling ribs. They were developed from the experience obtained in motor sport and constituted an important contribution to safety. Ideally, the brakes should be able to cope with about 120mph; this state had been reached with the new brakes which previous to that had definitely been 'slower' than the vehicle, apart from their tendency to fade.

The second innovation was the synchronized gearbox, including bottom gear. As long ago as 1945 and 1946 one of the Porsche designers, Leopold Schmid, had conceived an entirely new type of synchronizing system, and a gearbox on this system had already been fitted to the Cisitalia grand prix car. Although, as we know, the car was not raced as a whole, nevertheless the first practical experience had been made. This form of ring synchronization, so called because next to the gear wheels there were revolving steel rings which dealt with the equalization of the shaft revs, was a Porsche patent. It enabled the construction of a synchronized gearbox in a very limited space; mainly, however, the synchronizing time was materially shortened by this system.

In the autumn of 1952 the Porsche car was the first vehicle into which the ring system was fitted. In the years that followed licences for this system were sold to many large motor manufacturers and a number of grand prix cars of the new 1954 racing formula were so fitted, as were also several large sports cars successful at the time.

Not only did the house of Porsche export fair-sized quantities of cars to the U.S.A. but negotiations were started with a few American firms to fit the Porsche engine into specialized vehicles and also aircraft. In the autumn of 1952 negotiations took place in the U.S.A. between Ferry Porsche and Wendell S. Fletcher who owned the Fletcher Aviation Corporation in Pasadena, California.

Porsche — Super — Spyder — 550 — Formula 2

This company produced a jeep in 1953 called the 'Airborne' jeep, a very light cross-country vehicle with a body like a ship's hull made out of light alloy sheets. This airborne jeep had a wheel base of 6ft 6in. and weighed only about 1,480 lb and it could be adapted for river crossing. Fuel tanks were in the sides of the pontoon-shaped monocoque body. The engine was at the rear — a 1,500cc Porsche of 55bhp.

The Fletcher Corporation had changed the engine a little: the cooling fan had been replaced by Fletcher-designed so-called 'jet cooling'. In this arrangement, a funnel-shaped housing is fitted round each pair of cylinders, the hot exhaust gases create considerable suction in these funnels whereby cool fresh air is sucked in, passing the cooling ribs and taking off the hot air. This multi-purpose jeep was designed for American paratroops.

In the autumn of 1952, during a meeting of technical journalists at the Porsche works, an 'internal' competition was arranged: ten prominent rally drivers were invited with their own Porsche cars to attempt a fuel economy run over a circuit in southern Germany measuring about 290 miles and mainly situated in the mountains of the Black Forest. The idea was to keep to a minimum average of at least 37mph; it was permitted to switch off the engine going downhill and to increase the tyre pressures to reduce rolling resistance. A well-known technical journalist was to accompany each of the rally drivers in their cars. A Swiss, Charles Renaud, together with a motoring journalist, F.K. Wolff, won this competition with a 1,500cc car averaging 37.4mph and using 4.73 litres of fuel per hundred kilometres (approximately 60mpg). Second was Walter Engel (with Dr. Woltereck), also with a 1,500cc car, and he achieved 4.82 litres per hundred kilometres. Third was Count Einsiedel (with H.U. Wiselmann) in a 1,300cc car and he consumed 4.84 litres. The winning car was then tested for maximum speed, using the same carburettor setting. The catalogue stated a maximum speed of 103mph and 102.9mph was actually averaged on this test.

The new 'tame' engine with 55bhp was given the prosaic name of '1500 Normal' by the works, as opposed to '1500 Super'. The customers soon called this car 'die Dame' (The Lady) and this description spread abroad everywhere and is still used today.

Intensive participation in sport showed Ferry Porsche very clearly that the 'Super' engine with overhead valves and pushrods would soon no longer be able to compete with the sports cars manufactured elsewhere. A real sports engine for racing would have to have overhead camshafts, for the rev limit of the 'Super' engines was in the region of 6,000rpm due to the long pushrods and 6,000 was no longer enough.

This was the reason why in the summer of 1952 the first designs came into being for an engine destined for future race participation and with these first design concepts the real 'Spyder' story begins. The story of the Porsche Spyder which was destined to be so famous later is full of extraordinary happenings, the strangest being the name 'Spyder'. Today everyone uses this — as an attribute of the Porsche sports/racing car; but a number of Italian car makers also built a spyder — Lancia, Fiat and Alfa Romeo for instance — but to the Italians this word simply means an open two-seater in series production, whereas with the Porsche Company the word 'spyder' has a precise meaning concerned with motor racing. At Porsche's only the car specially built for racing and equipped with a four camshaft engine was ever called Spyder. At the time when it came into being there was an international concept 'sports/racing car' as opposed to a series-built sports car. Since, however, the series sports car no longer existed in the FIA regulations at the end of 1956, the sports/racing car of earlier days was only referred to as a sports car. The next step to the series-built car is the gran turismo.

The word 'spyder' arose in connection with the Porsche sports car in the autumn of 1953, but the story, or its prior history, started a lot earlier. The first legitimate precursor to the Spyder was not built in Zuffenhausen but in Frankfurt.

In the winter of 1949-50 Walter Glockler, the main distributor of Volkswagen in Frankfurt, who had not lost his motoring enthusiasm, began to develop a sports/racing

133

car together with his works manager Ramelow and a coach-builder called Weidenhausen whose works were opposite Glockler's. Although the development work started artisan fashion, it was by no means improvised or amateurish. The Glockler-Porsche was technically very good and sufficiently fast for those days. In the spring of 1950 they had an 1,100cc car ready in Frankfurt which developed 58bhp when run on alcohol fuel and it weighed about 1,000 lbs. It had a very light tubular chassis and the engine was turned round, in other words the engine was in front of the rear axle.

In 1951 Hermann Kathrein won the 1,100cc German championship driving the same car and in 1952 Hans Brendel — who shortly before the war became trainee driver at Daimler-Benz — drove the Glockner-Porsche which had been improved in a few small details and this good and faithful car achieved yet its third German championship. Its wheel base was a mere 6½ft — the shortest ever used in a sports car.

In the meantime Walter Glockler built another car which was fitted with a 1,500cc Porsche engine, and by winning the Freiburg hill climb and the Grenzlandring race he became German champion in 1951 in the 1,500cc class. The larger Glockler-Porsche was used in the autumn for record attempts at Montlhery and this particularly well designed vehicle (from the point of view of aerodynamics — it had a very small frontal area) had a top speed of around 130mph, despite the relatively low output of 90bhp which was obtained on alcohol fuel. During the Grenzlandring event Glockler drove the car with a perspex cowling over the driver's seat.

Max Hoffmann, the Porsche representative in New York, bought the Glocker-Porsche and competed with it successfully in a few American sports car races.

Glockler's activity showed two things: firstly, that with relatively simple means appreciable successes could be obtained under the competitive conditions of the time and secondly it became clear where the limits lay. Against the increasingly successful Osca, Gordini, EMW and particularly Borgward it was becoming difficult to score further successes. In the United States Osca in particular appeared as a very serious competitor and it seemed increasingly difficult to stay on top with the pushrod engine.

Ferry Porsche's motive in developing a new car was not only because he wished to compete more successfully in motor racing (a new chassis was not thought of at that time) but it was considered necessary to have a new research object. The 'normal' Porsche engine was an exceedingly reliable and robust motor and the class victories at Le Mans and Liege-Rome-Liege had clearly shown this, as had the 72-hour world record with the light alloy coupe. Air cooling had been tested and provided itself — albeit with a per litre output still within the confines of the sports touring car in the region of 40-50bhp/litre. How about air cooling on a real high efficiency engine, say in a sports/racing car with more than 70bhp/litre?

One of the younger designers, Dr. Fuhrmann, who had proved himself on the camshaft design, was given the job of the development. The new engine to be designed was given the Porsche number '547'.

As is usual in such cases, certain problems had first to be studied, especially those concerning valve operation. A decision was taken to operate the four camshafts by means of countershafts instead of chains. Ferry Porsche and chief engineer Rabe often stood for hours around the drawing board of Dr. Fuhrmann to take counsel about the engine. In the autumn of 1952, number 547 was sufficiently advanced on the drawing board to talk about building it. But the question was whether the high development costs would be justified in this small company — a serious point in those early days.

Eventually the engine was built during the winter of 1952-53 and project number '547' underwent its brake tests a little after Easter 1953.

In the meantime the 1953 racing season was getting near but the engine was nowhere near far enough advanced to be used in racing — the time it takes to develop a new engine tends to be underestimated very greatly by the average layman. If one but considers that almost every part has to be individually and specially made and that if a part, such as the crankshaft, breaks, another one must be made, based on the results of the test and improved to eliminate the risk of breakage, all involving intensive work on the drawing board, some idea of the time needed will be realized.

Porsche, however, did want to do something in the 1,500cc sports/racing car class in that year for it seemed that in view of the very strong opposition there was a certain danger that private initiative would no longer suffice. Thus they first of all built a very light vehicle, open and very good aerodynamically with the 'about face' engine arrangement (to improve weight distribution) and they chose a similar tubular chassis to that used by Glockler.

During the Eifel race of 1953 it rained cats and dogs and this car was driven by Walter Glockler's cousin Helm; it was equipped with the ordinary 1,500cc Super pushrod engine, running on alcohol fuel with a compression ratio of 10.5 : 1; he won by a small but sure margin from Borgwards. And then came Le Mans.

The Le Mans regulations prescribed a fuel which was commercially obtainable and apart from this it was necessary to ensure that the engines were running as well at the end of the 24 hours as at the beginning. It followed that the maximum safe power from the pushrod engines was limited to 77-78bhp, with which a top speed of about 125mph would have to be obtained. The two tubular-chassis vehicles which had in the meantime been made ready were fitted with covered-in cockpits which, though not particularly comfortable, helped the aerodynamics. Frankenberg drove one of the cars with his Belgian colleague Paul Frere, the other was handled by Hans Herrmann and Helm Glockler. At the end of the 24 hours there was an *ex aequo* double victory for the two cars in the 1,500cc class and on the Mulsanne straight they were timed at 123.6 and 122.4mph respectively. The ventilation of the tiny coupes was very poor, as was the visibility, but the end justified the means.

For the sports car race before the German Grand Prix on the Nurburgring, Hans Herrmann and Helm Glockler were entered by the works. They appeared with the two Le Mans cars but without the aerodynamic tops which would have been useless on the Nurburgring and for the short race distance and using alcohol, the engines were tuned to give 98bhp, probably the uppermost limit to which the 1,500cc Super engine could be developed. Herrmann won in a convincing manner with a fastest lap of 11 minutes 2 seconds, which for the car as it was then constituted, was a positively incredible time.

During practice for the race, Porsche had a third car running which had a racing number (131) and a T (training or practice) as is usual for practice cars. Externally it had some barely noticeable differences from the other two cars: the tail fins behind the rear mudguards were a little steeper and the air intake slots differently arranged but it would not have created any special attention had it not had an entirely different sound from the other cars, and had they not so obviously avoided opening the bonnet in public. Racing manager Huschke von Hanstein and number-one-driver Hans Herrmann put in a few practice laps with the 'peculiar sounding' car, but they were not particularly quick. Herrmann did not go quite so fast as the times he had put in with the old car and when it stopped Ferry Porsche was by its side and a discussion took place in undertones.

Secrecy could not long be maintained as the experts had got wind of four camshafts. This number '547' was first driven in a motoring competition but there was no question of permitting it to be photographed.

A week later they lent the car to Hans Stuck in recognition of his pre-war successes with Auto-Union, for the Schauinsland hill climb. This first event for the car did not, however, go according to plan, for Stuck was unable to familiarize himself with the characteristics of the engine which only produced power at the top end and seemed a little dull below 5,000rpm. Thus Hans Hermann won again with a terrific time using the pushrod engine, in front of Bechem in a Borgward and Stuck who just beat Hans Glockler

135

for third position.

The complete new vehicle was given a number — 550 — and the Porsche type 550 consisted of an improved tubular chassis with a special system of cross-bracing, an open light alloy two-seater body with a very low air intake for the oil cooler which was mounted in front; the mudguards were heavily profiled. The 4-speed gearbox with ring synchromesh was the same as on the production cars and fitted behind the rear axle with the clutch hydraulically operated. Suspension was the same as on the production car, two square, laminated torsion bars in front, two shorter and thicker round-section bars at the rear. The brackets for the shock absorbers were differently mounted and the length of the suspension arms had been altered. The 547 engine was fitted into this chassis and it was recognizable on first sight by three features: the air cooling blower had twin intakes; the four overhead camshafts (two per bank of two cylinders) had one distributor each, mounted at the rear end of the top shaft (which indicated that twin ignition was used); then there was the large separate oil tank which revealed dry-sump lubrication.

Since the Freiburg hill climb in 1953 there was therefore officially in existence a Porsche type 550 fitted with a 547 engine, and right from the start they considered building a small series for sale. This was particularly encouraged by Max Hoffmann, the American agent, who thought (correctly as was shown later) that a very high performance sports car could be sold more easily in the States than in Europe. Following considerable discussion as to whether a small series should be built or not and after a lot of experimentation with bodywork details, the 550 was finally shown at the Paris Salon in 1953, it being said that this was a works car and an exhibition piece, but that probably replicas would be on sale one day.

This car was called the 'hunchback' at the Porsche Factory, on account of its appearance. Their intention at the Salon was to exhibit an open two-seater which, whilst being reasonably aerodynamic, would accommodate both persons in comparative comfort and without enclosing the passenger's seat. To achieve this, a wide head-rest and fairing was formed behind the seats giving it the hunchback look.

If there had been only a European market for this car, it probably would never have been called anything but type '550,' but the American market was very important and the agent said that for his clientele it would have to have not only a number but a pretty and agreeable sounding name. They remembered that a few sports-bodied American cars towards the end of the 'twenties had been called 'Spyder' and the word was still familiar to enthusiasts; some found the appellation a little odd, for a spider was a thing that crawled and a sports/racing car hardly did that. But the Americans stuck to their guns and surprisingly quickly the car became known as the 'Porsche Spyder.'

Although many people knew that at the end of the 'twenties some forms of bodywork were called 'Spyder,' why they were so called and how that curious name arose nobody at first seemed able to explain.

The two-seater Auburn, Stutz, Cord, Kissel, Mercer, Duesenberg, Packard and Hudson made during the late 'twenties and early 'thirties — the so-called 'classics' of American luxury for the stars of the silent film — were sometimes called 'Spyder' or 'Spider.' Normally, however, in advertisements and brochures they were referred to as Sports Roadsters, or when the folding top was invisible, they were called Speedsters. Twenty years later, in the spring of 1952 to be exact, another Spider (or Spyder) was available in the U.S.A. — the Italian SIATA with a 730cc Crosley engine, very popular over there at that time.

Generally speaking, Porsche Spyder is spelt with a 'y', but this is entirely incorrect, for the word is really derived from the insect 'spider.'

The spider cars we know look unlike any creepy, crawly spider — yet the word in connection with a vehicle is much older than the motor-car. Before Daimler and Benz revolutionized our world, we rode in horse-drawn carriages. The horses set a certain maximum speed, but the endeavour to travel faster than others already existed. But how to achieve this? Very simply — either by using several fast horses or a light carriage — the principle was the same then as today.

In the 'sixties of the last century English and Irish coach-builders conceived the idea of building a particularly light four-wheeled carriage with a makeshift top. This vehicle was called a 'Tilbury-Phaeton' and the reason was this: a phaeton was a four-wheeled carriage with a folding top and a Tilbury a two-wheeled one — by calling it a Tilbury-Phaeton the coach-builders wanted to convey that the carriage was as light and handy as a Tilbury but still remained a Phaeton; but this designation was too complicated and as the carriage with its high rear wheels and thin single shaft coachwork looked a little like a spider, Holmes the coach-builders from Dublin coined the practical and simple word 'Spider.'

A contemporary description states: 'This type is exceptionally light in build, this being achieved by reducing the weight of all the elements — the frame, wheels, axis and seats, yet without reducing the strength of these parts....'

Even then the incorrect spelling of 'spyder' was used — perhaps the coach-builders were poor spellers, perhaps they really spelt the word with a 'y' in those days.

The first self-propelled spyder was mentioned in the brochure of Panhard-Levassor in 1901, an exceptionally smart two-seater without a hood, fitted with wheel steering and a front engine (rare in 1901) with an output of 7hp. It weighed about 15cwt, had a maximum speed of 27mph and cost 8,500 gold francs.

The next spyder in the history of the motor-car appeared in 1924 in England. There was a make of car called the G.N., owned by H.R. Godfrey and Archie Frazer-Nash. At the end of 1923 the G.N. company which had been founded in 1910 ceased to exist and Captain Frazer-Nash founded his own company under his own name. A well-known driver of the period, Basil Davenport, bought one of the last of the G.N. chassis and fitted it with an 1,100cc V-twin engine with overhead camshafts. This vehicle with its very narrow section wheels and narrow body, really looked like a spider and was so called. From 1926 to 1928 the G.N. Spyder held the Shelsley-Walsh record.

That then is our historical survey. One of the Spyders that was built for the motor show was once more loaned to Hans Stuck for two races in South America but still fitted with a 1,500cc pushrod engine and not the four-camshaft one. With it he won the 1,500cc class of the sports-car Grand Prix of Sao Paulo.

On the following day Stuck drove also in the Formula Libre racing-car class which was won by the Swiss de Graffenried in a 2-litre Maserati and Stuck managed to get into fifth place, a very good position considering he drove a sports car. Then it was sold in Brazil on the order of the works.

In the spring of 1954 the Swiss Racing Drivers' Association arranged their traditional 'racing school' in Campione on Lake Lugano. The House of Porsche had been invited to demonstrate a car for purposes of instruction and the 'pupils' were delighted when Porsche's not only turned up with a light alloy coupe but also with a 'hunchback' Spyder fitted with the four-camshaft engine.

Although Campione did not stage a race it was still the first appearance of the Porsche type 550 with the 547 engine in a sporting contest. Hans Herrmann drove several pupils in it around the circuit, which only measures 0.6 of a mile and at the end took part in a demonstration run in which Ascari and Taruffi drove 3.3-litre Lancia sports cars.

A little later the Spyder was entered for a proper motor race, the 1954 Mille Miglia. Porsche stated that they were going to run it experimentally, but they probably would not have let it start, had it not some chance in the 1,500cc sports car class. Again, the driver was Hans Herrmann and the passenger seat was occupied by Herbert Linge, an experienced racing and experimental mechanic who himself had raced on a number of occasions. In the first half of the race there was a sharp tussle with the 1,500cc Oscas, the fastest of which, however, dropped out with engine trouble, but Herbert Linge also had

137

to spend 20 minutes working on the car when the distributors got wet due to the heavy rain.

There was one very dangerous incident when Hans Herrmann approached a closed level crossing at such speed that there was no longer any question of braking (it is a fact that the Mille Miglia takes in public roads with level crossings and that railway traffic does not stop). The level crossing barriers remained closed for a very brief time and the sports cars had to wait, but Hans Herrmann could not stop and hitting Herbert Linge with the flat of his hand on his crash helmet to indicate that he should crouch down, he drove the Spyder underneath the bar of the level crossing whilst the train was still about 30 yards away. The Spyder was sufficiently low for this.

In this, the first important event of 1954. Hans Herrmann won the 1,500cc sports car class in the Mille Miglia with little opposition and became sixth in the general classification. This was the event in which Alberto Ascari won outright with a 3.3-litre Lancia in front of Vittorio Marzotto in a Ferrari and Musso in a Maserati.

New designs always have teething troubles and despite this very promising beginning there were two setbacks. During the Eifel race, Hans Herrmann appeared in the pits after the first lap. The engine no longer ran evenly and, far worse, trouble with the front suspension put him out of the race. Bechem and Hartmann in Borgwards won the 1,500cc class with little oppposition.

As an aside, let us mention that in the gran turismo class of up to 1,600cc a new name appeared, albeit with an old car and an engine which was not even entirely paid for — Wolfgang Graf von Trips. His first important event had been in the 1954 Mille Miglia when he acted as co-driver to the Wolfsburg engineer Hampel who owned a 1,300cc Super and the two achieved a class victory. Now he had appeared for the first time on the Nurburgring and got his car into second position after Josef Jeser. At the end of that season he was already gran turismo champion in the 1,600cc class and drove a works 300 SL Mercedes at the end of 1955 in Sweden and a 300 SLR in the Tourist Trophy in company with Fangio, Moss and Kling. In 1957 and 1958 he was in the Ferrari works team, being the only German grand prix driver collecting points for the world championship. Porsche-mounted he captured the title of European Hill Climb Champion.

But let us go back to the unpleasant happenings of 1954. After the Eifel races came Le Mans and three works Spyders were lined up at the start, all being equipped with a 1,500cc engine. Besides these an 1,100cc car was entered. One of the cars did not survive the first half-hour's racing and when it stopped at the pits it was found to have a holed piston. At first it was thought that the drivers had been too fast in the first laps and overdriven the vehicle. With half the race gone a second car stopped at the pits and faces grew longer. Five hours before the end the third 1,500cc car, driven carefully by the Belgians Claes and Stasse, came into the pits and stayed there for quite a while. Desperate measures were decided upon and they cut out one cylinder, letting the poor car bang along on three pots for the last four hours of the race. At that time an Osca was leading by 14 laps in the 1,500cc class, but the old racing rule was well-known to Porsche's men. Let's see who gets the chequered flag!

The Porsche Spyder won its class despite the two Oscas being so far ahead during the race. When only three cars remained in the 1,500cc class, the Oscas started an internecine battle between themselves, for both wanted to win — and both took a curve too fast in the pouring rain 1½ hours before the end, left the road and had to retire.

The fault which caused the retirement of the 1,500cc cars at Le Mans was a relatively small one: the ignition setting was wrong causing overheating due to which the pistons burnt through, but experience must be bought — the 1,100cc car ran without any trouble at all and won its class, it was driven by the American engineer Arkus-Duntove (development chief of Chevrolet) and the Frenchman Olivier.

To make up for the poor results at Le Mans, two Porsche Spyders appeared 14 days later in the 12-hour race at Rheims, where the Polensky/Frankenberg team easily won the 1,500cc class and thus the teething troubles had been definitely overcome. The sports car race preceding the German Grand Prix on the Nurburgring for instance saw four Porsches in first, second, third and fourth position. Now followed eighteen months during which the Porsche Spyder certainly was the leading and fastest vehicle in the 1½-litre class.

At the end of 1954 the first Spyders were sold to private owners and altogether more than 100 cars of the type 550 came onto the market, by far the larger part going to the U.S.A. The cars so sold were in no wise different from the works cars used in 1954, neither from the chassis nor the engine point of view. They produced about 110-115bhp and could be revved up to 7,500rpm.

In 1955 the Porsche Spyder at Le Mans won not only the 1,500cc class but also the Index of Performance; this had never happened before with a car in this class.

In the autumn of 1955 it became obvious for the first time, during the 500-kilometre race on the Nurburgring that other sports cars had more performance than the Spyder type '550.' The best lap time achieved with the 550 on the Nurburgring was 10 minutes 50 seconds and during practice for this race Edgar Barth with a very much improved EMW from Eastern Germany and also Jean Behra with a new 1½-litre Maserati got down to 10 minutes and 30 seconds. This was alarming.

The first improvement which was tried on the works cars consisted of a 5-speed gearbox besides a stiffened-up chassis. First gear of this box was for starting only and thus it was not really a 5-speed one in the proper sense. It was theoretically possible to change down into this starting gear which happened at a later stage during hill climbs, but being unsynchronised it was not particularly easy to engage via a special locking catch.

During all winter an improved model was developed for works racing, called the Spyder RS. This made a very promising debut during the 1,000-kilometre race at the Nurburgring and subsequently won the Targa Florio when driven by Maglioli. The Porsche RS (Rennsport) differed from the 550 in the following seven main points:

The engine, whilst basically similar, was made to produce 130bhp. The chassis was of an entirely new space frame arrangement, total weight was reduced by about 90 lb, and the rear axle was newly developed. It had two universals with a low mounted pivot point, whereas the front suspension remained the same; its wider brakes were already in use at Le Mans in 1955 and as previously mentioned, the 5-speed gearbox. Finally, for long distance races, the fuel capacity was increased to almost 28 gallons by using a side mounted tank, whereas previously 20 gallons were about the maximum.

The RS achieved lap times of 10 minutes 20 seconds to 10 minutes 25 seconds on the Nurburgring in 1956. Another car was built as a prototype in 1956, also a Spyder but with a shorter wheelbase of 200cm and narrower track. They also reduced the frontal area which helped top speed: this car was called the 'Mickey Mouse.' It was first seen during the Solitude race in 1956. The road holding was not 100% satisfactory and there was trouble with the brakes. Then the Mickey Mouse car was used in practice for the Nurburgring but not during the race. Finally it appeared in the last German event on the Avus where it shot over the top of the north loop banking in a most spectacular manner due to faulty material and burnt out completely. The Mickey Mouse type was not subsequently recalled to life.

In its stead, during the second half of 1957, a new prototype appeared at certain hill climbs with the same wheel base as the Spyder RS but with a different, slightly lower body with fins at the back and with a new front suspension — it was called the Spyder RSK. The 'K' originated from the shape of the front suspension because the two carrier tubes were at a 90-degree angle to the axis of the car and fitted in a sort of K-shaped manner.

The 1958-59 RSK models no longer had that 'K' front suspension, although the letters remained.

139

Porsche — Super — Spyder — 550 — Formula 2

After the works had used the Spyder RS for one season only, about thirty cars were built during the autumn of 1956 for sale to private owners and the same system was put into operation with the RSK. After one season the works car becomes the smaller series-produced car. This RSK which bore the internal type number 718, no longer had torsion bar suspension at the back but a low-pivot swing axle mounted on coil springs with double acting Koni shock absorbers fitted concentrically within them: thus for the first time the House of Porsche had abandoned its 'own' torsion-bar suspension, particularly because of a small weight saving and because road holding could be improved by the use of coil springs.

The RSK Spyder was also under consideration for modification into a Formula-2 car; steering could be centrally placed with suitable cowling of the driver's seat.

The RSK as sold was fitted with two Weber twin-choke carburettors of the type 46 IDM I; the engine had a compression ratio of 9.8 : 1 and delivered 148bhp at 8,000rpm; the rev limit was around 8,400rpm and maximum torque of 107.7 lb/ft was reached at 6,300rpm. The differential was of the limited-slip type.

The jump from 1,500cc sports to Formula-2 is not a big one, anyway that is what they said at Porsche's when a Formula-2 race was included in the 1957 German Grand Prix. They covered in the second seat in the Spyder RS — it was not yet the RSK, nor the central seater developed from it — and handed the car to Edgar Barth who had come to Zuffenhausen six months earlier from the Eastern zone because the management at EMW had decided not to compete in motoring sport any more. He had already put up good times when competing in the 1,000 kilometre race.

During grand prix practice, he achieved a time which was then thought well nigh impossible, 10 minutes 2.2 seconds, and during the race it soon became obvious that the timekeepers had not made a mistake. Barth joined battle wheel to wheel with the 'real' Formula-2 Cooper driven by Salvadori and once achieved a lap time of 10 minutes 5 seconds. During the second half of the race he could even afford to slow down because Salvadori had retired with a faulty transmission. Barth won the Formula-2 race on the Nurburgring in a convincing manner; the rest of the Coopers, all equipped with the 140bhp Climax engine, were considerably lighter than the Porsche but not so efficient aerodynamically with their exposed wheels.

The success and the times obtained by Barth were encouraging and in 1958 the works participated in two well-known Formula-2 races using the Spyder RSK. The first was at Rheims where Jean Behra was at the wheel, for he was to drive the marque in sports car events during the 1958 season. For Rheims the RSK was made into a central seater but apart from this it was still basically a sports car, even to having a starter and battery.

The RSK central seater certainly presented more frontal area than the low and small Cooper, but aerodynamically it had the advantage, and although it weighed some 2cwt more than the Cooper it had a few more bhp under the bonnet. The Cooper Climax would not produce more than 140-142bhp whereas Porsche's had developed engines which gave almost 160. These very highly tuned engines were not used in long distance events but only in hill climbs and short-distance Formula-2 races.

Apart from a whole field of Cooper and Lotus Formula-2 racing cars. a new Ferrari was also on the starting grid, driven at that time by Peter Collins. During the first laps there was a very tough struggle between the quickest Cooper driven by Stirling Moss (who had made fastest lap) Collins' Ferrari and Behra's Porsche. Whilst accelerating round the two hairpins on the Rheims circuit the lightweight Cooper managed to pull ahead a few yards, but at the end of the straight the better aerodynamics of the Porsche paid dividends and it seemed obvious to draw comparison with the 1954 G.P. when Mercedes made their debut in Formula-1 at Rheims, using aerodynamic all-enclosed cars which were faster than all the other competitors.

During the first half of the race Moss had to retire his Cooper, seemingly due to gearbox trouble. Collins with the Ferrari kept up the good work, but Behra gained one second per lap on him, until taking first place; he could even slow down towards the end of the race and yet win by a safe margin. No Cooper or Lotus — some twenty had started — could keep up with Behra's speed.

It seems remarkable that Behra's average was as high as Fangio's with a Formula-1 Mercedes in 1954; the Formula-2 vehicles of 1958 were therefore as fast on a high-speed circuit, such as Rheims, as the Formula-1 vehicles of 2,500cc in 1954. Such comparisons show clearly the technical advance in motor engineering — motor racing is a very accurate yardstick for this.

The second Formula-2 participation happened again on the Nurburgring when Formula-2 cars ran at the same time as the Formula-1 and for that reason Behra did not drive a Porsche as he was signed up with BRM for Formula-1 events. Porsche's had Edgar Barth, however, a particularly fast man on the Nurburgring, and his Formula-2 times deserve to be noted. His fastest lap took 9 minutes 42 seconds. On medium to fast circuits the Formula-2 cars of 1958 were already speedier than Formula-1 of 1954, for the 2½-litre cars could not better 9 minutes 55 seconds; Fangio in 1956 made his fastest lap in the Formula-1 Ferrari in 9 minutes 41 seconds, but, after all — he was Fangio!

Barth did not win the Formula-2 event which fell to Bruce McLaren in a Cooper Climax, who astonishingly enough drove for the first time on the Nurburgring that day and got down to lap times of 9 minutes 37 seconds. Phil Hill from America in a Formula-2 Ferrari was quite close at first but dropped back later with brake difficulties.

For the Avus race in September 1958 the central seater was loaned to the American, Masten Gregory, whereas Behra and Barth drove the RSK sports. Here on the Avus, where maximum speed is still more important than at Rheims even, there was never a doubt that Gregory could vanquish the Coopers and Lotuses. The spectators were astonished that this American grand prix driver should suddenly appear at the wheel of a Formula-2 Porsche but it must be appreciated that Gregory was no stranger to Porsches; as long ago as 1955, together with his countryman Carroll Shelby, he had handled a Spyder 550 works car in the Tourist Trophy on the Dundrod circuit near Belfast when they had won the 1,500cc class. The more successful Porsche became in the general classification of the big races the more did the grand prix drivers want to drive them. Equally it was realized at the works, that it would be necessary to use grand prix drivers because lap times for the 1,500cc cars were getting down to the values which a few years ago had been the exclusive province of the grand prix stars.

Stirling Moss had also driven a Porsche on several occasions: during the 9-hour race at Goodwood and the sports car Grand Prix of Portugal in 1955; then again in January 1958 during the 1,000 kilometres of Argentina where he was due to drive a 3-litre Maserati which became damaged during the first practice day and could not be got ready in time. Racing manager Huschke von Hanstein offered Moss and Behra a 1,586cc Spyder for that race, the type which had already been used for the last events of the European hill climb championship in 1957 (there had even been a 1,700cc version, but this was only used in three hill climbs because the crankshaft did not seem to be sufficiently strong for longer distances — the 1957 championship was for 2-litre sports cars).

Moss and Behra did not agree immediately but wanted to try the car first, and the British ace put up a time on his fourth lap which the Porsche people had not thought possible even in their most optimistic forecasts — in fact it was good enough to put him in the middle of the 3-litre sports cars; Behra's time in practice was only a second slower. During this 1,000 kilometres of Buenos Aires, Moss and Behra drove the 1,600 Spyder RS into third position in the overall classification behind the leading two 3-litre Ferraris, the second of which only overtook Porsche during the last five laps.

In connection with grand prix drivers handling Porsche cars the question is often raised 'why are the aces faster than very good sports car drivers?' During the Argentinian race the answer became very obvious: Moss and Behra gained their decisive seconds not on the slow 75-80mph bends but on the very fast curves, where it was a question of taking them at 130 or 135mph. To grand prix drivers, accustomed to maximum speeds of around 165-180mph and used to handling power/weight ratios of 4½-6 lb/bhp, a car with a maximum speed of 145 to 155mph and a ratio of 6½-9 lb/bhp does not exactly seem small beer, but at least its handling is far less problematical.

As the little Porsche sports cars did so well in the general classification of the big events during 1958 and 1959, a lot of useful points were acquired towards the sports car world championship and the firms who fielded the 3-litre cars, Ferrari and Aston Martin, treated Porsche's points with considerable respect; the Zuffenhausen works were second after Ferrari in 1958 having acquired the same number of points as Aston Martin.

The greatest post-war success of Porsche was the Targa Florio of 1959. Although neither Aston Martin nor Jaguar appeared at the start, Ferrari fielded a whole battle order. Despite that, none of the 3- and 2-litre cars of the Italian works finished this traditional race of 1,008 kilometres; Porsche occupied the first four positions and some will have recalled the Targa Florio of 1924 when Christian Werner was victorious with the 2-litre Mercedes, developed and refined by Professor Porsche: in the years between, German vehicles had twice won there, Mercedes with Moss and Collins in 1955 and Porsche with Maglioli in 1956. The 1959 winners were Edgar Barth and Wolfgang Seidel with a 1,500cc RSK.

In the spring of 1959 Porsche took the next step towards Formula-2: a car with exposed wheels was developed, firstly because a fully enveloping car was not so suitable for circuits with many slow corners on account of extra weight and secondly because they wanted to have a design study object, in view of the future 1½-litre racing formula due to begin in 1961.

When a journalist asked Ferry Porsche in 1953 whether the firm had any intention of constructing formula racing cars, Ferry Porsche replied in his own particular way: 'The name of Porsche, as you know very well, has been closely associated with grand prix racing for decades. It follows that we shall always be interested in it in the future, as far as economic possibilities permit. But at the moment no racing car is being built here.'

The economic possibilities arose five years later helped by the fact that the 1½-litre engine had been so successful in the sports car. One could therefore suppose that success was likely also in the racing car formula, and for this reason they built an experimental car that was tested a few days before Monaco by Count von Trips at the Nurburgring. It had exposed wheels, a chassis that had been developed from the RSK and weighed some 10cwt with 160bhp. Trips got down to 9 minutes 29.8 seconds on the third lap and so it was decided to enter it in the Formula-1 race at Monte Carlo.

In this race only 16 of the fastest cars, according to practice times were admitted. Trips managed to qualify the Porsche and he, with the Formula-2 Ferrari and Lotus, were the only Formula-2 cars on the grid — but the experiment ended in the second lap when Trips spun, hitting a wall and damaging the car extensively. But for the Formula-2 race at Rheims on the 5th July 1959 it was rebuilt and Joakim Bonnier, who was signed up with Porsche for sports cars during 1959 and with BRM for Formula-1, managed to get it into third position. Second man in that event was Hans Herrmann in another Formula-2 Porsche which however had not been built at Zuffenhausen. Jean Behra had obtained an engine from Ferry Porsche and Collotti of Modena had built a chassis and body for it. This 'Behra-Porsche' or 'Collotti-Porsche' was a little lighter than the works cars, weighing about 90 lbs less and Hans Herrmann, to whom Behra lent the car, was able to keep up with Moss. He even took the lead on several occasions.

The Cooper which Moss drove at Rheims had a Borgward engine. Cooper's had noted during the 1958 season that the Climax engine would probably not be potent enough in its 1½-litre version to cope with all the competition. Then Borgward stated that for the time being they would retire from motoring sports and Cooper's tried the very powerful Borgward engine in one of their chassis in the late autumn of 1958. The Borgward engine gave 165 bhp and now in 1959 they were using the very fast Cooper-Borgward.

The duel between Herrmann and Moss resolved itself to the advantage of Moss when Herrmann had to use the escape road at the Thillois hairpin, which put him back a few seconds. Anyway, he managed a good second place and Trips, with the central seater RSK got into fifth position. Thus Porsche played an ever increasing part in the great sporting events of the last years and it is to the credit of the Zuffenhausen works that they had so participated without a break since 1951 — in this they were alone in German sport, a sport which not only served to advance technical development and sales of their own products but brought prestige in foreign countries to German companies.

26 The Speedster – Type 356A – Carrera – Carrera GT

LET us go back to series-production developments. Right from the start the Porsche factory used two body types, the coupe and the drophead. In the autumn of 1954 a third type came about, especially for export to America and particularly for the Californian climate, a body shape called 'speedster.' This could be obtained with all the engines available at Porche's at that time: 1,300cc, 1,300cc Super, 1,500cc and 1,500cc Super.

The speedster was almost 135 lb lighter than the coupe and was equipped with lightweight racing seats in lieu of the comfortable. thickly-upholstered ones. There were no wind-up windows, a different facia board, a lower front screen and a folding top which could only be considered as makeshift. When it was up, visibility was very poor and weather protection could hardly be called perfect — to put it frankly the rain entered somewhere on most cars!

Porsche did not hide any of these facts: the car was designed for good-weather motoring in a warm climate and it was very popular in the States. Apart from this, sporting motorists esteemed it highly — because of its low weight.

The speedster had a certain history, for the prototype of the 356 built in the spring of 1948 in Gmund could really be referred to as a sort of speedster. The wish for an open two-seater with a more sporting character than the drophead coupe was always present. In the spring of 1951 a sporting motorist from Stuttgart had such a car built, which, with a steel body, weighed almost a ton. This vehicle was seen during the Eifel race of 1951 with a tuned 1,500cc engine. Heinrich Sauter put up second fastest practice time with it but had to give up with engine trouble during the race. During August the car was used in from Liege-Rome-Liege and subsequently it was taken over by a French driver called Francois Picard, who called it 'le petit tank.' It was last seen in the sports car race of Monte Carlo in the spring of 1952.

In 1951 Johnny von Neumann, who had the Porsche agency for the West Coast of the United States, built himself a roadster or speedster; he simply cut off the top of a light alloy coupe which had been sold to the States. With this car, fitted with a small aero screen, von Neumann won the Torrey Pines Trophy race in California.

All these, however, were 'home-made' single examples, but in the early summer of 1952 there was a 'legitimate' speedster precursor of which only fifteen were built. It was called 'America-Roadster' and had a flat wind-screen which was removable so that a racing aero screen could be fitted. It only weighed about 12cwt and with the 70bhp Super engine provided a power/weight ratio of about 18 lb/bhp and thus accelerated much better than the coupe.

In the States this car won a considerable number of races and good positions in others. Prominent people who drove it included Briggs Cunningham, the creator of the Cunningham sports car, who had tried very seriously from 1951 to 1953 to do well at Le Mans with an American sports car. His cars were usually equipped with 5.5-litre Chrysler or Cadillac engines and generally finished the race but could never really hold a candle to the much lighter, smaller-capacity Ferrari and Jaguars; yet they were an interesting facet of the racing scene and deserve a place in post-war sporting history (the biggest Cunningham success was his third place in the 1953 24-hour race at Le Mans).

Only one American roadster ran in Germany, in the hands of Kurt Zeller, brother of the well-known motor-cycle racer Walter Zeller.

In 1954 there was another new item for all Porsche types — a crankcase, in three parts. Until then Porsche's still used the VW crankcase, even for the 1,500cc, but suitably modified. This was only discarded in September 1954 and then as before, all castings were ordered from outside contractors, as Porsche's had no foundry. A third novelty for 1954 was the fitting of an anti-roll bar in front which improved road holding and slightly reduced the oversteering tendency.

A decisive step towards the improving of the chassis was taken for the motor shows of 1955. After 1952, when the big brakes and synchronized gearbox were first fitted, this was the second important milestone in the technical history of the Porsche car. The innovations concerned both engine and chassis.

Now the type number was no longer 356 but 356A and the 'A' refers to the new chassis. The rear shock absorbers were now fitted vertically and not at an angle; the front anti-roll bar was increased in diameter from 14 to 15mm, and a whole number of details in the steering and suspension were modified to such a degree that the 356A could hardly be said to oversteer any more. Its road holding was so near neutral that in negotiating many-cornered mountain roads the Porsche could almost be considered to understeer, tending to 'go' in front; this did in fact happen in certain borderline situations on wet roads. Apart from that the 356A depended more on differing tyre profiles, in other words with certain types one could bring about over- or understeer.

The construction and profile of tyres has far greater influence on a fast car than is generally realized. Not only are there tyres which are better on wet roads than others but there are differences in the achieved top speeds which can vary by as much as 10mph from tyre to tyre. Such wide differences are only marked on really fast cars.

The Porsche engineers had tested the car's road holding very accurately on a small aerodrome near Stuttgart. It is a mistake to think that road holding cannot be measured and that one is dependent on the sensitiveness of the driver; on this aerodrome there are circles with certain radii, along which cars are tested with different tyres, spring rates, torsion bars, etc. They are driven faster and faster until there is a tendency to slide or rear-wheel breakaway. The relative speed with which one can drive the car on these circles can be measured accurately, and on an aerodrome where there are no curbs or ditches, skidding out is entirely without danger.

The 1,500cc engine of the 'Dame' and the Super was increased to 1,600cc in the autumn of 1955 (bore 52.5mm, stroke 74mm) and the exact cubic capacity was now 1,582cc. The 'Dame' had a compression ratio of 7.5 : 1 and the Super's was increased to 8.5 : 1, providing the former with 60bhp at 4,000rpm and the latter with 75bhp at 5,000rpm. Maximum speeds were 100 and 110mph respectively. The type Dame had a softer camshaft than the Super. The type reference of the Super engine was previously 528 and the Dame 546, now that further development had taken place it was referred to

145

as 616/1 and 616/2.

Apart from the two 1,600cc cars the autumn programme of 1955 still contained the 1,300cc and 1,300cc Super engines, but both of these ceased in the spring of 1956. The 1,300cc Super engine which had been used for the first time in the 1,000 kilometre race in 1953 on the Nurburgring, had put up creditable performances in the following two years in the 1,300cc gran turismo class and was quite popular with the competition drivers (1,290cc, 60bhp at 5,500rpm, compression 8.2 : 1), but when Alfa Romeo developed the Sprint Veloce with 90bhp from the Giulietta Sprint (all this from 1,300cc), there was no longer any chance for the 1,300cc Super in competition. In 1955 two 1,300cc Supers (Count Trips and R. von Frankenberg) still won their class in the Mille Miglia, but in 1956 this was no longer possible. Porsche did not develop the 1,300cc engine any further for they wanted to concentrate on the 1,600cc class.

But a new star had appeared on the sporting horizon of the private owner: the Porsche Carrera, or as it was known in the works, the type 356A/1500 GS with the 547/1 engine.

The Carrera owed its name to the Carrera Panamericana. Carrera is a Spanish word and means 'race' and the Carrera was the short name for that famous long-distance event that used to be run in Mexico from its southern to its northern frontier, on the one and only road joining North and South America. Officially this race was called the Carrera Panamericana Mexico, and it was held for the last time in 1954. A year later the Mexican Automobile Club could no longer organize it because landslides and floods had so damaged sections of the road that it could not be put into a raceworthy condition.

Porsches participated privately in that race for the first time in 1952, the entrants being Count Metternich and Count Berckheim with a 1,500cc coupe and a drophead. Berckheim retired with gearbox trouble, but Metternich finished as the fastest 1,500cc in eighth position in the general classification. Two Mercedes 300 SL's, driven by Karl Kling and Herman Lang won this event outright.

In the following year Karl Kling drove a Porsche Spyder (Daimler-Benz did not participate) and a second Spyder from the works was driven by Hans Herrmann. Neither of these finished, Kling suffering engine derangements and Hans Herrmann having to retire because of rather worrying front-axle trouble.

After the Porsche retirement, Hans Hugo Hartmann in a works Borgward took the lead in the 1,500cc class, but was later overtaken by Jaroslav Juhan from Guatemala in a Porsche. Juhan's car was one of the Le Mans 1953 models with a 1,500cc Super engine which had been sold independently. Juhan did not finish, but Hartmann's chance seemed to be very good until, 130 miles from the finish, he had to slow down very considerably, having broken a valve spring.

For each stage of the Carrera there was a maximum time limit which could not be exceeded without the car being disqualified. Hartmann was unlucky and crossed the finishing line a few seconds after the maximum time allowance and so was deemed a non-finisher leaving the Mexican private owner Jose Herrarte, who had also bought a Le Mans Porsche, to win his class in the 1953 Carrera, first over all being Fangio at the wheel of a 3.1-litre Lancia in front of Taruffi and Castellotti.

The fifth Carrera Panamericana, in November 1954, resulted in a convincing victory for Porsche. Hans Herrmann drove a works 550 Spyder and so did Jaroslav Juhan. At the beginning of the race things looked a little doubtful for Herrmann as he had two bouts of tyre trouble on the first stage and had to drive the last 40 miles on the canvas. Gunther Bechem in a Borgward won that sector and Juhan was second. During the third stage Herrmann began catching up, Bechem had suffered an accident and Juhan was in the lead. On the last stage but one, Herrmann had caught him up and was satisfied to take the lead by only a small margin, thus giving Porsche's a double success in the 1,500cc class, apart from being third in the general classification with an average speed of 99.3mph after that the winner Maglioli on a 4.9-litre Ferrari and Phil Hill on a 4.5-litre Ferrari, Juhan followed in fourth position.

In remembrance of the Porsche successes in this Carrera Panamericana a new, faster Porsche was type-named 'Carrera.' To be quite accurate, this model had really nothing to do with the Central American race; it had not run there for the simple reason that at the time the car was designed the Carrera itself was no longer run. On the other hand, there was every justification for naming a competition model after a specific and famous racing venue.

It was certainly meant primarily for sporting purposes, to be accurate for the gran turismo class of up to 1,600cc in which, for a number of years it really had no equal. It is a phenomenon in itself that no other company tried at that time to field a car to compete with the Carrera, which became the classic sports car for the fast owner/drivers in races all over the world.

During motor races there is no call for a car-heater and on the Carrera the problem of heating the inside was solved in a most unsatisfactory manner, which earned it the title of 'the most expensive refrigerator in Europe.' Engine accessibility was also not so easy as on the normal Porsche types. On the Spyder the whole rear decking could be removed to work on the engine; the same engine, however, on the Carrera had to make do with the normal rear 'bonnet' so that changing plugs for instance needed a certain amount of time and dexterity. But touring-car standards cannot be applied to cars which achieve 125mph from 1,500cc, can be revved up to 7,500rpm and produce 70bhp per litre.

The engine of the Carrera was in principle exactly the same as in the Spyder but it had been made a little 'tamer' so that it could be used in town traffic. Its bore and stroke were 85mm by 66mm, i.e. 1,498cc, but compression ratio was only 8.7 : 1 instead of 9.5 or 9.8 : 1; it gave 100bhp at 6,200rpm. Whereas the 1,600cc models in normal and Super form had a tyre size of 5.60in by 15in. the Carrera had 5.90in. by 15in. super-sports tyres, in other words fatter ones, all the better to transmit the 'horses' onto the road, apart from which the Carrera weighed a little more than the 1,600cc models. With a full tank it weighed 17½cwt against about 17cwt for the normal car. Externally it looked exactly like the other cars apart from the small 'Carrera' at the back in gold letters.

Later it was available in two versions, so that the exacting fast-touring owner could have a 125mph motor-car with reasonable comfort — the Carrera de Luxe included the normal fittings of the rest of the range and even had useable heating. For competition drivers on the other hand, the car was made lighter, sliding instead of wind-up windows were fitted and it had racing seats instead of the heavy upholstered ones; also the engine was given a few more horses. This then was the Carrera GT (gran turismo). The 1,500cc logically became the 1,600cc for it came into the 1,600cc class. Just as on the 1,600cc Super they abandoned the roller-bearing crankshaft and fitted a plain bearing one — the reason being that the roller bearing tended, in certain cases, to have rather a short life.

The Carreras that raced in the 1959 season in the class of 'improved gran turismo vehicles up to 1,600cc' had between 120 and 130bhp, in certain cases even a little over 130. On the Nurburgring they achieved lap times which under favourable conditions lay between 10 minutes 45 seconds, and 10 minutes 55 seconds — the same times as were achieved during 1954 and 1955 by the Spyders. On the other hand the Spyders of that period were not particularly light and weighed around 13½cwt for 110bhp, so that a power/weight ratio of 11.8 lb/bhp resulted. The Carreras with their 130bhp weighed about 15½cwt and therefore had a power/weight ratio of about 13.7 lb/bhp. That was still a little worse than the Spyder during the first year, but on the other hand, the road holding of the 1959 Carrera was better than that of the 1954 Spyder which compensated for the small disadvantage in power/weight ratio.

As far as top speed was concerned the Carreras provided about 128-130mph whereas the Spyders with a 15-20bhp less got up to 138 or so, no doubt owing to the considerably smaller frontal area. On the Nurburgring however, out and out maximum speed is not so important, on circuits such as Hockenheim the Carrera could never match the times of the Spyder.

On many European circuits interesting battle developed in the 1,600cc class. Just to mention a few names, Max Nathan, Hans Joachim Walter, Paul Ernst Strahle and Sepp Greger won championships in Germany; Hammarlund won the Swedish gran turismo championship on several occasions, and Claude Storez, who crashed fatally in 1958, became French champion. Storez, in company with his countryman Buchet, won the Liege-Rome-Liege rally outright in 1957 at the wheel of a privately owned Carrera Speedster.

Liege-Rome-Liege should have its own chapter in the sports history of Porsche. Beyond doubt it was the toughest rally in Europe, 3,300 miles non-stop with many speed sections on which the prescribed average of 31-37mph could not even be maintained by the fastest cars and the best drivers. Some special stages had to be covered at 44mph averages and these took the drivers over very steep, curving and narrow alpine roads which were closed to ordinary traffic during the event. This rally, which had been run also before the war and which the Belgians and the French call the 'marathon of the road,' had German participation from Adler and Hanomag in those pre-war days.

The Storez/Buchet success of 1957 was the third Porsche victory in the general classification of this very difficult event and the fourth one came in 1959 through Paul Ernst Strahle and Buchet who again won it outright at the wheel of a Carrera Speedster. This was a particularly significant success because Strahle had to cover more than a third of the whole distance without second gear until this could be put right. Despite this he managed to keep to the 31mph average on the feared Gavia pass.

27 Pages from the past – Diesel tractors

DURING March 1956 Porsche's celebrated the 25th anniversary of the founding of the firm and about the same time the 10,000th car was produced. Let us cast our minds back: in December 1930 Ferdinand Porsche had moved into the Kronenstrasse in Stuttgart to establish his own design office, but only in the spring of 1931 did this office become officially registered and therefore this date was chosen as the anniversary. It was a cheerful occasion particularly because the beginning of 1956 saw the old Porsche works being handed back. It was called Works No. 1 and contained the repair section, the entire design office, management and the experimental and racing department. Hans Kern, called the 'minister of finance' of Porsche and who joined them in 1933, became solely responsible for finance in 1942 and submitted a very interesting production statement in respect of the years that had passed:

Year	Staff Employees	Workers	Total	Turnover in D. Marks	Production	Place
1931	13	–	13	–	–	Stuttgart
1938	66	49	115	1,602,000	–	Stuttgart
1944	299	289	588	5,852,000	–	Stuttgart
1945	39	119	158	2,068,000	–	Gmund
1946	53	169	222	1,319,000	–	Gmund
1949	9	3	12	625,000	–	Stuttgart
1950	48	60	108	4,438,000	298	Stuttgart
1951	93	121	214	12,511,000	1,103	Stuttgart
1953	175	262	437	24,271,000	1,978	Stuttgart
1955	232	384	616	38,000,000	2,952	Stuttgart
1959	–	–	1,100	90,000,000	7,600	
1973	–	4,280	–	397,000,000	15,415 (911)	Stuttgart
					(914)	Ludwigsburg
1975	–	3,750	–	353,000,000	9,224 (911)	Stuttgart

A new man in a leading position was Claus von Rucker, who took over the technical management of production and experimental departments. Before the war he had worked at BMW — among other things he looked after the German team during the Six-Day trial — after the war he worked first in Canada, then in the U.S.A. as vice-chief of development at Studebaker's. As before, Walter Schmidt was in charge of sales, Huschke von Hanstein the public relations boss and racing manager and in the latter department Wilhelm Hild was in charge of sports car development and Kirn was chief buyer.

There had been a change at the very top and new perspectives arose from this. On 1st January 1956 Professor Dr. Prinzing was put in sole charge at Friedrichshafen of an entirely new company called Porsche-Diesel-Motorenbau GmbH who, under their own flag, began to produce tractors which until that time had been built on the basis of Porsche licences by Allgaier in Uhingen.

Thus we arrive once more on the subject of tractors, a subject at first seeming a little remote and uninteresting to the motorist, but so important from the point of view of economics that it is not solely of interest to farmers — besides which the Porsche diesel history is quite a fascinating one.

Let us be quite clear about Friedrichshafen — Porsche's contribution to these works consisted of ideas, designs and patents; they supplied the production experts, tractor experts and those who sold them, also the service engineers. The money came from Mannesmann. The first contact with Mannesmann, or to be accurate, with its managing director Dr. Hermann Winkhaus, came about in the autumn of 1950. At that time no one thought about tractors let alone Friedrichshafen, nor did Dr. Winkhaus or old Professor Porsche, as they sat opposite each other in Stuttgart to discuss the 'rain-cannon.' At Mannesmann's they were busy developing a 'cannon' capable of dosing large farms with enough 'rain' to take away the fear of drought: accumulated water was to be made to fall by way of rain at predetermined intervals.

'You are able to design everything,' Dr. Winkhaus said to Dr. Porsche. 'You have not only designed cars and aeroplane engines but also wind machines and turbines. You should be able to advise us how to control this 'rain-cannon'.' Professor Porsche started discussion with Winkhaus and made a few suggestions which were very welcome at Mannesmann's. In all probability this talk with Winkhaus was one of the last technical discussions held by Professor Porsche, for a few days afterwards he had a stroke which put him to bed and later he had to be taken to hospital. He died on 30th January 1952, as we already know.

Five years later the Mannesmann-Porsche discussions were revived. Allgaier in Uhingen, who in the meantime were building the Allgaier tractor 'System-Porsche' especially the type AP 17 with the 17bhp engine tended to return to their own special field in which they had specialized for many years: the manufacture of machine tools. The tractor business seemed to be slowing up, for competition amongst the manufacturers was getting very tough and sales were faltering.

Under the protective umbrella of Mannesmann a new works was built in Friedrichshafen for the manufacture of tractors, and in the first months of its existence the new company produced the same types as Allgaier had made; at the beginning these were still called Allgaier but a gradual change-over to a new type and to their own name took place.

To be accurate, the Porsche-Diesel factory was not in Friedrichshafen itself but in a suburb of the town made famous by the development of the Zeppelin air ships and through the work of Maybach and ZF; the Porsche works are in Manzell, about two miles north-west of the centre of Friedrichshafen on the road to Meersburg, directly on the shores of the lake Constance. From the point of view of engineering history the works at Manzell are on historic ground. Here, on the spot where tractors were produced, used to be a jetty which extended into the lake. From there in the year 1900, the first Zeppelin airship, the 'LZ 1' designed by Count Zeppelin took to the air. For this airship they built a floating hangar which was tied up to the jetty at Manzell; later this ground belonged to the Dornier aircraft factory and from here at the end of the 'twenties and early 'thirties, started the big Dornier flying boats which had quite a place in the history of German aviation.

In the middle of this area there is a curious, somewhat derelict small building which was once a chapel. The roads on which the tractors and the lorries of the suppliers and construction companies travel are carefully arranged to go round this chapel which stands on a little hillock in the middle of this modern technical world. Its existence is closely allied to the name of Manzell, a name even older than Friedrichshafen or Buchhorn (which was the first name of Friedrichshafen). In the year 826 of our era, during the reign of Ludwig the Godfearing, son of Charles the Great, this very ground is mentioned and so is the little chapel.

A monk from the monastery of St. Gallen, called Manus, founded there a hermitage, the 'Zelle des Manus' from which the name of Manzell is derived. Some of the foundations of the old chapel seem to go back to the tenth century and where the 'cell' of Manus had stood, some small chapels were probably built a little later.

At first the Allgaier programme was taken over and four tractors of 12, 22, 33 and 44hp were built, but at the same time a programme for a simplified system was worked out. First was the little 12hp tractor with a single cylinder. The next bigger types simply had an extra cylinder added with the same cubic capacity and identical pistons, connecting rods and pushrods. This obviously simplified service and of 87% of all spare parts were interchangeable among all the tractor types. Only the steering and axles were not the same in all the types.

In the meantime the horsepower output of all types was increased, the single cylinder giving 14hp and called Porsche-Diesel Junior, the twin cylinder 25hp ('Standard'), the 3-cylinder ('Super') providing 38hp, and the 'Master,' a 4-cylinder with 50hp. All of them are air cooled by means of a radial fan driven by gear wheels from the camshaft and not by V belt. The amount of cooling air can be regulated from the driving seat. Tractors must be foolproof: if they overheat the horn sounds.

The motorist would find unusual the fact that all these tractors have adjustable track width and some have four and even seven different positions, making them suitable for particular agricultural purposes and soil conditions. The job is simply done by pulling out the half-shafts in front. All have lockable differentials and the 'Standard' and 'Super' also have a hydraulic Voith anti-stall clutch, apart from the normal single dry-plate clutch. With it the tractor can be started in any gear without stalling and even if one were to start with the handbrake on, this clutch would automatically disconnect the power from the drive shafts and the engine would continue running — the dream of all driving school pupils! Bottom gear in these tractors is a 'crawler', one in which it can move with the speed (if that is the right word) of 0.6 miles per hour.

From time to time the Porsche clubs have visited the Porsche-Diesel works in Friedrichshafen and it is a particular delight for the drivers to try their prowess at the wheel of a tractor — unless, of course, they are farmers. Even the former world champion Fangio, when visiting the tractor plant, drove one of them when he was interested in their representation in Argentina.

From the end of 1950 to the end of 1955 Allgaier in Uhingen had built 34,000 tractors. The production figures in Friedrichshafen continued to climb and in 1956 they were 9,465, in 1957 — 11,027, and in 1958 as many as 16,927.

The tractor plant was sold to another manufacturer in 1962.

28 Stationary, boat and aircraft engines

NOW that we have visited Friedrichshafen, let us again return to Zuffenhausen, but this time not to the car factory, for in connection with the 25 years' jubilee in the spring of 1956 it is time to consider developments taking place in the quiet of the design office: stationary engines, boat and aircraft power units were taken into the manufacturing programme. As far as the industrial engine was concerned the first numbers were built in 1953 in agreement with the Volkswagen works which had brought out an industrial engine the previous year. In its construction and special equipment the Porsche was similar to the VW industrial engine and accordingly sold by those agents who also sold the VW engine and serviced it. In this connection the output of the 1,500cc Porsche engine was reduced to 43bhp at 3,600rpm.

In the autumn of 1955 the industrial engine of 1,600cc saw the light of day and the further development of the car engine was incorporated in the industrial one, although the latter was only fitted with one carburettor and had the relatively low compression ratio of 6.5 : 1. Thus Porsche engines in the last few years have powered fire engines, generator welding sets, self-propelled harvesters, and threshers, donkey engines, snow-clearing machines, compressors and 30 kVA electrical generators.

The first boat engines ran during the autumn of 1955; to be more exact one experimental boat privately owned by Mr. Porsche operated on the Worther See and the Swiss importer of Porsche had one on the lake of Zurich. But a good while had to elapse before Porsche boat engines were produced in larger numbers, and even then they were supplied to governmental departments for such uses as rescue launches, rather than to private buyers. The conquest of the water is still to come but the conquest of the air is proceeding apace. After the different aero engines (type number 678/0 up to 678/3) had been tested and pronounced airworthy by the government, they were fitted into two aircraft, the 'RW3' of Rhein-Westflug in Krefeld and the 'Elster' by Putzer. Experimentally, the Porsche engine was also fitted to a tailless aircraft by Horten and into the 'Motorraab.' The different types varied in their power output between 52 and 65bhp and some were equipped with magnetos, yet others with coil ignition. In the autumn of 1959 an RW3 with Porsche engine made a good showing in an air rally at Baden-Baden. This first appearance in the sport of flying was noted with considerable interest for the Porsche 1,600cc engine was the first aircraft engine developed after the war in Germany.

In its basic concept it was almost identical, just as the stationary ones, to the engines used in the car and it was air-cooled. Only the reduction gearing for the air screw and the twin ignition, prescribed for aircraft engines, distinguish it.

29 Mountain Championship
– Targa Florio

BETWEEN 1957 and 1959 the Porsche Company was particularly active in contesting the European Hill Climb championship and considerable successes were achieved. This European championship was first competed for in 1930; in the sports-car class Caracciola then won with a Mercedes SSK and in the racing-car class Hans Stuck became champion at the wheel of the Austro-Daimler ADM-R. In 1932 it was no longer called the European mountain championship but the International Alpine Championship - this ceased in 1933 but was revived in 1957 for sports cars up to 2 litres capacity.

Porsche fielded Edgar Barth and Umberto Maglioli in the first two events (Mont Ventoux and Schauinsland) first with a 1,500cc and then the 1,600cc Spyder RS; opposition came from the 2-litre works Maserati driven by the Swiss champion Daetwyler and the Borgward 1500 of Hans Herrmann and Cabianca. In Freiburg in 1957 the Porsche was for the first time used in its 1,600cc guise. This 1,600cc version of the Spyder engine was employed in the following years in several races; in fact wherever Porsche wanted to compete in the 2-litre class and where they had to face cars of bigger cubic capacity. Increasing the cubic capacity brought about only a small advantage in maximum bhp but the improved torque curve showed up to advantage.

Whilst practising for the Gaisberg event, the third heat of the championship in 1957, there was a regrettable accident in which both Barth and Maglioli were involved: they were together in a Carrera studying the track the day before practice. They were driving quite slowly, tourist fashion, for learning a new track can only be done at a slow pace. It was early in the morning, shortly after sunrise, and they were running downhill through a blind and long-drawn-out right-hand curve on the right-hand side of the road. They were met by another driver roaring uphill in a tuned-up touring car entered for the race. He was attempting to practice at racing speed prior to the official practice period and in cutting the curve disregarded the possibility of other traffic on the road. This resulted in a head-on collision with Barth and Maglioli, and Barth was out of the running for the following four weeks with a broken jaw, whereas Maglioli sustained a complicated fracture of the leg, so complicated in fact that he was away from the racing wheel for a year and a half. This emphasizes that unauthorized practising must be stamped out. In one fell swoop this accident stopped both hill-climb experts of Porsche's and the points they had already gained were nullified for they are always awarded to the driver and not to the make of car.

Porsche tried to make up for this unfortunate occurrence in the further heats of the championship but no one could keep up with the Swiss Daetwyler who was already at an advantage due to the greater cubic capacity of his Maserati engine. The two Spyder RS with the 1,600cc engines were therefore driven at Gaisberg by Huschke von Hanstein and Richard von Frankenberg and at the next event in Switzerland, at Lenzerheide. Von Trips was also fielded as well as Frankenberg. The former had been driving Ferraris in that season but the Italian Scuderia 'lent' him to Porsche's for the mountain championship.

In the Swiss event, Trips was seen at the wheel of a 1,700cc version of the Spyder engine — a logical further development within the framework of the 2-litre class. This 1,700cc engine was only used for very short events such as hill climbs, since it was feared that not only the crankshaft but also some parts of the transmission would be unable to cope with the increased power and torque of this engine. In the 1958 season the 1,700cc engine did not appear again, but it was briefly seen in 1959 during the Targa Florio and at the Tourist Trophy at Goodwood.

Frankenberg's car, at the Lenzerheide event in 1958, was no longer the Spyder RS but the prototype of the RSK which was due to be used the following years. Such a prototype had also been used in 1957 at the 24-hours of Le Mans by the Barth/Maglioli team. It did not finish the race then because Maglioli had a slight accident with it: Tony Brooks with the 3-litre Aston Martin had a broadside skid at the Tertre Rouge right-hander just in front of Maglioli's car. (Brooks at that time had only fourth gear available on his Aston Martin due to transmission trouble and thus not enough power to correct a small skid.) The resultant minor collision damaged the car, but fortunately Maglioli was unhurt.

The Frankenberg car in Lenzerheide had a 1,600cc engine and he tied for second place with Daetwyler. Trips made fastest time for Porsche and Hans Herrmann, who during that season had changed over to Borgward after driving a Porsche at Le Mans, was in fourth position only two-tenths of a second behind. In hill climbs tenths of seconds often play a decisive role and some drivers are better 'sprint' drivers than others. Trips proved himself to be a 'sprinter' in the first hill climbs that he essayed and consolidated this in 1958 to an even greater degree.

The last but one event of the 1957 season was in Italy. The Aosta-Great St. Bernard hill climb is the longest of its type in Europe and starts at the end of the village of Aosta, the finishing line coinciding exactly with the top of the St. Bernard Pass, a total of 33.8 kilometres (about 21 miles), the last 4 miles of which having a loose surface. Porsche wanted to enter Barth besides Trips and Frankenberg after both the German and Austrian doctors expressed no worries regarding his fitness, but the Italians had him examined by their own doctors and refused to let him drive, therefore the third Spyder RS was driven by the Italian Munaron who had already driven the works car experimentally at Freiburg. Daetwyler won this event in front of Trips and thereby became Hill Climb Champion of 1957 even before the last event in Greece. This, on Mont Parnes, just outside Athens, was won by Trips in front of the 1,500cc Borgward of Herrmann. The international regulations, however, prescribed that the drivers would have to participate in at least four of the six championship events for their points to count towards the championship. Even though one driver might achieve a notably higher number of points in three events than some other drivers in four or five, these did not count; this somewhat curious interpretation showed that regulations are sometimes thought up by people who no longer have sufficient contact with the sport. It followed that the points of Trips and Barth were not counted for they had only competed in three events. Runner-up in the championship was Hans Herrmann in the Borgward and Richard von Frankenberg in a Porsche was third.

In 1959 the capacity limit for the mountain championship was fixed at 1,500cc and it resulted in a tough duel between Borgward and Porsche. The Breman works had signed up the Swedish grand prix driver Joakim Bonnier to reinforce Hans Herrmann and Cabianca.

Porsche had also looked for a grand prix reinforcement and engaged the French ace Jean Behra. However, the latter was more of a grand prix driver than a hill climb expert. The Porsche team therefore consisted of Behra, Trips and Barth and whilst struggling for those elusive fractions of seconds Trips and Barth both left the road at the Schauinsland, fortunately both were only slightly injured; Hans Herrmann also hit a protruding rock and arrived at the finishing line with a flat tyre. Bonnier was the outright winner. At the Gaisberg event, which was the decisive one, Trips managed to turn the tables and beat Bonnier by a hairs-breadth, thus becoming European mountain champion of 1958.

Edgar Barth collected the title the following year at the wheel of a Porsche. For the first event two RSK's were entered, one for Barth and the other for Bonnier who was also driving the BRM in grand prix races that season. But he drove a little too fast in one of the curves during this event and the car looked anything but pretty after its accident, though fortunately he was unhurt. The works then decided only to enter Barth for the further events and since Borgward were no longer competing that year and had lent the 1,500cc racing engine to Coopers, the championship became just a Porsche affair. Private Porsche owners now moved up into the forefront and two things became obvious very quickly. Firstly, that some of them, such as the Swiss Walter and the Austrian Vogel were brilliant drivers and in fact equal to the works drivers, and secondly that the engines of the privately entered RSK cars were as powerful as those of the works cars.

The year 1959 brought altogether remarkable successes for private teams. Beginning with the first world championship for sports cars, the 12-hour sports-car race at Sebring provided the Americans Sesslar and Holbert and their RSK with victory in the 1,500cc class in front of the works RSK driven by Barth and John Fitch. The Americans also achieved fourth position in the overall classification behind two 3-litre Ferraris driven by Hill/Gendebien and Behra/Allison and the works RSK of Trips and Bonnier.

Then came the Targa Florio which gave the house of Porsche a 1-2-3-4 victory, after all the works Ferraris had retired, the second and fourth places going to private owners; one was a Spyder RS and the other one a Carrera GT, both owned by Paul Ernst Strahle and driven by three drivers in relay, Strahle, Mahle and Herbert Linge. The RS achieved second place behind the outright winners Barth and Seidel, the privately owned Carrera getting into fourth position. Third place was occupied by the works-entered Carrera driven by the Porsche racing manager, Huschke von Hanstein, together with the Sicilian Baron Pucci. As a matter of fact Hanstein competed in quite a number of events in 1958-59 with a works Carrera and achieved remarkable results in the events counting towards the European championship.

In 1959 the Swiss driver, Walter, with his privately owned RSK, became German champion in the 1,500cc sports car class. The basis for this was his victory (together with his compatriot Heuberger) in the 1,500cc class during the 1,000 kilometre race at the Nurburgring. In 1958 and 1959 the regulations of the German sports-car championships were so arranged that it could also be won by a non-German driver. Behra achieved this in 1958 and Walter in 1959.

30 Disc brakes – Rear engines for racing

THE Porsche sports cars in 1959 were always equipped with drum brakes as was the Formula-2 car, despite the fact that in that year everywhere sports/racing cars and racing cars were fitted with disc brakes. The English manufacturers having used disc brakes for some years past, Ferrari also changed over to them in 1959, at least for racing. The technicians have argued about this problem a great deal and disc brakes were introduced to the series production cars. This tendency clearly originated in England where Jaguar showed the way with the Le Mans cars and their disc brakes as long ago as 1953, even when other firms thought this development premature.

Stirling Moss tried the Porsche Formula-2 car in September 1959 at Goodwood and after three laps managed unofficially to lower the Formula-2 lap record; he explained that the road holding and brakes (drum-type) enabled him to achieve this. It is not yet clear if disc brakes will prevail on series-production cars, for the drum brake battles hard for survival with the result that the designers keep thinking up improvements which perhaps would not exist had they not been spurred on by the disc brake. Today, in 1977, this statement is of course superseded. Thus, competition in engineering acts as a spur and the ultimate consumer being the buyer of the series-produced car, benefits by the improvements.

The year 1959 certainly showed a number of new tendencies, for instance an unmistakable move towards the rear-mounted engine, particularly so in racing cars, but also in the series-production vehicle. Since Porsches have ever been the protagonist of rear engines, we must touch on this subject again within the framework of Porsche history.

As is well known, the first grand prix car designed by the old professor was rear-engined, the 16-cylinder Auto-Union of the 750-kilo formula which was current between 1934 and 1937. This was the first rear-engined car ever to be used in grand prix racing and it was victorious in a number of classic events, showing itself to be on a par with other, orthodox racing cars of the period. Despite its success, the rear engine used in a car of such nature was received with a certain amount of scepticism and it was said at the time that although the rear-engined racing car was the equal of the front-engined in respect of road holding it was much more difficult to handle, so that only a few top-class aces were able to master it completely in grand prix driving, whereas the merely good or very good racing driver could not achieve exceptional times with such a car. They said that

157

with a 'normal' racing car there was a far better chance of getting near the times put up by the great aces. Only the real geniuses of the wheel such as Rosemeyer, Varzi and Nuvolari were then able to cope with a rear-engined car to the ultimate degree.

After the Second World War and within the duration of the 1½-litre supercharged (and 4½-litre unsupercharged) formula, there was only one orthodox racing car design: the Alfettas, the four CLT Maseratis, Gordini, the 4½-litre Talbot, the entire Ferrari battle force and the johnny-come-lately BRM, all had the engine in front. Again there was only one exception — the Cisitalia, now designed by Porsche junior, but, of course, remaining an outsider, for it never appeared on a circuit.

When Formula-2 appeared on the scene (at that time for 2-litre cars) there was still no rear-engined racing car. The models which had the most success were the 2-litre 4-cylinder Ferraris and the 2-litre 6-cylinder Maseratis, supporting roles being played by Gordini, HWM, Cooper-Bristol and Cooper-Alta. Even when the new Formula-1 of 2.5 litres appeared in the spring of 1954, no rear-engined racing cars were seen on the starting line albeit with one exception: Bugatti, which only appeared ephemerally once at Rheims in 1956 and never again.

Rear-engined cars only existed in Formula-3, the smallest of the racing cars, but much as the performance of these 500cc devices was admired, they were still not taken seriously from the point of view of constructive tendencies. The cars, with their 50bhp engines and weighing only about 550 lb, were allocated to a special sphere of racing, but without connection to racing car construction on a grand scale — at least that is how it was in the beginning.

When Porsche again appeared with the Spyder works cars in 1953 it seemed as if the Stuttgart works would once again be the lone voice in the wilderness, as indeed they had been in 1934 and 1947; although admired they were thought of as outsiders, albeit outsiders with genius. Further rear-engined sports cars only appeared in the 1956 international competitions — the Coopers — and even for them an explanation was ready at hand. The Cooper company had done great things in Formula-3 and their cars all had rear engines. It was therefore logical that this little English company should take advantage of the experience gained with rear-engined vehicles and also equip its sports cars in a like manner. In 1956 the Porsche had about 125bhp but the Cooper, which was much lighter, only about 105. For this relatively small output (small in relation to the bhp output of grand prix cars) the rear engine was admitted as showing some advantages.

In the following years Porsche increased engine output up to 160bhp; the 1,600cc and 1,700cc engines gave even more power than that and the power/weight ratio got to be as high as 6.6 lb/bhp, which approached the grand prix car values of the 1954-55 season. At Coopers they had developed a Formula-2 1,500cc racing car of a like power/weight ratio, for it weighed just over 880 lb and produced some 140bhp. Porsche and Cooper then kept to their rear-engine layouts and achieved good results; particularly, the handling question was now easier than in the days of the Auto-Union. The modern rear-engine designs showed perfectly reasonable handling and could easily be corrected when they started to slide. They could also be managed quite well by drivers who were not necessarily of world-championship stature.

Cooper's Formula-1 car at Monte Carlo in 1957 was the first real break-through of a rear-engined racing car into big-time racing. Jack Brabham appeared at the start in a Cooper, in fact a Formula-2 chassis, slightly modified and fitted with an engine of only just 2-litres, yet with it he lay in fourth position for about half the race amongst a number of international aces — on the 96-100th laps he was even third behind Fangio (Maserati) and Brooks (Vanwall). On the 100th lap he had to give up due to engine trouble, but by pushing the car to the finishing line he achieved sixth position, being five laps in arrear. In January 1958 Moss, in a Cooper, won the Argentinian Grand Prix despite the fact that his engine was only of 2.2-litres and that the Ferrari works team was present; this was the first post-war victory of a racing car with a rear engine.

In the 1959 season when the Climax engines for the Cooper were finally increased to 2.5-litres, it almost became the rule that Cooper won the grands prix: Brabham won at Monte Carlo and Aintree, Moss at Lisbon and Monza. A rear-engined car was the world championship vehicle and in Formula-2 Cooper won the manufacturer's championship with a Borgward engine.

When these successes became obvious, BRM developed a rear-engined experimental car as did Lotus and even Ferrari. In other words, all the racing-car manufacturers in Formula-1 either went over to the rear engine or at least developed rear-engined experimental cars; a development which even experienced technicians would have called futuristic five years previously. It is not even very easy to state clearly what advantages there are in having a rear-engined grand prix car. One thing is sure though: the rear suspension of a front-engined car is less heavily loaded when the rear-mounted fuel tank is half empty or almost empty (this being a reason why Ferrari and Lancia had experimented with cars fitted with side-mounted tanks). The progressive lightening due to fuel being used up tends to bring about increased spinning of the rear wheels during acceleration.

Another equally clear advantage is the absence of the propeller shaft, for with a rear-engined layout, engine, transmission and rear drive are in one block, saving weight and removing one source of trouble. To say that a rear-engined car always tends towards oversteering, whereas a front-engined one always understeers because of the different weight distribution, is an idea which is fixed in the minds of many laymen. It is however incorrect, firstly because in a racing car the weight distribution (between front and rear axle) is not so different and secondly because even if a car has 60% of its weight on the rear axle it can be made to understeer, as the latter characteristic does not only depend on weight distribution but also on the spring rates, roll centre and steering geometry.

As far as the construction of standard cars is concerned, there was a surprising fact to be noted. We know that the Porsche designs for the Volkswagen go back to the years 1931 to 1934 but shortly after the war the Volkswagen acquired a rear-engined 'cousin' in the shape of the little 4 CV Renault. It must be stated here that the rear-engined layout was already decided upon when Professor Porsche gave advice at Renault's in Paris. Renault's then developed a larger car, the Dauphine, which was still small like the VW. Neither Europe nor America had ever produced medium-sized cars with rear engines (although we must mention the Tatra, which could hardly be called a quantity produced vehicle for the world market). When the Chevrolet 'Corvair' appeared in the autumn of 1959, a rear-engined car of some 80bhp, it soon became apparent that the medium-sized rear-engined car was now also accepted.

31 Production figures 356B

THE Porsche works in Zuffenhausen continued to increase their production; in 1951 they exported 25% of their production, three years later this figure amounted to 60% and then it stabilised at over 70%, 40% of which being exports to the United States. The relationship between turnover and number of workers and employees is particularly advantageous, due to the fact that Porsche have remained assemblers, neither pressing, forging nor operating a foundry.

If we look up the personnel notices for the year 1959 we find that Ferry Porsche reached the age of 50 and received the large Cross of Merit. We must also mention another decoration: together with Professor Nordhoff, the managing director of the Volkswagen works, he received the Elmer A. Sperry medal in the U.S.A., one of the highest engineering honours which America has to offer, Ferry Porsche receiving it also for the work done by his late father. The ties with the Volkswagen works in the last years have become closer than ever. Despite the fact that the Porsche car itself contains very few VW parts today, it had used many in 1950 and 1951. The marriage between Porsche's grandson, Ernst Piech — the son of Mrs. Louise Piech and her husband Dr. Anton Piech who died in 1952 — and Nordhoff's daughter, Barbara, may well be called symbolic. Professor Porsche's widow died at the age of 82 in the autumn of 1959 and was buried at the Schuttgut near Zell am See, the Porsche family property, in the little chapel in which the Professor also rests.

The Frankfurt motor show in 1959 brought about more improvements on the Porsche car. Since Frankfurt, it was no longer the '356 A' as it was since 1955, but the '356 B'. Externally it was distinguishable by slightly higher and more vertically-mounted headlights and a different and higher-mounted bumper. Below the front bumper on the right and left there were now air intakes for the brakes which had undergone improvement and which now had 72 axial cooling ribs and different linings, all due to racing experience.

Inside there was a new dished steering wheel and a shorter gear lever which was closer to hand. The rear occasional seats had been lowered by 2½in. and in addition to the 'Dame' and 'Super' engine types there was now also the 'Super 90', so called because from 1,600cc it provided 90bhp at 5,500rpm. It had higher compression, different carburettors and was tuned to a higher degree. The Carrera series finished during the autumn of 1959.

32 Ferry Porsche's forecast in 1961

MOTOR cars, like all technical products, are being developed year by year – but, if one were to stand in the design office, one might even say from day to day and hour to hour. To conclude in 1960 this history of the house of Porsche, which at the same time is also an important piece of automobile history, let us appeal to the boss, to Ferry Porsche, to give his opinion on the direction that automobile development will take over the next few years.

'The first idea that comes into my mind of the layman during discussion about the line of development of the motor car of the future – is the turbine car! Due to the appearance of a few prototypes and the publication of a number of articles concerning this subject, opinion has become strengthened that the turbine car is just around the corner. I often hear the question: Surely you have been working on the turbine car for quite a while?

'But nature and engineering do not progress in leaps and bounds. Ten years have now elapsed since the first turbine car appeared in public and in the last five years a number have shown surprising achievements – I am thinking about Rover in England and the Renault "Etoile filante" in France. About ten years having elapsed since the prototype; surely one ought to assume that a car, fit for series production and for everyday operation, should have been developed. But this has not been the case with the turbine-powered car. Even in aircraft production where the problems concerning turbine power are not as complicated as in car manufacture, it took no less than 20 years; for the first prototype Heinkel flew in 1938 yet only in 1958 did a turbine powered passenger plane fly the Atlantic. One thing stimulates another. When the turbine-powered prototypes appeared they acted as an incentive to the designers of normal passenger-car engines to improve their products. I want to emphasize here that in my opinion we are not at the end of the development of the piston engine. The turbine engine will only have a chance in the series-production car when the two lines of development cross, in other words when turbine power will fulfil the special demands of a passenger car in a more advantageous manner than a piston engine. To achieve high speeds on flat surfaces alone is not sufficient proof. Apart from this, turbine engines will probably first be used in large motor coaches and heavy vehicles.

'When we have a racing car formula which includes also turbines then we shall get around to the competition between the piston engine and the turbine – but it is too soon for a turbine engine formula. As long ago as 1957 the race organizers of Le Mans put up a prize for a turbine powered vehicle which would have had to compete in the race for 24 hours and cover a certain minimum distance. Yet none of the prototypes was entered; the prize had been put up too soon.

'It seems very important to me that designers of everyday cars make them as foolproof as possible, which in itself calls for the piston engine even for a relatively conservative vehicle. If you think about the Volkswagen you know that the fact of its being foolproof is an important, correct and legitimate sales argument. In the last few years, in the U.S.A., a lot of experiments were made which did not increase the tendency towards being foolproof. For instance in 1957 there were more new cars there with fuel injection than in 1958 — here in Europe it is the other way round, development is not as stormy but on a more level plane.

'I am sure that the bhp/litre output of our piston engines will continue to grow in the next few years, without too much worry about teething troubles. Compression ratios, as in America, are tending to get higher and higher here (9 : 1 and 10 : 1 are becoming normal for ordinary cars). This will necessitate further improvements in fuel techniques, which is very desirable.

'The construction of cars will level out to a minimum size in the region of the Volkswagen and not below; to be more specific: a car which can be comfortably driven without worrying about too little power in the mountains or insufficient acceleration for overtaking, and which can be used for 350 miles a day, four people up, without fatigue.

'On the other hand, road building does not keep up with our future programme of vehicle development. It is in a state of dreadful "retard". It seems to be forgotten that motor manufacture and road building must be closely allied, otherwise the inventive spirit of the designers is hindered.

'I have often talked of sport, a theme which has been discussed a very great deal of late but with this "arriere pensee": is motor sport still essential to the designers or is it a game that attracts the masses? I am sure that proving grounds can be built today where everything necessary can be tested on a vehicle for series production. I am equally sure, however, that a series of tests on a proving ground subsequently condensed into a sober test report will not provide as much incentive for the designers and experimental technicians as a motor race. A hundred-metre sprinter sometimes achieves prodigies of power beyond his normal self when running against five other first-class runners, yet he would not achieve such speed when practising on his own.'

Ferry Porsche is very much on the side of the sport: 'Prior to a motor race a certain number of problems have to be solved because otherwise the other manufacturers would win. This impulse is exceedingly important for progress and particularly the quick progress of engineering. It should not be said that ours is an exceptional position because we only build cars that have a sporting tendency and which bear an obvious relationship to sporting success. We also design for other companies, and our experience drawn from sports cars in this manner fructifies also other designs.

'In the United States the large companies do not participate in races but their experimental departments are full of almost all European sports and racing cars which can be purchased — so as to profit also by their experience.

'The sport contributes materially to the safety of the modern series-built car. Let us consider only brakes and road holding. Whilst I point out first and foremost the question of the mechanics of driving, I particularly want to stress that the subject of safety should be tackled at the root and more so than is done at the moment. All I hear these days is that the safety of a motor-car depends very largely on the softness of the foam rubber padding on the dashboard or how well the sun-blind is padded and how deeply the steering wheel is dished. But these are only secondary factors. The first question should not be: what do I do or what will happen to me if I have an accident? No, the first question should be: how do I avoid an accident? What can I do to my vehicle to prevent it skidding, to have good brakes, tyres and shock absorbers?

'To make a car safe means firstly to design it with so much built-in road safety as is possible according to today's state of design — sport, once again supplies decisive impulses in this field. The problems are however interlinked, for road safety must not only be seen from the car's point of view but also from the road-building point of view. To alleviate the results of accidents is an important job; but to try and prevent them happening seems to me to be even more important.

'The next five years are hardly likely to show revolutionary changes in the design of motor vehicles, only a steady refinement already noticeable here and there towards more power, safety and greater driving comfort.'

Part 2

Porsche becomes an important manufacturer with world-wide markets for the 911, and a dominant force in sports car racing

1   A return to Formula 1

THE tradition of motor racing had gone hand-in-hand with the growth of the house of Porsche and in the climate of the early 1960s it was almost inevitable that the company would become a Formula-1 manufacturer in its own right. As it happened Formula-1 came to Porsche. For in 1959 and 1960 Jack Brabham won the World Championship for Drivers in a rear-engined Cooper-Climax and set the pattern for all future Grand Prix cars — a pattern that Ferdinand Porsche had favoured since 1934!

A further stroke of fortune came when the *Federation International d'Automobile* announced that from 1961 the World Championship would be contested by 1½-litre cars. During 1959 and 1960 Porsche had become dominant in Formula-2 events with such outstanding drivers as Hans Herrmann, Edgar Barth, Graham Hill, Jo Bonnier and Stirling Moss regularly winning European events, in spaceframe rear-engined single-seater Porsches powered by highly tuned 160bhp versions of the Super Carrera four-cylinder engine.

Porsche had by now entered a new phase in its history. The Zuffenhausen factory employed more than 1,100 workers to produce almost 8,000 cars per year, the annual turnover exceeding 90 million Deutschmarks. In addition, the research and development office clearly benefitted by the fact that since 1945 the Volkswagen factory had produced some 3,500,000 Beetles, each one reputedly worth 10 DM to Porsche, so everywhere the theme was expansion and progress.

In July 1960 the A.v.D. organised the German Grand Prix at the Nurburgring to Formula-2 regulations, and the race was won most convincingly by Porsche although, unfortunately, the race lost its Grande Epreuve status because of the alteration to the regulations. But it was, in name, Porsche's first Grand Prix victory and one which gave the management a good deal of encouragement to get on with the development of an eight-cylinder 1½-litre engine for the new Formula-1.

At the 1960 race, works Porsches were entered for Bonnier, Hill, Barth and von Trips, while Herrmann had an older car. These five cars dominated the first two rows of the starting grid, the race being held on the short South Circuit, only Brabham's F2 Cooper-Climax challenging the German marque. The race was held in dreadful weather conditions, with rain and low cloud making the event a misery for everyone, and the result was a very satisfying Porsche victory with Bonnier and von Trips a full two minutes ahead of Brabham's Cooper, followed by Hill, Herrmann and Barth.

A return to Formula 1

During the winter of 1960/61 Porsche pressed on with the development of the new flat-8 engine, which had two overhead camshafts on each bank of cylinders and a horizontal cooling fan, similar to that on the Chevrolet Corvair engine on which Porsche had collaborated. Driven by a belt, shaft and bevel gears, it forced the air through glass-fibre ducts over the eight separate, finned cylinder barrels. Kugelfischer petrol injection was being experimented with, but the unit was tending to be unreliable and was giving 'only' 170 horsepower which compared unfavourably with Ferrari's claimed 190 horsepower for the Dino engine, though the true figure for the Modena engine was thought to be nearer 178bhp.

Disc brakes were being experimented with, although the intended Formula-1 car still had drum brakes, and the chassis had been extensively modified in having conventional double wishbones and coil springs at the front end.

Monaco, the first Grand Prix of the 1961 season and the first to be held for the 1½-litre formula, heralded Ferrari's almost invincible Dino and proved something of a disappointment for Porsche fans. The eight-cylinder engine was not ready, and the four cars sent from Zuffenhausen missed the first practice session. Two were the latest chassis, with wishbone suspension, for Bonnier and Herrmann, Gurney drove an older F2 model and the fourth was held in reserve. Significantly though, all four had Kugelfischer injected engines which allowed a good spread of power, from 2,000 to 9,000rpm according to the drivers, although they were handicapped by the fitting of four-speed gearboxes (the F2 cars ran regularly with six-speed boxes, but these were deemed unsuitable for Monaco and unnecessary anyway with the improved power band). The race gave Moss' Lotus a truly memorable victory over the Ferraris which were second, third and fourth, while Dan Gurney finished fifth to give the house of Porsche its first Constructors' points. Encouragingly, Bonnier had chased hard after Moss for many laps until a vapour lock in his petrol injection system made the engine die, so the latest Porsche clearly had a lot of potential.

At Zandvoort, only a week later, the works Ferraris were going faster than ever, von Trips and Phil Hill scoring a 1-2 victory in the Dutch Grand Prix ahead of the Lotuses of Clark and Moss, while the works 4-cylinder Porsches of Gurney and Bonnier were rather sadly trounced; the official verdict of the German team was lack of experience with tuning the petrol injection system, and at Spa a month later the Porsches had reverted to Weber carburettors, and F2 chassis. Again the race was a Ferrari benefit, the Dino models filling the first four places while Gurney gained another championship point, finishing sixth behind Surtees' Cooper-Climax.

At Reims on July 2nd four works Ferraris were entered and everyone resigned themselves to another walkover victory. Spirits were low in the Porsche camp because there was still no sign of the flat-8 engine, which was not giving more than 160bhp reliably, and Bonnier and Gurney were to run the old F2 chassis once again.

The best laid plans sometimes go awry, and in the course of this very hot, slip-streaming race three of the Ferraris retired, Ginther and von Trips for mechanical reasons and Phil Hill after a spin. This left the two works Porsches very well placed against the fourth Ferrari, that of Baghetti, and Moss' Lotus which then pulled up with brake trouble.

With only three laps to run, Gurney drew alongside Baghetti to lead the race with Bonnier right on his tail, and it was an unforgettable moment for everyone at the French track. Unhappily Bonnier's engine succumbed to the pace with only two laps to run, and he limped home in seventh place. All eyes turned to the Thillois hairpin, and Gurney's silver Porsche was the first to turn onto the finishing straight with Baghetti's red Ferrari in its slipstream. Then, with 300 yards to run, Baghetti pulled out in a perfect passing movement and took the flag less than a car's length ahead, and the Porsche so narrowly failed to achieve what had seemed impossible two hours before.

Porsche again entered the Weber carburated F2 cars for the British GP at Aintree, but Bonnier caused a surprise when he equalled the Ferrari times — in fact the three Ferraris and Bonnier all practised at 1 minute 58.8 seconds and the silver car was on the outside of the front row of the grid. The race was another Ferrari 1-2-3 benefit though, and Bonnier's reliable Porsche was beaten to fourth place by Brabham's Cooper-Climax, while Gurney finished seventh.

The experimental chassis appeared for the first time at the Solitude Grand Prix, a non-championship Formula-1 race, entrusted to Edgar Barth. Bonnier and Gurney raced the older cars, and were narrowly beaten to the flag by Ireland's Lotus, but the new Porsche was attracting a good deal of interest. It still had a four-cylinder engine but with the horizontal cooling fan, a longer chassis to accommodate the eight-cylinder engine when ready, and ran Porsche disc brakes for the first time, these incorporating some Dunlop patents. The outing was strictly for test purposes, and Barth finished no higher than eighth. For the German Grand Prix which followed, Gurney's works car was fitted with disc brakes, but otherwise the cars were unchanged since earlier in the season; the experimental chassis was abandoned, and while Moss trounced the Ferraris for the second time in the season, Bonnier retired with mechanical trouble and Gurney could only finish seventh, after bending his rear suspension in a collision with Hill's BRM early in the race.

Another second place was the reward for Gurney and Porsche at Monza, the last European round of the 1961 World Championship, where the Californian and Bonnier both ran old chassis with the latest horizontal fan four-cylinder engines. That was the day of the fateful collision between Clark and von Trips, leading to the death of the German driver and 11 spectators; Ginther's Ferrari retired and Phil Hill won the race to clinch the World Championship for himself and the Constructor's title for Ferrari, and he was followed to the line by Dan Gurney who had had a splendid duel with Moss until the Englishman's Lotus retired with wheel bearing failure.

The final Grand Prix of the season could have brought Porsche more success, for the Ferrari team withdrew its entry for the American GP at Watkins Glen following the Monza tragedy. Two 'normal' Porsches were entered for Bonnier and Gurney, but they were just not quite fast enough on the day to beat Innes Ireland who chalked up Team Lotus' first factory GP win, Gurney finishing second just 4.3 seconds behind.

In the final analysis, Porsche finished third in the Manufacturers' Championship behind Ferrari and Lotus-Climax, and Gurney finished third in the Drivers' Championship. No doubt it had been a disappointing season, but everyone felt that if they could do that well with old chassis, four-cylinder engines and (in most races) drum brakes, 1962 could only be better.

The new flat-eight cylinder engine finally made its race debut not in a Grand Prix, but in the Targa Florio held in May 1962. It was of 2-litre capacity, and, fitted with four twin-choke Weber carburettors, developed 210 horsepower. Each bank of four cylinders had two chain driven overhead camshafts and twin-plug ignition was employed, using Bosch coils. An open-two-seater was entered for Bonnier/Gurney and a Le Mans Coupe for Graham Hill/Vaccarella, both cars using the six-speed Porsche gearboxes. Gurney soon went off the road, as a result of brake trouble, so Vaccarella was quickly paired up with Bonnier. Although their car ran reliably and it could be called a satisfactory debut, the Porsche was beaten into third place by the new 2-litre V6 Ferrari sports cars.

A sleeved Formula-1 version of that engine, of 1½-litre capacity and developing 180 horsepower, was fitted into an entirely new chassis for Gurney and Bonnier to handle in the first World Championship race of the 1962 season, at Zandvoort on May 20th. The chassis was narrower than the 1960/61 version, still a space-frame design, but with torsion bar suspension all round — what could that be, but a Porsche design! The longitudinal torsion bars were mounted alongside the top chassis rails, pivoted by the top wishbones, and were fully adjustable for ride height. Conforming with Formula-1 practice the driver's

167

seat was the main petrol tank, a subsidiary tank being mounted in the nose alongside the oil tank. Disc brakes were now a regular feature of the Porsche Formula-1 cars.

By this time the 'kit car' trend established by Cooper Cars had extended, notably to Lola and Lotus, and the new Coventry Climax V8 engine developing 180 horsepower was now ascendant. The marque BRM too was becoming dominant, the reliability of the Bourne engines narrowly overcoming the brilliance of Jimmy Clark and the remarkable new Colin Chapman designed Lotus 25 monocoque which also made its debut at Zandvoort.

Throughout the year BRM and Lotus thoroughly eclipsed even Ferrari, which was a surprise to everyone, and the greatly improved Porsche chassis had to work hard for their results. But still, there was one splendid Grand Prix victory, and a 1-2 result in the non-championship Solitude GP to show for the effort.

When the Porsches made their debut in Holland, it became apparent that the unraced chassis needed some adjustments, but the Weber carburated power units were excellent. Gurney, though only eighth fastest in practice, and looking untidy, was a full two seconds faster than he had been the previous year. When the race began the Californian was holding a promising third place until the gear lever came out of its mounting (Gurney was quite good at doing that, being a powerful man). He retired, and Bonnier made a pit stop to have the rear suspension checked, eventually finishing in seventh place.

The debut race was a disappointment for the Porsche factory, and team manager Huschke von Hanstein virtually decided to withdraw the cars from the Monaco Grand Prix to carry out further development. However, the 2-litre flat-eights went extremely well at the 1000 Kilometre sports car race held at the Nurburgring, though beaten by larger-engined Ferraris, and Gurney persuaded von Hanstein to enter the Monaco GP after all. He handled the eight-cylinder model while Bonnier drove the older four-cylinder car, both having six-speed gearboxes this time. Gurney's optimism was misplaced, for having qualified fifth fastest (though only one second slower than Clark's Lotus on pole position) he was involved in a multiple accident caused by Mairesse at the first corner, and retired with a broken gearbox casing. Bonnier was badly outpaced but finished fifth, the last survivor, seven laps behind.

Following that disaster, Porsche decided to miss the Belgian Grand Prix and concentrate on some serious development of the new cars at the Nurburgring. When they next appeared at the French GP, held at Rouen, the cars were substantially altered. The gearchange system had been modified, and suspension improvements included radius rods from the front top wishbones back to the chassis frames. Rear anti-roll bars were fitted, and Bonnier's car had fibre-glass filling the top rear wishbones to provide extra stiffness. The driving seats were lowered and made to recline more, and the bodywork lowered around the cockpit.

Clearly the cars were more competitive, and Gurney (now established as one of the quickest Grand Prix drivers, along with Clark, and certainly one of the best on Rouen's fast downhill swerves) was well up with the leaders. Bonnier was less fortunate, damaging his gearchange mechanism after bumping over the kerb at the hairpin bend, and eventually retiring with fuel feed trouble.

It was a race of attrition, with retirements coming thick and fast for all sorts of reasons. But Gurney remained in contention, and following the retirements of Clark and Hill he took up the lead, and won the race by a full lap from Tony Maggs' Cooper-Climax.

The Porsche had run perfectly, while rival makes did not, and for the first time a Grande Epreuve had been won by a car bearing the name of Porsche. A great day indeed, though the post-race publicity dwelt on a lamentable incident which happened after Gurney had taken the flag, when the gendarmes stopped Surtees from entering the pits and causing a chain reaction which wrote-off the cars of Trintignant and Taylor. The British monthly journal *Motor Sport* commented: "It was a victory for Porsche by default of others, but if any driver deserved it, it was big Dan Gurney. From the first appearance of the 8-cylinder Porsche he has done all he could to encourage the designers."

That may sound a bit like faint praise, but in the context of the Porsche story it must be admitted that Gurney's victory, though still remembered many years later, did not constitute the beginning of a glorious era for the German make. Indeed, it was the only Grande Epreuve success for Porsche, as Graham Hill and Jimmy Clark really established their ascendancy. The fuel injected four-valve per cylinder BRM and Coventry Climax engines were, by the end of 1962, giving over 200 horsepower and the Porsche drivers were handicapped by a small but significant power deficit, not easy to overcome because by the nature of air cooled engines. Because of their relatively high cylinder head temperatures, no more than two valves could be designed into each combustion chamber.

But still, the Porsches were very light and handled well, and good results could still be expected at the slower circuits. Following the splendid Rouen result, two Porsches were again fielded at the Solitude GP, again a non-championship race, and with their eight-cylinder cars Gurney and Bonnier were a full six seconds quicker per lap than they had been the previous year. Clark was on pole position, but it was Gurney who led the race from start to finish and Clark's challenge failed when a shower of rain caught him out and he spun off the road, damaging the rear suspension. Trevor Taylor wasn't really happy with his Lotus 24 and there was nothing left to match the works Porsches, Gurney finishing almost two minutes ahead of Bonnier whose car lost power with a broken exhaust pipe.

Porsche's fortunes were riding high now, and the tremendous effort being put into the Formula-1 programme seemed justified. At the British Grand Prix held at Aintree, Gurney was among the leaders until a slipping clutch dropped him back to ninth place, and Bonnier retired with transmission trouble. Then in the German Grand Prix which followed, the highest prize, a Grande Epreuve win on home ground, seemed to be within grasp when Gurney dominated the practice sessions and took pole position in a sensational 8 minute 47.2 seconds, a full three seconds quicker than Graham Hill's BRM.

A cloudburst of rain before the start made driving conditions exceedingly difficult, but Gurney was master of the situation and for two laps he led the BRM in masterful fashion. Then on the third lap Hill slipped past and Surtees closed on the leaders with his new Lola-Climax, and the wet but enthusiastic 60,000 strong crowd was treated to a rare motor racing duel.

Unknown to all the Porsche supporters the battery broke loose in Gurney's cockpit, and as the American hesitated for a moment Surtees slipped past him. For the entire duration of the race the three cars ran almost nose to tail, each driver waiting for the others to make the slightest mistake on the slippery road. But when the chequered flag came out Gurney was third, 4.4 seconds behind Hill with Surtees between them. And that, regrettably, was as close as the Porsche got to victory for the rest of its career.

At Monza the Porsches' lack of power was important, and the two BRMs outpaced the field; Gurney ran in third place for a while, but retired with an oil leak leading to transmission failure, while Bonnier finished sixth a lap down. Interestingly, an attempt was made to streamline the cars by fitting discs over the wheels and fairing the suspension, while Gurney's Porsche had a cooling fan clutch which enabled it to 'windmill' at high revs thus saving engine power on the fast straights. The device did not prove satisfactory, and was not seen again.

In America, Gurney finished fourth with a failing engine, never having challenged Clark or Hill, and the Porsche factory decided not to enter any cars for the last Grand Prix of 1962, the newly instituted South African GP, as it was well out of the hunt for any title.

A good deal of heart-searching was going on in Zuffenhausen about the future of the

169

Grand Prix effort, for it was realised that at least another 20 horsepower would be needed to compete on level terms in 1963. During the winter Bonnier and Gurney were invited to look elsewhere for their Formula-1 drives, and that was indeed the end of Porsche's valiant effort to conquer the world of Grand Prix racing.

Rumours persisted for many years that Porsche would return, but the official company line was always that too much emphasis was given to the driver-personality cult, and too little to the technical aspect of Formula-1 racing. Except for 1975, every World Championship from 1965 onwards was won by a 'kit car' manufacturer using bought-out engines, and decreasing emphasis was given to the make of car.

Since 1962 Porsche has not built a single-seater, concentrating from then onwards on sports and GT racing where useful development is speeded by competition, technical progress more valuable and more readily applicable to the production cars.

2 The Porsche 911

THE STORY of the 911 model is really synonymous with the growth and prosperity of the Porsche company. As early as 1956 it was appreciated that the 356 model would have to be replaced eventually, and a number of designs and prototypes were scrutinised and rejected. There could be no question of launching a flop, such as the Ford Edsel, because the company simply could not afford to fall back from the success of the 356.

As history shows, the 911 was not merely a success but a shining achievement which took the Porsche company from its minor but significant production role to the status of an established motor manufacturer with world-wide markets. Six years after the model was launched production was increased to 15,000 cars per year, and it continued to be difficult to satisfy the demand. America continued to be Porsche's biggest market, even ahead of Germany, and what the customers appreciated more than anything else was that every car continued to be built to exacting standards. The standard of engineering was exemplary, and improved each year, so that each succeeding model was better to drive than the last. The new body shape survived that difficult test of time successfully in its first decade, while power outputs rose with increases in engine capacity. The 911 won virtually all the major classic rallies, competed strongly in endurance events and even won the 1973 Daytona 24-Hours and the Targa Florio in 3-litre Carrera form. In 1964, such success could only be dreamed of!

By the time the 356 model was phased out in 1965 no fewer than 76,303 cars had been made, and considerable development had taken place. The 356 (7,627 cars) was replaced by the 356A in August 1955, and in the next four years 21,045 examples were made. The 356B model also ran four years in production and 30,963 cars were made, including the Carrera 2 version which had a 1966cc four-camshaft engine developing 130 horsepower. Then in 1963 the 356C was introduced, with disc brakes — the rear brakes had integral handbrake drums to ensure maximum efficiency on hills — and 16,668 cars were made before the 911 finally engulfed all production facilities. Coupe, Cabriolet, Speedster, Roadster and Convertible versions were all made, though the expensive 2-litre engine was soon dropped from production in order to concentrate on the 75 and 95bhp versions of the 1.6-litre unit.

In the early 1960s the entire factory was being prepared for the new 911, and in 1963 just prior to the first announcement the neighbouring Reutter coachwork plant was taken over to allow expansion of production. A completely new car is quite a rarity in the motor industry, most so-called new cars normally relying on new engines in old bodies, or new bodies with old engines, so phasing the cost and time interval of the development period.

But the 911 was to be entirely new, virtually every nut and bolt of it, though the general concept was similar in that the new model would have torsion bar suspension, and the air cooled engine overhanging the rear wheels. It was the concept of Ferry Porsche II that the design department carried out, and Ferdinand (Butzi) Porsche III who sculpted a body style that was still reminiscent of the wind-cheating 356, yet entirely modern in design.

Requirements for the new model were simple. The car had to resemble the 356 in style and in character. It would be compact; Ferry Porsche insisted that the wheelbase should be no more than 87 inches, less than five inches greater than the 356's, but interior space should be generous for two people and two children. The car would be a true Grand Touring model, with extremely high performance for its size and capacity. Some advantage would be gained from careful aerodynamic study, more from the high output six-cylinder engine of 2-litre capacity which was designed by Ferdinand Piech.

Placing the engine in front of the rear wheels was considered, but the theory was rejected on the grounds that it would restrict interior space to an unacceptable degree. Front-wheel drive was rejected on grounds of relatively high power losses through the transmission, so when it was eventually decided to mount the power unit in the 'traditional' position behind the rear wheels it was time to work on the body profile. In three distinct stages young Ferdinand transformed the 356 outline by removing the bulbous curves and making the profile cleaner, sharper and more purposeful. The windscreen was deeper, side and rear windows enlarged, and the roofline dropped at a constant angle to the rear lights. The doors were larger, interior space greater although the overall width of the car was *reduced* by 2.4 inches. The height was the same, due mainly to the retention of 15-inch wheels in the interests of a smooth ride on poor surfaces, but luggage capacity was significantly improved. Overall length was increased by a mere six inches, the 911 saving space by having integral bumper bars with good shock-absorbing ability. The front wings were to be detachable, to save repair bills.

Only steel could then be contemplated for a car in regular production, and the body was designed to be completely integral with the platform chassis, quite a departure from established Porsche designs using platform chassis to which the bodies were attached.

The 911 would retain torsion bar suspension at the front and rear, would have high geared ZF rack and pinion steering and Porsche specification ATE disc brakes, but the rear suspension was substantially different in that the swing axle design, which took some mastering, was replaced by a longitudinal trailing arm system which minimized changes of camber and track as the car went along. This in itself transformed the roadholding, making the Porsche one of the safest cars to drive quickly.

The heart of any car, though, is the engine. The Volkswagen-derived four-cylinder was right at the end of its development, and concurrently with the eight-cylinder racing engine of 1961/62 the experimental department was putting the finishing touches to the production six-cylinder unit. Six cylinders for smooth running, horizontally opposed in banks of three for balance and compactness were used, and air cooled because everyone at Porsche had unshakeable faith in this concept. Pushrod engines were now antiquated in design, and dual overhead camshafts as in the Carrera 2000 GS were deemed too expensive to produce and unnecessarily complex, so it was eventually decided to compromise with one overhead camshaft on each bank with chain drive.

The individual, finned cylinder barrels were made of aluminium with chrome-plated bores, and the crankcase was made of aluminium alloy. A large bore (80mm) and short stroke (66mm) gave a capacity of 1991cc with plenty of scope for enlargement, and ten years on the capacity had been increased by 50% while the original power output of

130bhp DIN rose as high as 200bhp in the 3-litre 911 Carrera of 1975, and over 500 horsepower with turbocharging for the 1976 prototype competition cars.

Each individual alloy cylinder head had two valves per cylinder, inclined in a penthouse roof combustion chamber, and carburation was by means of one triple-choke Solex on each bank. The forged steel crankshaft was short and sturdy, running in seven main bearings, and dry sump pressure lubrication was adopted. The horizontal fan was driven by a vee-belt direct from the crankshaft, drawing air through the horizontal grille in the engine cover.

As in the 356 the gearbox was mounted ahead of the wheels, below the back seats, but again it was a new design with five forward ratios, first and reverse gears on the left plane of the gate, second, third, fourth and fifth in the usual H-pattern.

Prototypes of the 901, as it was originally called, performed extremely well. Despite the car's superior appointments and extra weight (it tipped the scales at 1,080kg, 2,384 pounds 'dry') it equalled the acceleration of the Carrera 2000 GS and had a higher top speed, timed conservatively at 210kph/130mph. It accelerated from rest to 60mph in nine seconds and to 100mph in 22 seconds, and could cover a kilometre in 29.9 seconds from a standing start.

The 901 was shown as a prototype at the Frankfurt Show in September 1963, and it was appreciated straightaway as a milestone in Porsche's history. If it would go as well as it looked (as if anyone doubted that!) it was going to be a winner. Encouraged, the company directors pressed on with factory modernisation, and prepared to switch production to the new model.

It had been decided to keep the 356C in production a little longer, as a cheaper alternative, until the line could be rationalised and the 1600cc four-cylinder engine put into a new version called the 912. So from August 1964 the old and new models were produced alongside. Before the new six-cylinder car went into production, though, Porsche were obliged to rename it 911 because they found that Peugeot had the rights to type numbers with a zero (the Peugeot 404 was followed by the 504, 304, 204 and 104), so the car was launched commercially in September 1964 as the 911. The price in Germany, 22,900 marks before taxes, compared with the 14,950 marks charged for the basic 356C model and as much as 23,700 marks for the 356 Carrera 2 Coupe with which it compared best.

The 911 was given a most enthusiastic reception, and motoring writers in every country bestowed praise on the highly efficient car, then a rarity in having a five-speed transmission which enabled it to accelerate strongly and cruise quietly in 'overdrive' fifth. The torsion bars, longitudinal at the front combined with MacPherson struts, and transverse at the rear, allowed a really supple ride while the trailing link rear suspension was markedly better than the discarded swing axle arrangement. Most important, the smooth six-cylinder engine proved extremely strong and reliable as it was to show in competitions later on.

The international competitions debut was in January 1965, when Porsche development engineers Herbert Linge and Peter Falk ran a car in the Monte Carlo Rally. Conditions were bad, with heavy snow delaying all the competitors before the Chambery control on the *route communale*, but Linge and Falk pressed on to earn the 2-litre class victory. It was a satisfying rally for Porsche, because Eugen Bohringer drove outstandingly well in the extremely unsuitable Porsche 904 four-cylinder prototype to finish second overall in the event, a plucky drive talked about long afterwards.

There were two developments during 1965. The 356 model went out of production during March and the following month it was replaced by the Porsche 912, which had all the mechanical components of the 911 but with less expensive specification and with the trusty 1582cc four-cylinder engine developing 90bhp DIN. A maximum speed of 115mph was claimed for the car, with a 0-60mph acceleration time of under 12 seconds. The second development was the announcement, at the Frankfurt Show in September, of the 911 Targa convertible model. This broke entirely new ground, because instead of having a conventional folding soft top just the metal roof over the occupants' heads detached, leaving the strong stainless steel hoop in place as a safety measure, and the plastic rear window could be unzipped and removed or left in place, preventing strong drafts from attacking the driver's neck! Full convertibles were going out of fashion anyway, except in Britain where the traditional sportscar manufacturers continued to offer soft tops, and the new Porsche Targa soon became a favourite, particularly in America.

Porsche's experimental department, headed by Ferdinand Piech and including Linge, Falk, Helmuth Bott and Hans Metzger, well occupied with developing the 904 and 906 models, also found time to develop the 911 for competitions. As a circuit racing car it would be handicapped by weight compared with the specialised lightweight models, though as time went on a Grand Touring category virtually built up around the 911 in classic long distance events, and it became a feature of the Nurburg 1000 Kms for instance to see a dozen Porsche 911 drivers duelling hard for honours in the wake of the prototypes.

It was the rally scene where all the potential lay to begin with. Overall victories in the Hesse Rally and the German Rally in 1966, coupled with a GT class win in the Alpine Rally, laid the foundations for a big rally programme in 1967 when British rallyists Vic Elford/David Stone were officially engaged to drive the works' car.

At their disposal they had the newly announced 911S version, the highlight of the 1966 autumn motor shows. At that time the range was enlarged: a cheaper version of the 911 became the 911T priced at 19,000 marks, this six-cylinder engine now having cast iron cylinder bores and developing 110bhp to give the model a top speed of 125mph; the 911 became the 911L (Luxe) still with 130bhp, and the new 911S had the engine developed to produce 160bhp DIN, giving a top speed of 140mph. The weight was reduced by 107 pounds by simplifying the interior equipment and fitting attractive forged magnesium wheels; an anti-roll bar was added to the rear suspension and Koni adjustable shock absorbers were fitted all round. Another important innovation was the fitting of ventilated disc brakes, which rapidly cooled the discs and pads when the car was being driven competitively.

Further modified for competitions, the 911S soon became a winner. A class win for Elford/Stone on the Monte Carlo Rally was followed by outright wins for the pair on the German Rally, the Tulip Rally and the Geneva Rally, and the Polish driver Sobieslaw Zasada triumphed on the Polish Rally. It was certainly a tremendous year for Porsche, the company winning the Grand Touring category of the European Rally Championship.

No year went by without some improvement to the Porsche 911 range, and in 1967 the Sportomatic automatic transmission was introduced. Mainly for the American market, Porsche adopted the Fichtel and Sachs system, which incorporates a torque converter, a four-speed gearbox and a normal but servo operated vacuum clutch with an electrical sensor in the gear lever, and tailored it specifically for the 911. There was no clutch pedal, of course, and the torque converter enabled the driver to move off in any gear, though each gear could be selected in the normal way. It was reckoned that this gave the user all the fun of a normal sporting gearbox without the chore of footing the clutch all the time in heavy traffic; demand for the Sportomatic transmission was so great that one car in five soon had this equipment.

Typically, before they offered it for sale, Porsche decided to demonstrate the Sportomatic transmission on a race circuit — and there's no finer track for testing gearboxes than the Nurburgring! The factory did not pick any old race but the toughest of all, the Marathon de la Route, which was driven off the public roads in 1965 and returned in another guise a couple of years later, as an 84-hour endurance event. Three drivers were assigned to the Porsche 911S Sportomatic, Hans Herrman/Jochen

Neerpasch/Vic Elford, and they demonstrated the transmission in the best possible way by taking an outright win.

The years 1968, 1969 and 1970 were golden ones for Porsche in rallying, with innumerable successes to enhance the prestige of the 911. In January 1968 Porsche brought off a notable achievement when Vic Elford/David Stone won the Monte Carlo Rally outright, followed in second place by Pauli Toivonen/Martti Tiukkanen who were just 76 seconds behind. Then Bjorn Waldegard/Lars Helmer won the Swedish Rally brilliantly, and one success followed another throughout the year. Toivonen/Vihervaara won the East German Rally; Andersson/Svedberg won the rough forestry stage Gulf London Rally; Kremer/Kelleners/Kauhsen won the 24-hour endurance GT race at Spa-Francorchamps; Toivonen/Tiukkanen won the Danube Rally; Kremer/Kelleners won the Brno 4-hour event; the Marathon de la Route again fell to Porsche, this time a manual transmission 911R driven by Linge/Glemser/Kauhsen; Toivonen won the Geneva Rally, Doncel the rough Firestone Spanish rally, and a 911 also won the GT class at Le Mans.

A few words should be said about the 911R, the predecessor of the 911 Carrera, which was developed specially for racing. The weight was reduced to only 800 kilogrammes by stripping out the interior and fitting glass-fibre doors, bonnet and boot lids, while the engine was further developed to 210 horsepower. Only a limited number were made for competition purposes, and with flared wheel arches to accommodate wide wheels and racing tyres they were extremely effective on the circuits. Significantly too, the 911R had the Bosch petrol injection system also used on the 906 Carrera, which was to become a feature of the 1969 production models.

The Bosch system gave the six-cylinder engines fitted in the 911E and 911S models plenty of advantages, though at higher cost. It made the engines more efficient, thus more economical and more powerful. It also made them smoother, and allowed a better power band. The double-row, six plunger injection pump was driven from the left camshaft by a spur belt. A camshaft forced the fuel through six equal length pressure lines to nozzles located in the cylinder heads, discharging the fuel at 220 to 265psi against the inlet valves just as they were beginning to open.

Thus equipped, the 911E model went up from 130 to 140bhp DIN (with a top speed of 134mph) and the 911S from 160 to 170bhp DIN, while the 'basic' 911T continued with Solex carburettors. The Bosch injected engines were able to cope with the American emission laws of the time (though they became increasingly stringent later on), and apart from the power increases the torque curve benefitted too.

There were other improvements to the range, notably a rearrangement of the rear suspension to increase the wheelbase by 2.24 inches. This was done to counteract the oversteering tendency in extreme conditions, and at last it could be claimed that the rear-engined cars *understeered*, at normal speeds anyway. The front/rear weight ratio was changed from 40/60 to 42/58, which does not sound very much but made an appreciable difference, and the ride quality also benefitted.

Altogether there were 20 improvements across the range. Wheel arches were flared to accommodate 6 inch section rims used on the 911S; hydropneumatic self-levelling struts were fitted to the front suspension of the 911E model to provide better damping and a smoother, shock-free ride; bigger brake alloy calipers and pads were fitted front and rear to increase the braking power and improve pad life; a completely new heating/ventilation system was deemed to be a major improvement, incorporating a three-speed fresh air blower (the swivelling quarterlights then became fixed, as it was thought that the ventilation system could keep the car cool in all conditions); electric window winders became available as an option; there were many more detail improvements, including things like a smaller but thicker, leather covered steering wheel, thicker rubber strips on the bumpers, a new rear light design, chrome alloy strips under the doors, a more powerful horn, a heated rear window, a dipping mirror, and so on.

The Porsche 911

It is worth pausing for a moment to say that by 1968, twenty years after Professor Porsche's VW based prototype had taken shape, the house of Porsche was employing 3134 people, and 14,395 cars were made that year. The 100,000th Porsche, a 912, had been sold in 1966 and now the company was well on its way to the 150,000 mark, a target achieved in September 1970. Turnover had increased from 3.4 million marks in 1950 to 108 million marks in 1960, and to a staggering 300 million marks in 1968, and all the while the company was still privately owned on a 50:50 basis by the families of Porsche and Piech.

In 1969 the 911 model continued on the wave of success, while the experimental department was busy perfecting the 917 racing car which took the world by surprise. In January there was another 1-2 victory in the Monte Carlo Rally, Bjorn Waldegard/Lars Helmer leading Gerard Larrousse/Jean-Claude Perramond. Waldegard made it a fine double when he won the Swedish Rally for the second time. On the race circuits the 911R was doing well, winning the Grand Touring category in the Daytona 24-Hours and the Sebring 12-Hours. The Acropolis Rally fell to Toivonen's Porsche, another victory in the Spa 24-Hour endurance event to Guy Chasseuil/Claude Ballot-Lena; the Polish Rally to Zasada again; the Danube Rally to Poltinger; the Tour de France to Larrousse/Maurice Gelin, who followed up that success by winning the Tour de Corse; and Etchebers won the Firestone Spanish rally to round off the season.

The Porsche factory had another trick up its sleeve for the 1970 season, lighter engines to improve handling and an increase in engine capacity which benefitted both the power and torque bands. The extra capacity was derived from increasing the cylinder bores from 80 to 84mm, the stroke remaining at 66mm, thus increasing the capacity for all the six-cylinder models from 1971 to 2195cc. The 911T went up from 115 to 125bhp DIN, still with two triple-choke carburettors though Zenith were now specified; the 911E went up from 140 to 155bhp, while the Weber carburated 911S went up from 170 to 180bhp with a top speed of 143mph. Additionally, the 911R was phased out in favour of a homologated, lightweight version of the 911S which could run in the Grand Touring category at 200 pounds below the normal production weight. Clutch diameters were increased in size to cope with the extra power and 10 per cent more torque, and there were other modifications of a minor nature. Significantly here, the crankcase construction was changed from alloy to magnesium alloy (AZ 91), which reduced the engine weight and benefitted the cars' handling.

Three very notable hat-tricks crowned the 1970 season, confirming the all-round capabilities of the 911 beyond all doubt. Bjorn Waldegard/Lars Helmer again won the Monte Carlo Rally, their second time and Porsche's third. The pair then went on to win the Swedish Rally for the third time running in a Porsche, then later in the year the 84-Hour Marathon de la Route fell to Porsche for the third time, on this occasion a 911S driven by Gerard Larrousse/Claude Haldi/Helmut Marko. On top of these successes, Waldegard also won the Austrian Alpine Rally, Janger won the Danube Rally and Ruiz-Giminez won the Sherry Rally.

Despite these victories, success was becoming harder to achieve as the ultra lightweight Alpine Renaults were becoming increasingly competitive. By now Porsche's experimental department was changing direction, increasingly concerned with the American safety and emission laws though at the same time developing the Carrera and the turbo Can-Am models, so at the end of 1970 the Zuffenhausen company temporarily stopped supporting the rally programme. Privateers continued to run Porsches in rallies, with the blessing of the factory if not with active support, and in 1971 Finnish importer Antti Aarnio-Wihuri surprisingly won the Arctic Rally.

The homologated Carrera model of 1973 put Porsche back on a more competitive footing, and a limited programme was organised to assist Bjorn Waldegard. He appeared in the East African Safari and the 1000 Lakes Rally, without success, but in 1974 he came

Jean Behra in the centre-seat Porsche Formula 2 car at the Nurburgring, in 1958

Two years early for the newly announced Formula 1 of 1961 was the single-seater Porsche which appeared for Wolfgang von Trips at Monaco in 1959. It had drum brakes and a 6-speed gearbox. After setting the fastest Formula 2 time in practice, von Trips crashed on the second lap

Debut of the flat-8 cylinder Porsche F1 car was at Zandvoort in 1962, in the hands of Dan Gurney

Dan Gurney led the rain-soaked German GP at the Nurburgring in 1962, but Graham Hill (BRM) and John Surtees (Lola) scraped past during the race, less than five seconds covering the three cars at the finish

The first, and only, World Championship Grand Prix victory for the Formula 1 Porsche flat-8 cylinder fell to Dan Gurney at Rouen in 1962

The 1968 version of the Porsche 911 S (left) and T (right). Note the flared wheel arches

Open and closed. The 1968 Porsche 911T Targa has the best of both worlds

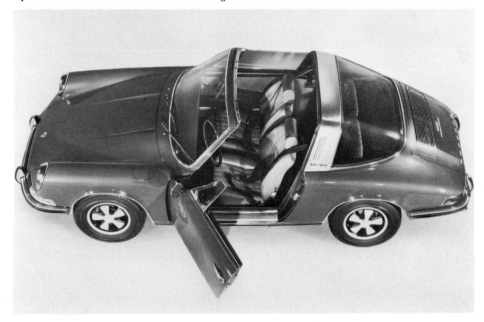

The Porsche production line in the old Reutter coachbuilding factory, before the main factory was modernised and centralised

The interior of the 1969 911S. For this year there was a smaller steering wheel, upholstered horn button, new heating and ventilating system and a new safety mirror which releases upon collision

Bosch fuel injection on the 911 six cylinder engine

A right hand drive Porsche 911 Targa of 1969

Bjorn Waldegard has consistently been one of Porsche's top rally drivers, here winning the Swedish Rally of 1968 with Lars Helmer

Shock absorbing bumpers, 1974 Carrera

Compare this photograph with the 1969 version of the 911S. This is five years later

Porsche have always used very pleasing wheels. These are perhaps some of the best, here on a 1976 911

1973 Porsche 911 Carrera 2.7 litre; the 911 at its best

1976 model Turbo. Note the use of black coachwork trim

A surprise win in the 1973 Targa Florio was earned by Herbert Muller and Gijs van Lennep in the Martini Racing/Porsche System prototype 911 Carrera. A similar car also won the Daytona 24 hours driven by Peter Gregg/Hurley Haywood

Bjorn Waldegard led the 1974 East African Safari in a works prepared Porsche 911 Carrera until, in the closing stages, his rear suspension gave trouble. Waldegard finished second

Turbocharged flat-6 power unit in the 1974 Martini Racing/Porsche System Carrera 911 increases the output of the 2140cc engine to 480hp. The car weights 800kg

The Martini Racing/Porsche System Carrera 911 raced by Herbert Muller and Giys van Lennep pictured at Monza, where it finished fifth overall

186

A 1977 Carrera. Despite possibly excessive safety regulations Porsche have managed to retain the classic 911 line

For 1977 Porsche can supply a Martini colour scheme even for the interior. Here is the Turbo at the London Motor Show of 1976

The 911 road going turbocharged engine installed. Nothing could be less complicated

The special tachometer for the Turbo gives boost pressure as well

Turbo in Martini colours for 1976 London Motor Show

Nino Vaccarella in the Porsche Coupe shared with Jo Bonnier in the 1962 Targa Florio. It was the debut of the 2-litre 8-cylinder engine, and the car finished in third place behind two Ferraris

The Abarth bodied Porsche driven by Herbert Linge/Hans Herrmann to sixth place on the 1962 Targa Florio

Edgar Barth was the established hillclimb champion of the early '60s, winning the 1964 title comfortably in the 8-cylinder prototype RS Spyder. Pictured winning at Gaisberg

Herbert Muller drove the lightweight Elva chassis Porsche in European hillclimbs in 1964, finishing second in the championship. Pictured at Trento Bondone

An unexpected victory fell to the new Porsche 904 in the 1964 Targa Florio, Colin Davis/Antonio Pucci succeeding after the faster prototypes dropped out

Eugen Bohringer/Rolf Wutherich accomplished a brilliant second place overall in the 1965 Monte Carlo Rally, driving a Porsche 904

Gerhard Mitter, Hillclimb Champion in 1965, at the wheel of the eight-cylinder Spyder pictured at Trento Bondone

close to success in East Africa, leading the marathon event by a wide margin until his rear suspension failed in the closing stages, dropping him back to second place. Some consolation was gained from the international circuit of Ireland Rally, also taking place over Easter, which gave Porsche Carreras the first two places overall, Cahal Curley leading Ronnie McCartney's similar 2.7-litre model.

The production of the 150,000th Porsche in September 1970 (it was sold to an American who had owned seven Porsches before), coincided with a much needed expansion of the production facilities. In only 18 months a completely new factory complete with the latest type of paint shop had been put up close to the original factory, creating 450 new jobs and increasing the central production quota from 28 to 50 cars per day. In addition, the Karmann coach-building company had its own production line making between 20 and 25 bodies per day, so the potential now was 17,500 cars a year. The new paint shop enabled Porsche to offer a greater range of metallic paint finishes which were becoming popular.

Continuing expansion called for heavy investment. In 1969 52.4 million marks were allocated for the new plant at Schwieberdinger Strasse, the following year 30 million marks were invested, and in 1971 a total of 35 million marks was invested, bringing the total to over 110 million marks. However there were a couple of setbacks in 1971, a two-week general strike by the metal workers (the first in Porsche's history) and a decline in sales caused by the American emission regulations, lowering the year's profits from 420 million to 315 million marks. By this time, the company employed 4,000 people.

The cheapest 911T version was the most successful commercially, accounting for 64.8 per cent of the production, followed by the 911S with 17.3 per cent and the 911E with 14.9 per cent. The VW-Porsche, described in a later chapter, declined seriously because the 2-litre engine could not meet American regulations and accounted for three per cent of the production, and the 912 ceased production altogether with the advent of the VW-Porsche. Exports to the States declined only a small amount in overall terms, from 40 per cent in 1970 to 38.2 per cent in 1971, while the German home market picked up from 29 to 33.9 per cent. The Targa models were still gaining in popularity, accounting for 44 per cent of the production compared with 31.5 per cent the previous year.

Further technical improvements were on the way for 1972, notably another increase in engine capacity and a lowering of compression ratios making the exhaust emission problems easier to handle. The bore dimensions remained at 84mm but a new crankshaft was fitted increasing the stroke to 70.4mm, and the capacity to 2,341cc.

On the 911T when the compression ratio was lowered to 7.5:1, the power rose by five horsepower to 130bhp DIN at 5,600rpm, and torque improved from 148 lb.ft at 4,200rpm to 166 lb.ft at 4,000rpm. The cheapest model in the range now had a straight-line performance approximately equal to the original 911, with a top speed of 128mph, but it was considerably more flexible in mid-range acceleration and, like the new 911E and 911S, would run on commercial grade 91 octane petrol.

The 911E was given an 8:1 compression ratio and power rose from 155 to 165bhp DIN, with a similar gain in torque. The car was now endowed with a maximum speed of 137mph and would accelerate from rest to 60mph in under 7 seconds. The 911S also gained ten horsepower, to 190bhp DIN, though the top speed was still quoted rather conservatively at 143mph while contemporary road tests reported a maximum of 145mph.

For the first time since the introduction of the 911 something was done about the aerodynamics, an air dam being fitted across the front of the 911S below the line of the bumper bar. Superficially this would seem likely to slow the car down, but experience with the 908/3 in racing had proved that the extra drag was almost insignificant, but that high-speed stability was greatly improved. Also changed, to the regret of purists, was the gearchange gate to the more conventional pattern, with 1-2-3-4 in the H-plane, fifth and reverse away to the right. The dry sump oil tank was relocated behind the driver's door for easier access and better weight distribution and the filler, like that of the petrol tank, was covered by a sprung flap operated from inside the car. Upper and lower rear shock absorber mountings were also relocated to improve damping efficiency, and the 911E was no longer equipped with self-levelling pneumatic struts, Boge shock absorbers becoming standard equipment except on the 911S, which still had Koni equipment to order.

Although Porsche's efforts in rallying were curtailed, the new European Grand Touring Championship gave the 911 a fresh lease of life on the circuits. Private owners increased the engine capacity to 2,687cc by increasing the bore to 90mm, and by further tuning the engine power was increased to the region of 270 horsepower.

If anything, the new championship got off to a poor start due to the invincibility of the competition versions of the 911S. Grids comprised almost entirely of this model, with the rare intervention of a de Tomaso Pantera or the less competitive Alpine-Renaults, and Erwin Kremer's team soon became the one to beat. At the end of the nine-race series the English driver John Fitzpatrick, Kremer's lead driver, was a clear winner of the championship with five victories, ahead of Claude Haldi and Jurgen Neuhaus. 'Fitz's' record was good enough for him to win the coveted Porsche Cup, awarded annually since 1970 to non-works teams using Porsche cars, ahead of Willi Kauhsen and Sobieslaw Zasada. The Porsche Cup is not merely a trophy, either, for a prize fund of 250,000 marks is also donated by the company. It is worth mentioning that while practising for the GT round at the Nurburgring Fitzpatrick became the first touring car driver to break nine minutes around the tough Eifel circuit, lapping in 8 minutes 54.7 seconds.

The revival of the name 'Carrera' was one of the most exciting moments in the story of the Porsche 911. In the Autumn of 1972 the Porsche factory launched the new model with the increased bore and a capacity of 2,687cc, developing 210 horsepower in standard form — and still running on commercial grade fuel. While the standard range continued unchanged at 2.4-litres the Carrera broke new ground, and a production run of 500 cars was planned for homologation into the Group 4 (modified GT cars) category. Three versions were offered, the RS, RST and RSR depending on trim and specification: the RS was the basic road version, the RST had luxury touring equipment installed, and the RSR was the full competition model weighing 900 kilogrammes, a saving of 60kg compared with the RST. In fact the cars were so much in demand that the initial production run was increased to 1,000 cars, and the Carrera was homologated into Group 3 (standard GT cars).

Gas filled Bilstein strut shock absorbers were fitted at the front, and the Carrera RSR models had such sophisticated features as lateral drilling holes in the ventilated disc brakes to reduce weight and improve heat dissipation, alloy front suspension cross members and forced lubrication gearboxes. It was not difficult to distinguish the Carreras on the road, for they had upturned wings on the engine cover lid and, on the standard white painted cars, the name 'Carrera' was sign-written in bold letters along the sides of the car.

Because the new Carrera would not be homologated into the Grand Touring category until April 1st, two cars were sent to America as prototypes to run in the Daytona 24-Hours in February. One was assigned to Roger Penske's team to be driven by his Can-Am duo, George Follmer and Mark Donohue, while the second was assigned to privateers Peter Gregg/Hurley Haywood. But the factory was one jump ahead of the customer again, taking advantage of the prototype rules to increase the bore again, from 90 to 95mm, and increase the capacity to 2,992cc. Power went up from 210 horsepower in standard form to just over 300 horsepower (a reliable 309bhp was usual as the season progressed).

Opposition was not very good, Ferrari staying out of the contest, and the race was expected to be won by a lone Matra 670 driven by Larrousse/Pescarolo or by one of the

Gulf-Mirage prototypes, driven by Derek Bell/Howden Ganley and Mike Hailwood/John Watson.

However the prototypes proved to be unreliable, the Matra retiring with a blown engine and the Gulf-Mirages going out with broken suspension and clutch troubles. To everyone's amazement the Porsche 911 Carreras were leading the race 1-2 on the Sunday morning, Penske's car ahead of Gregg/Haywood!

Unfortunately the Donohue/Follmer Porsche succumbed to piston failure, but Gregg and Haywood kept going without any problems to win the race, no less than 22 laps ahead of a Ferrari Daytona driven by Milt Minter/Francois Migault. So after the first round, Porsche led the 1973 World Championship for Makes! Gregg/Haywood followed up this fine win with another in the Sebring 12-Hours, though the event was reduced from title status because the Florida airfield was deemed by the CSI to be unsuitable for prototype racing.

For the European season in the summer the cars were brought back to Germany, and prepared in the colours of the Martini and Rossi vermouth company which sponsored the factory team. One 'prototype' was driven throughout the year by Herbert Muller from Switzerland and Gijs van Lennep from Holland, with the intention of letting private owners race their homologated cars while the factory would run against the lightweight purpose-built prototypes to continue the development programme. A second car was run in most races for different drivers, in the early rounds by Follmer with Willi Kauhsen or Reinhold Jost.

Clearly even in prototype form the 3-litre car could not keep up with the 650 kilogramme, 450 horsepower Ferraris, Matras, Alfa Romeos and Gulf-Mirages, but in tradition with Porsche's past history they maintained a very good record of speed and reliability, in other words finishing further up the list than one would expect.

The second stroke of good fortune came at the Targa Florio, where Ferrari and Alfa Romeo entered two cars each; Porsche's prototype, handled by Muller/van Lennep, was becoming very effective with brakes and wheels from the 917 model, and a full width rear wing which helped even more to make the car stable at high speed. A second Carrera was entered for former Targa Florio lap record holder Leo Kinnunen with Claude Haldi, while a third car was entered for Gunther Steckkonig/Giulio Pucci.

Clay Regazzoni wrote off one of the Alfa Romeos during practice, and the other three Italian cars failed early in the race; Merzario was the first to go, with a flat tyre leading to suspension damage on the first lap. Then Ickx went off the road, and on the fourth lap de Adamich also went off the road, helped by a slower car with a driver who had not seen the Alfa Romeo coming up behind him.

With four laps competed the van Lennep/Muller car was safely in the lead, followed by a Ferrari Dino engined Lancia Stratos prototype driven by Sandro Munari/Claude Andruet. The Lancia's challenge faltered slightly when the driving seat mounting broke and needed to be fixed, and after 11 laps of the gruelling event the Porsche beat the Lancia by more than six minutes, and Kinnunen/Haldi followed up in third place.

This was Porsche's eleventh victory in the classic Targa Florio, the first having been Maglioli's win in 1956, making the German factory the most successful of all on the Madonie course. Ferrari has seven victories and Alfa Romeo nine, and the score-sheet was worth taking note of after the 1973 race because it was the last time it would count for the important World Championship for Makes series — again, because the CSI thought it too dangerous for the lightweight prototypes which were being used. The Targa Florio continued as an Italian national event, but of course lost its prestige.

With the 1973 World Championship more than half way through, Porsche was second only to Ferrari in the points and ahead of the Matra team, which went on to take the title. Van Lennep and Muller went on to take fourth place overall at Le Mans (a race which forecasters said could fall to Porsche if the prototypes were as unreliable as they had been earlier in the season), and in the final tally the Porsche Carrera model was placed third in the World Championship.

The European Grand Touring Car Championship limped along year after year, never attaining the status achieved briefly by the European Touring Car Championship, when Ford and BMW had their titanic battles in 1972/73. Despite occasional sorties by such rivals as de Tomaso and Lancia (with the Stratos) the GT series was invariably a Porsche domain, and the contest was between two entrants, Erwin Kremer and Georg Loos. In 1973 the championship resulted in a tie between Claude Ballot-Lena and Clemens Schickentanz, in 1974 John Fitzpatrick swept the board in a Loos Carrera, in 1975 it was Hartwig Bertrams who took the title after a year marred by disputes, then in 1976 Dutchman Toine Hezemans won the title, again in a car entered by Loos, this time the Gp4 934.

Huschke von Hanstein confirmed the claims made for the 911 Carrera 2.7 with speed records at the Wolfsburg test centre, the runs observed by the FIA and later confirmed as class records. In a slightly modified RSR the former Porsche competitions manager established a new standing start 10 kilometre record with a terminal speed of 152.9mph, and a new standing start 10 mile record with a terminal speed of 161.5 mph.

The 2.7-litre engine was proven beyond doubt, and in the Autumn of 1973 the Porsche 911 range was equipped with this power unit. The 911T was dropped from the line-up, the basic model now being the straight 911 (again!) with a power output of 150bhp DIN. The 911S dropped back slightly to 175bhp DIN, but the Carrera was given a further production run and became the top model of the range, developing 210bhp DIN.

While the Carrera continued with the Bosch mechanical manifold injection system, the 911 and 911S adopted a new type of injection developed by Bosch called the K-Jetronic system. Giving a constant petrol/air mixture, K-Jetronic is more precise than the mechanical system and even more efficient, enabling Porsche to keep up with the American emission laws which were becoming more stringent all the time.

Engine flexibility improved with each increase in capacity, and the K-Jetronic system improved the torque curve still more. Whereas the original 911 in 1964 developed 144 lb.ft of torque at 4,500rpm, the 1974 model produced 197 lb.ft at 5,700 rpm, an increase of over 33 per cent. Importantly, the 2.7-litre engine gave a minimum of 180 lb.ft of torque from 3,250rpm; customers found that the Porsche could be quite a 'lazy' car, pulling strongly in high ratios if they wished, a very different proposition from the old 2-litre engines which demanded to be driven briskly.

Another advantage of the K-Jetronic system was that it further improved the petrol consumption, despite the extra engine capacity, but to give the new 911 a really good range a 17½ gallon petrol tank was standardised. This was done without decreasing the luggage space, because a deflated B.F. Goodrich emergency tyre made the spare wheel much more compact (this type of tyre was used on the 907 and 908/3 racing cars, and proved reliable as a 'get you home' standby). An electrical air compressor which plugs into the dashboard cigarette lighter became part of the standard equipment on the 911S and Carrera.

Showing what attention is always paid to detail, Porsche also increased the capacity of the windscreen washer fluid bottle to almost two gallons, realising that their clients would not be calling at petrol stations so often!

On the technical side, alloy trailing arms were fitted to the rear suspension to reduce weight and increase strength, the rear wheel bearings were enlarged, and shock absorber and anti-roll bar mountings were modified. A modification was also made to the clutch pedal mechanism to reduce the pressure by approximately 30 per cent. Also to meet the American safety regulations, improved bumper bar standards were introduced so that the car could withstand a 5mph impact without sustaining body damage. The 911 and 911S had tubular structures which would crush progressively to take the impact, but the Carrera had optional small shock absorbers which would rebound after an impact and leave no visible damage at all.

In November 1973 a further racing development was announced, a full 3-litre version of the homologated Carrera RS. Like the factory prototype which did so well during 1973 it had the bore dimension increased to 95mm (the stroke remaining at 70.4mm) and power was increased from 210 to 230bhp DIN. This model, which formed the basis of the 1974/75 Group 4 car, accelerated from rest to 60mph in 5.4 seconds and to 125mph in a mere 21.5 seconds, and had a top speed of 155mph. Like the factory development model, the 1974 RS had ventilated disc brakes similar to those on the 917 racing car, a limited slip differential, wider wheels and tyres, and a larger wing on the engine cover, but the weight was unchanged at 900 kilogrammes. In RSR Group 4 trim with twin-plug heads this model developed 330bhp ex-factory, and other than its European successes it eventually gave Peter Gregg/Hurley Haywood their second Porsche-mounted Daytona 24-Hours win, early in 1975.

Before turning to the factory programme in 1974, mention should be made of Bjorn Waldegaard's incredible run in the Safari Rally, ending in second place after leading for most of the distance. The factory prepared a special 911 RS for the purpose, powered by a 210bhp 2.7-litre engine and including many special options such as raised suspension, sintered clutch, and full protection for the battering it would receive on the rough Kenyan roads. The car was entered by a London Porsche dealer and former Safari winner, Bill Fritschy, head of Chipstead of Kensington, and Hans Thorzelius was the co-driver. Waldegaard, probably one of the best rally drivers ever to handle a Porsche, drew out a 38-minute lead in the major part of the rally, only to lose this advantage when the car's rear suspension broke during the third and final leg. The Swede was finally classified second overall, after a sensational showing.

For endurance racing Porsche prepared a new version of the Carrera RS making use of the Eberspacher/KKK turbocharging system fitted so successfully on the Can-Am cars. Under the CSI's equivalency formula, supercharged and turbocharged cars have their capacity multiplied by 1.4 so, to keep within the 3-litre regulation for prototypes, the engine capacity had to be kept down to 2,140cc, effectively returning to the production engines made from 1969 to 1971. Turbocharging increased the power to 450-500 horsepower, depending on how much boost was applied. Although the basic steel body was retained, extensive use of lightweight metals and fibre-glass for the doors, engine and boot lids, reduced the car's weight to 820 kilogrammes. Such a car, in the hands of Herbert Muller and Gijs van Lennep, was not expected to beat the 480bhp/650kg prototypes from Matra, Alfa Romeo and Ferrari, but as in 1973 it was expected to be sufficiently close to snatch surprise wins if the other prototypes should prove fragile.

After extensive testing at the Ricard circuit in southern France, two turbocharged prototypes made their debut at the Le Mans trials and 4-Hour race in March. The weekend was not a success, for the engine oil was overheating, transmissions were showing signs of strain, and both cars retired from the 4-Hour race with over-revved engines. At the Monza 1000 Kms race a month later, further development had been carried out and larger air coolers fitted between the turbochargers and inlet manifolds, making the engines run cooler and develop more power ('almost 500 horsepower' was claimed). One car was entered in the race, and it was completely reliable finishing in fifth place behind a trio of Alfa Romeos and a Gulf GR7.

From that point in the season the car proved quite reliable, notching up a run of high placings: third in the Spa 1000 kilometres, sixth at the Nurburgring behind a quintet of 3-litre prototypes, then an unexpected failure at Imola; of the two cars entered, one was delayed by tyre trouble and a defective gearbox, while the other had turbo fanblade problems. Did this indicate the possibility of a failure at Le Mans?

Just one turbocharged 911 was entered for the 24-Hour race, pitted against no fewer than four Matra 670 machines and two Gulfs, a hare-and-tortoise situation for the Germans. True to form the prototypes went ahead, and one by one they fell by the wayside. Jarier had an accident in the pits' lane, the second Matra blew its engine, the third was seriously overheating almost from the start. One Gulf retired with a broken driveshaft, the other also had driveshaft lubrication problems and was constantly in the pits.

The usual Le Mans cliff-hanging drama was seen at 10 o'clock in the morning, with six hours to run. Pescarolo's leading Matra stopped with a broken gearbox (a special transmission designed and built by Porsche, incidentally) and limped slowly back to the pits. Now Muller/van Lennep were in second place and closing fast, and in the hour that the Matra was in the pits the Porsche closed to within one lap of the lead.

That was as close as the Porsche got, though. The Matra roared back into the race, and drew away as the turbocharged Porsche itself developed a gearbox fault, losing fourth gear, the drivers settling down to consolidate second place overall in the final results.

Continuing the 1974 programme, the Martini sponsored 911 turbo was sixth at the Osterreichring, then second place at Watkins Glen brought the marque up to second place in the World Championship table, ahead of Alfa Romeo and Gulf. An uncharacteristically low seventh placing at the Paul Ricard circuit, followed by a fifth at Brands Hatch, completed the season for the Porsche factory, for an announcement had already been made that there would be no official racing programme the following year. By missing the final round of the 1974 championship, at Kyalami, the Martini Porsche team managed by Norbert Singer dropped to third place in the points table, behind Matra and Gulf, but ahead of Alfa Romeo, Ferrari, Chevron, Lola, Ligier-Maserati and March.

Frankly, the season had been a technical exercise which proved everything that Porsche wanted to know about turbocharging applications on road cars, but with no prospects of winning outright there was no point in going on. So far as competitions were concerned, 1975 was treated as a year of preparation for 1976 when the new World Championship for Manufacturers (Group 5) would be introduced.

The respite from competitions was not unwelcome from a marketing point of view, since the oil crisis of 1974 had resulted in a sharp downturn in orders. The 1973 total of 15,415 cars sold in 1973 dropped to 9,915 in 1974 and again to 9,224 cars sold in 1975, while the number of employees was trimmed from 4,300 in 1973 to 3,750 a year later.

There were no panic measures under consideration at Stuttgart-Zuffenhausen, however. Dr. Ernst Fuhrmann, by now the Managing Director, commented in an interview with Edouard Seidler: "The crisis didn't modify anything fundamental. Why should it have? To change everything today would mean admitting that we were wrong previously.... sports cars like ours are good cars, they keep a total justification, both technically and energetically."

Porsche's answer to the crisis, in fact, was to manufacture even faster, even more expensive cars for the customers! In August 1974 the Turbo (type 930) was announced, a full production model with the KKK turbocharger unit boosting a 3-litre flat-six engine, and a year later a full 3-litre version of the Carrera (the Carrera 3) was announced. Like the Turbo, it had a new aluminium crankcase developed during the 1973 racing season, accommodating a 95mm bore and retaining the 70.4mm stroke.

The 3-litre Carrera was given new, four-bearing camshafts with a rather peaky profile allowing a healthy surge of power at 4,000rpm, bigger valves and a development of the K-Jetronic petrol injection, the result being a really high-performing GT car worthy of the name. This Carrera, developing 200bhp DIN, was the most powerful road car yet offered in the 911 series and had a top speed of 145mph, accelerating from rest to 100mph in a mere 18 seconds. Thanks to the Bosch injection system and technical development by Porsche, however, the six-cylinder engine was highly efficient and economical. All the

911 range engines (but not the Turbo) would now run on 91-octane petrol, and even the Carrera would return 19-24mpg (Imperial), remarkable figures considering the car's performance on the road.

When the 928 was introduced in March 1977 it was on the same production line as the 911. Although its days were numbered the management committed Porsche to the 911 'until the early 1980s', by which time further development would presumably be uneconomic. Possibly the final stage of 911 development was announced in August 1977, when the 2.7 litre and Carrera was dropped, and the sole version was the 911SC powered by a 180 horsepower 3-litre engine. This had the Carrera's flared arches, five-speed gearbox, and (for the British market) a 'Sport' package of wide wheels, front air dam and rear wing.

The period from the introduction of the 911 to the end of 1976 saw vast changes in the Porsche organisation, not least in the management. Chairman Dr. Ferdinand Porsche could see quite clearly by 1972 that the company had outgrown family status, and invited the Porsche and Piech family members to join a holding company in non-executive positions. Appointed joint managing directors were former experimental chief Dr. Ernst Fuhrmann and financial boss Heinz Branitzki, Dr. Ferry Porsche himself remaining as chairman of the company.

The newly constituted board now controlled some 4,000 employees and an annual turnover of 397 million marks in 1973. But so far as the customer was concerned nothing changed — every car remained a hand-built, highly engineered product making no concession whatever to mass production techniques.

Professor Ferdinand Porsche still seems to dominate the Zuffenhausen works, and everything he believed in is perpetuated. The slogan: 'only replace something good with something still better' is observed to the letter.

A showpiece of the factory today is the comprehensive experimental centre at Weissach, 15 miles north-west of Stuttgart. Wholly owned by Porsche and virtually finished in 1972, the Weissach centre is the envy of all other manufacturers, for here prototype components and complete cars can be designed, built and tested right up to production stage. Apart from doing essential test work for the factory, the Weissach centre works in secrecy for other manufacturers, mainly Volkswagen, while its complex of test tracks is used extensively by tyre manufacturers; virtually all the testing of the 917-10 and 917-30 Can-Am cars was carried out on a 1.6-mile track.

To begin with a skid pad was the main feature of the Weissach centre, and it helped Porsche's experimental engineers to evaluate different tyre compounds and suspension settings for the racing cars. Then a complex of road circuits was built, including a 1.8-mile hill course with blind brows and jumps, plus 'tortures' such as a water splash, a wavy surface portion, a strong camber, potholes, and rough asphalt with railway lines.

Every part intended for production has to complete 100,000 kilometres without failure, and even the racing cars have to complete 50,000 kilometres by which time every possible weakness is discovered and rectified. Buildings, which now house 500 workers, were added to the centre, and research in them includes crash testing, emission control, climatic tests and chassis dynamometers, acoustics, engine dynamometers, transmission tests, tyre test rigs, a hydropulser which allows static durability tests on suspension components, static performance testing, and testing of materials. There is also a foundry, smithy, plastics workshop, woodworking shop, assembly plants, a paint shop, and a data processing centre.

One of the most important features of the 1976 model range onwards was a six-year anti-corrosion guarantee for the underbody, a by-product of the Longlife concept. This was achieved by adopting Thyssen galvanised steel for the main chassis member....an expensive, rather difficult solution in manufacturing terms due to the obnoxious zinc fumes given off at the welding stage, but still one that was worthwhile in marketing terms.

3 Sportscars, from 1½ to 3 litres

THROUGHOUT the decades of the 1950's and 1960's the Porsche management stuck resolutely to the basic principle of developing and racing cars which had some technical bearing on road cars. This had the advantage that success benefitted the 356 and 911 models technically and commercially, but it also meant that Porsche regularly competed in international events with engine capacities of up to 2.2-litres and not more than 270 horsepower, whereas rival makes such as Ferrari and Ford had two or even three times the engine capacity. As a result, Porsche relied on light weight and manoeuverability to dominate the Targa Florio, and on reliability to produce impressive though not conquering results in endurance events such as Le Mans.

Late in 1967 the FIA ruled a 3-litre limit on prototype sports cars, and only then did Porsche develop 3-litre and 5-litre engines which swept the marque right to the forefront, making it almost completely dominant in the World Championship for Makes in 1969, 1970 and 1971. In this chapter we will follow the progression of sports-racing car development through the 1960's and the 3-litre cars to 1971, devoting separate chapters to the all-conquering 917 and the turbocharged 917-10 developments.

Porsche's first Targa Florio success was in 1956 when Umberto Maglioli single-handedly drove a 1500 RS Spyder to victory, and three years later Edgar Barth/Wolfgang Seidel again won the classic event in a Porsche RSK, when the race was extended to the full 1000 kilometre duration — their win was achieved in just over 11 hours! In 1960, when the race was reduced to 11 laps (720 kilometres) on the Little Madonie course, Jo Bonnier and Hans Herrmann drove a 1,588cc, 165 horsepower RS60 model to another fine win, following up victory in the Sebring 12-Hour race by Herrmann with the Belgian driver, Olivier Gendebien.

Stirling Moss joined the Porsche team for the Targa Florio in 1961, and he and Graham Hill came close to victory over the new 2.4-litre Ferrari Dino sports car. With a comfortable win in sight, Moss was forced to retire with seized transmission only three kilometres from the end, letting the Ferrari through; Porsche's reputation was saved by the second-placed RS60 driven by Bonnier and Gurney.

The four-cam four-cylinder engine had clearly reached the end of its development, and real technical progress began in 1962 when the new flat-eight cylinder engine made its debut on the Targa Florio. For sportscar application the engine was of full 2-litre capacity

200

developing 210 horsepower. Fitted into a developed version of the RS tubular frame chassis, the model also had disc brakes fitted for the first time and they did not quite have the staying power of the well-proven drum brakes in the early days. Gurney slid off the road and hit a wall on the second lap of the race, so Bonnier transferred himself to the previous year's Le Mans coupe version, also with the flat-eight engine fitted, and finished in second place sharing the car with Nino Vaccarella. The race was won by the Ferrari driven by Willy Mairesse/Ricardo Rodriguez/Olivier Gendebien, this car using a 2-litre version of the V6 engine which was to become dominant in Grand Prix racing that year.

However Porsche's flat-eight engine was successful in the French Grand Prix, and although the company withdrew from single-seater racing during the winter, the power unit was retained in 2-litre form for long distance racing, and was avenged on the Targa Florio in 1963 when Jo Bonnier and Carlo Abate took a splendid win in record time. Another victory seemed likely in the Nurburg 1000Kms that followed when Ferrari drivers Mike Parkes and Willy Mairesse both spun off the road, but unhappily Porsche's first major sportscar win on home soil was denied when Graham Hill missed a gear and slid off the road, and the Barth/Linge car broke its driveshaft.

The type 550 competition car ran for 11 seasons in Spyder and Coupe forms, its power increasing from 110bhp to 210bhp with the eight-cylinder engine installed, but chassis development now seemed to be holding back Porsche's sporting programme and the completely new 904 model was developed and ready for testing in the summer of 1963. It broke away from all the traditions in having a heavy box-frame chassis and a fibre-glass body which was bonded to the frame. From the beginning it was meant to utilise the new production six-cylinder engine, but in fact most of the early examples were fitted with the four-cylinder engine to keep the cost down. The reason for this was that Porsche intended to build 100 cars straight off, on production line principle, to obtain homologation to run the cars in the Grand Touring category. A total of 120 were built, 100 actually sold and 20 retained by the factory for development and racing. Of these 20, ten had the six-cylinder engine initially and six had the flat-eight racing unit.

Porsche's decision to put racing cars on the 'production line' was certainly popular with customers, and the batch of 100 could have been sold twice over at the asking price of less than 30,000 marks. In the spirit of homologation the Carrera GTS was sold with steel wheels and road tyres, and customers were recommended to change the engine oil every 2,500 kilometres if using the car mainly in towns!

The main criteria for the 904 were simplicity, strength and, of course, reliability, but due to the weight of the chassis it was not light, and but for the outstanding road holding qualities should not have been competitive even with the RS61. The tubular frame RS60 and RS61 models, with 1,588cc/165bhp engines fitted, weighed a mere 500 kilogrammes dry (1,060 pounds) and had a power to weight ratio of 348bhp per ton.

The box-frame 904 GTS, with a plastic body bonded to the chassis to provide torsional strength, weighed 1,430 pounds dry and even with the 1966cc/180bhp Carrera engine fitted it had a power to weight ratio of only 280bhp per ton. As a Grand Touring car this was fine, but for serious competitions work the Porsche team would have to rely on the 2-litre eight-cylinder version which developed 230 horsepower with only a slight weight penalty (some 60 pounds) and had a power to weight ratio of 345bhp per ton; this could not, of course, run in the GT class but competed as a prototype.

Development of the 904 GTS was completed in only six months and before homologation was confirmed two cars ran at Sebring as prototypes, with mixed results; the works car of Barth/Linge had some clutch trouble and dropped to 20th place, but another driven by Briggs Cunningham and Lake Underwood finished in ninth place and won the 2-litre category.

A month later, and homologated in the GT class, two cars were sent to the Targa

201

Florio for Colin Davis/Antonio Pucci and Herbert Linge/Gianni Balzarini as back-up cars to the spearhead effort, a pair of eight-cylinder (1963 model) Spyders for Jo Bonnier/Graham Hill and Edgar Barth/Umberto Maglioli. Interest at this race centred on the 7-litre AC Cobras, which proved to have an abundance of power and an inadequacy of road-holding, and the two works Porsche Spyders were going nicely until the driveshaft broke on the Bonnier/Hill car and suspension troubles dropped Barth/Maglioli back to sixth place.

Meanwhile the 904s had outlasted, even outpaced the Cobras and an unexpected but very welcome win was recorded by Davis/Pucci with Linge/Balzarini following up in second place. This was Porsche's fifth Targa Florio victory, but, as happened nine years later, it was not achieved quite as expected!

No more outright wins were recorded in 1964, either by the 904s or the Spyders, but in the 2-litre category the 904s were quite untouchable and, as Paul Frere records in his book *The Racing Porsches*, were almost totally reliable: at Spa eight started and seven finished (the eighth was black-flagged because the driver was not competent), at Le Mans all five cars finished, and at the Rheims 12-Hours all eight cars finished.

In rallies too, the 904s proved their strength. In the revived Tour de France Automobile, four Porsches finished in runner-up positions to a pair of powerful Ferrari GTOs, which were distinctly favoured by the race circuit content of the event, and then in January 1965 Eugen Bohringer caused quite a sensation in the rally world by finishing second overall to Timo Makinen's Mini in the Monte Carlo Rally, a tough, snow-bound event which caused scores of far more suitable touring cars to fall by the wayside.

The feat was all the more remarkable because Bohringer, a Stuttgart hotelier who normally drove Mercedes saloons in rallies, came to terms with the mid-engined layout. Time and again since then the world's top rally drivers have attempted to put mid-engined cars on to the map, but failed. On race circuits or anywhere that drivers can practice and perfect their racing line, mid-engined cars are naturally better balanced and have higher cornering power than other types. Rally drivers go 'blind' much of the time, even on known roads, flinging their cars sideways to dissipate forward speed, bringing the tail round if the corner is tighter than it looks, and on icy and loose surfaces particularly they prefer the cars with engines overhanging the rear wheels, cars in which they can change direction instantly. Later on, VW-Porsche and Ford tried to go rallying with mid-engined cars but met with a damning lack of success; in that light, we rate Bohringer's success on the Monte Carlo as one of the outstanding feats in rallying.

At the end of the 1964 season Barth and Davis finished third overall in the Paris 1000Kms at Montlhery to a pair of 3.3-litre Ferraris, driving the now developed 904 GTS/eight-cylinder. For 1965 a spyder version was made, using the 904 frame and the eight-cylinder engine developing 235 horsepower, but the change from coupe bodywork which approximately doubled the torsional stiffness did nothing for the handling. For the Targa Florio the car was offered to Bonnier but he did not like it, opting for the similarly powered but coupe bodied car which weighed 170 pounds more. Bonnier was proved wrong on that occasion, for while Vaccarella and Bandini won the race in their Ferrari second place was taken by the 904 spyder driven by Mitter/Davis, followed by Linge/Maglioli in a 904/6 and Bonnier/Graham Hill finished fourth in their 904/8. Fifth, and GT class winners, were Gunther Klass/Antonio Pucci in a 904 GTS.

The unique 904 spyder was written off by Gerhard Mitter, practising for the Nurburg 1000Kms, and while the Ferraris went on with their winning ways Bonnier/Rindt picked up third place in the German endurance event, driving the 904/8. At 235bhp though, the eight-cylinder engine was deemed suspect for the really long-distance races, and at Le Mans the 904s were fitted with six-cylinder engines from the 911 model, to finish fourth and fifth.

In 1966 Dipl-Ing Ferdinand Piech (Professor Ferdinand Porsche's nephew) became head of the experimental department, and the pace of racing developments in particular began to grow rapidly. The 904 had served its purpose, and with a slightly more powerful engine was continuing to dominate the 2-litre GT class, but the weight of the car offended Piech and he planned to concentrate on developing the 906.

Development was accelerated when Lodovico Scarfiotti brought a Ferrari to the Mountain Championship to challenge Porsche's absolute supremacy. The hillclimb scene carried a lot of importance until the late 1960's and ever since 1957, when it became a contest for 2-litre sportscars, Porsche had won consistently, Edgar Barth being the undisputed champion in 1963 and 1964 before an illness ended his life.

In 1965 Mitter led the hillclimb onslaught but Scarfiotti's Ferrari was clearly quicker, and at Ollon-Villars Mitter's eight-cylinder engine was mounted in a completely new spaceframe chassis which was considerably lighter and far more competitive using Lotus suspension and wheels. Mitter was still unable to beat Scarfiotti, and the Italian team took the title away from Porsche for the first time in seven years.

That spaceframe chassis was basically the framework of the 906 model introduced for the 1966 season, but the mountain championship was used in later years for developing new racing cars, notably 910 in 1966, the 907 in 1967 and the 909 in 1968, the latter model having the body of the 908 and the chassis of the 908/3.

The Carrera 6 (catalogued as the 906 although the six-cylinder 904 GTS had also been referred to in the factory as the 906) had very little in common with the 904. The steel spaceframe chassis was considerably lighter and contained all the torsional stiffness needed, the plastic body panels merely being the clothing. It had the 904's suspension, brakes and 15 inch wheels, but it was designed to accept the six-cylinder production engine and did so from the beginning. Most important of all, it was 255 pounds lighter than the 904/6 at 1,235 pounds and had a power to weight ratio of 380bhp per ton with the 210bhp six-cylinder engine, and 450bhp per ton with a 260bhp, 2.2-litre version of the eight-cylinder engine installed.

Only 50 cars needed to be made to obtain FIA homologation, and these were duly completed in time for the 1966 racing season. They caused quite a sensation when they appeared, for the Carrera 6s had gullwing doors, and were considerably more efficient aerodynamically with a drag co-efficient of 0.350 (the 904 was never tested in a wind tunnel, but the drag co-efficient was certainly higher than 0.400).

Like all subsequent Porsche competition cars (even the turbo 917s) the Carrera 6 underwent trials on a 'destruction course', running almost 700 miles on a closed track including pave, a sharp brow and a banked corner; unlike earlier models the new Carrera had metallic Rose jointed suspension which proved completely reliable in arduous conditions.

A total of 65 Carrera 6s were made, 52 of them with 2-litre six-cylinder engines for homologation, nine prototype versions using Bosch fuel injection which boosted the power output to 220bhp, and four with 2.2-litre eight-cylinder engines developing 260bhp also with Bosch injection.

The Carrera 6 seemed right from the word go, and at its debut race in Daytona, Hans Herrmann/Herbert Linge had a completely trouble-free 24-hour race finishing sixth overall behind the 7-litre Fords and 4.4-litre Ferraris. Then at Sebring a month later a factory Carrera 6 driven by Mitter, Herrmann and Joe Buzzetta finished in fourth place behind a trio of 7-litre Fords.

The big effort, as always, was saved for the Targa Florio and four cars represented the factory, plus the Scuderia Filipinetti entry for Willy Mairesse/Herbert Muller. The newly homologated works Carrera 6 was entered for Pucci/Arena, two more had Bosch injection for Mitter/Bonnier and Herrmann/Glemser, and the fourth works car for Davis/Klass ran the 2.2-litre flat-eight for the first time, though on carburettors.

During practice Klass was the quickest, returning a time inside Vaccarella's lap record, but the two 4-litre Ferraris were turning in very comparable times and a needle match was easy to forecast. Race day was predominantly wet, though, and at the end of the first lap Vaccarella's Ferrari led Mitter's Porsche. The lead see-sawed until it rained again, and the lead Ferrari lost time on the fifth lap allowing Klass to go into the lead with Mitter just behind him. But Mitter tried too hard to catch his team-mate and went off the road, then a couple of laps later Klass' car also retired with broken rear suspension. In the end it was the Filipinetti car driven by Mairesse/Muller which earned the victory, leaving the works' drivers rather red-faced.

Four cars were entered for the Nurburg 1000Kms, but all sorts of troubles set in and the best result was a fourth place for Bob Bondurant/Paul Hawkins behind the American 7-litre Chaparral and a pair of Ferraris; Glemser crashed his works Porsche from third place, Rindt burned his clutch lining at the start and Klass had a driveshaft break. This was a bitter reminder to Piech and his team to preserve the Porsche reputation for reliability, and from then on it was decided to run only new cars in important races.

Five cars were run at Le Mans in June, three of them with aerodynamic long tails which reduced the drag co-efficient of 0.326 and two of them standard, homologated Carreras running with carburettors. One of the carburated cars broke a connecting rod an hour before the finish, but the other four cars proved totally reliable once again, though beaten by the 7-litre Fords which scored a crushing 1-2-3 victory. Ferrari's challenge faded during the night, and at the end the Porsches were fourth, fifth, sixth and seventh in the order of Jo Siffert/Colin Davis, Hans Herrmann/Herbert Linge a lap behind, Peter DeKlerk/Udo Schutz a further lap down, and Gunther Klass/Rolf Stommelen in seventh place winning the GT/sports category outright.

Porsche only made one more official sortie in 1966, to win the non-championship Hockenheim race, and meanwhile Gerhard Mitter was regaining his Mountain Championship title from Scarfiotti, despite having his foot in plaster for some weeks after an accident in Spa. For most of the season he ran a developed version of the 906 model which made its debut at Ollon Villars the previous year, but towards the end of the season he ran a new chassis, the 910. This was quite similar to the 906 chassis but the front track was increased, and 13-inch diameter magnesium alloy wheels with centre stud fixing were employed. The rear chassis frame was altered slightly to allow a bracing strut to be used in the engine bay when the eight-cylinder unit was fitted, this having proved useful in stiffening the six-cylinder 906 versions.

A notable improvement was gained in weight, the first version saving 75 kilogrammes (later on the weight was pared still further to 410 kilogrammes, under 900 pounds, by using an aluminium frame). Every possible means was used to reduce unnecessary weight, even to the extent of taking oil from the front cooler to the engine through the chassis tubes; anti-roll bars were tubular, saving weight without reducing stiffness, and light-weight materials such as fibre-glass and even titanium were being used in place of alloy and steel. The only concession was fitting front-hinged doors, which though heavier than the gull-wing versions were safer for long-distance racing, when a door might not be latched properly after a quick pit stop. A total of 28 cars were made, there being no intention to homologate the 910 as a sports car, but in 1968 the requirement was lowered from 50 to 25 cars so the 910 was homologated, replacing the 906 then as the 2-litre class winner.

The debut at Daytona in 1967 was a good one, Siffert/Herrmann finishing fourth in the 24-Hour race behind three 4-litre Ferraris, though the two factory back-up Carrera 6s both retired, one with engine trouble, and the other due to an accident. At the Sebring race which followed there were no works Ferraris, but Ford's big 7-litre cars were rolled out again to finish first and second, though Gerhard Mitter/Scooter Patrick in the six-cylinder Porsche finished on the same lap as the second Ford, in third place, followed by Siffert/Herrmann in the sister car. At Monza the Porsches were placed third and fifth, and at the Spa 1000Kms which followed Siffert/Herrmann finished second to Jacky Ickx's Gulf-Mirage Ford GT40, which the Belgian driver drove outstandingly in the rain.

The big effort was again reserved for the Targa Florio, and six 910 models were entered: three had Bosch injected six-cylinder engines for Schutz/Maglioli, Cella/Biscaldi and Neerpasch/Elford, and three injected 2.2-litre eight-cylinder engines for Stommelen/ Hawkins, Mitter/Davis and Herrmann/Siffert.

Principal opposition came from the Vaccarella/Scarfiotti Ferrari P4 and as expected the Palermo lawyer went rushing into the lead, but on the second lap he crashed at Cerda, then Gunther Klass crashed his Ferrari Dino which was also a threat, and the Muller/ Guichet Ferrari broke its differential. Later Andrea de Adamich's Alfa Romeo 2-litre broke its front suspension, and the way was clear for Porsches to make a clean sweep of the leader board, Hawkins/Stommelen winning in the 2.2-litre car followed by Cella/ Biscaldi and Neerpasch/Elford.

Victory in the Nurburg 1000Kms had so far eluded Porsche, but the Zuffenhausen marque made up for this in 1967 with the first four places outright. Three eight-cylinder 2.2-litre fuel injected cars were entered for Siffert/Herrmann, Stommelen/Ahrens (this car with ventilated disc brakes, which were found to reduce pad wear considerably) and Mitter/Lucien Bianchi; three six-cylinder cars, also with injection, were entered for Schutz/Buzzetta, Neerpasch/Elford and Koch/Hawkins.

The 7-litre Chaparral was quickest in practice followed by John Surtees' Lola-Aston Martin, then Siffert's 2.2-litre Porsche. In the race however the Lola soon retired with suspension trouble and the Chaparral went from the lead with transmission failure, leaving the Porsches to decide on the order amongst themselves. Then the 2.2-litre cars hit a patch of unreliability, both Siffert and Stommelen retiring with broken valves. The Mitter/Bianchi car was well in the lead but it began to have electrical trouble, the alternator having failed, and it ground to a halt on the final lap. Second string drivers Joe Buzzetta and Gerhard Koch had a real race right to the finish, ending the race less than half a second apart, with the Neerpasch/Elford car four minutes behind with a broken valve spring.

A new type of Porsche, the 907, was run at Le Mans for the first time, the two six-cylinder cars entered for Siffert/Herrmann and Mitter/Rindt. Basically it was very similar to the 910 but it had right-hand steering, the first racing Porsche so built, as a concession to the usual right-hand direction of the circuits, and it was considerably narrower above the waistline to lower the frontal area, down to a remarkable 0.273 co-efficient. The front suspension was revised to give more progressive damping with shorter, lighter springs, and ventilated disc brakes were standard equipment. Although six-cylinder engines were fitted at Le Mans in the interests of reliability, the 907 was normally fitted with the eight-cylinder engine.

Again the big Fords and Ferraris made the running, but again the 2-litre Porsches gained honourable results with Siffert/Herrmann finishing in fifth place in the new 907, averaging over 125mph for the 24-hour duration; the Rindt/Mitter car retired during the evening after the engine had been over-revved. Stommelen/Neerpasch in the 910 finished in sixth place seven laps behind the newer car.

At Mugello, a non-championship race on a mountainous course in central Italy, Porsche scored a sweeping victory with eight-cylinder 910 models with Mitter/Schutz leading Stommelen/Neerpasch, with Elford/Gijs van Lennep placed third in the new Porsche 911R, ahead of Jo Schlesser's Ford Mk2 model.

With Ford and Chaparral breaking up the scoring, Ferrari had a very slender lead over Porsche in the World Sports Car Championship when it came to the final round, the BOAC 500, at Brands Hatch in September. It worked out that if Porsche, with 2.2-litre cars, could beat the 4-litre Ferraris the German make could win the coveted World title, something that had never seemed possible before. It was a tall order, and against all

205

expectations the high-winged Chaparral of Phil Hill/Mike Spence lasted the distance to take a splendid victory; the real race was going on behind, between the Ferrari driven by Chris Amon/Jackie Stewart and the Porsche 910 eight-cylinder of Jo Siffert/Bruce McLaren.

It was a really hard race, the Chaparral, the Lola, Ferraris and Porsches fairly evenly matched. Graham Hill had been brought back into the Porsche team and was going well with the leaders until he missed a gear and damaged his engine. The Lolas retired and Elford's Porsche went out with engine trouble, and behind the Chaparral at the end, the Amon/Stewart Ferrari just managed to clinch second place, and the World title, by a single lap from the Siffert/McLaren 910, with the 907 driven by Neerpasch/Herrmann placed fourth.

That was the last time the factory ran the 910 models, having proved that the 907 would be a better bet for the 1968 season, and the 910s were all sold to private customers. On the hillclimb scene, Mitter won three hillclimb titles in a row, in 1966 with the 906, in 1967 with the 906 and the 910 prototype, and in 1968 with the 910 and latterly the 909 bergspyder which was reduced to an incredible 410 kilogrammes and was the fore-runner of the 908/3 Targa Florio car, though it still had a 2-litre eight-cylinder engine to conform with the rules. By this time it had titanium springs and hubs, and expensive but extremely light beryllium brake discs. The latter version of the 910 was interesting in that it had suspension operated lever flaps at the rear of the tail cover, rising into the air stream as the suspension rose in order to exert more downforce. On the hills this device was of little value, but like so many other development items it was seen later on circuit cars, and was to create a good deal of controversy. A particularly interesting feature on the 909 was the placing of the differential *behind* the gearbox, reducing the wheelbase and improving the polar moment of inertia, a distinct advantage on twisty roads.

For Porsche, the big turning point of the whole racing programme came late in 1967 when the Commission Sportive Internationale of the FIA decided to eliminate the 7-litre Fords and Chaparrals by the simple expedient of bringing in a 5-litre limit for 'production' cars, of which 25 identical examples had been made, and a 3-litre limit for prototypes. As it happened the decision had already been taken in Zuffenhausen to construct a new 3-litre machine, the 908, with what was basically an eight-cylinder version of the well proven production six, and it was already well on its way to the development stage. Had the change of rules been announced earlier, (as it should have been, and the subsequent rumpus forced the CSI to announce that in future it would give 12 months' notice of any changes), the 908 would never have been born, for the idea of the 917 model was now germinating.

But the 908 did come, and for Porsche it marked the beginning of a new era. At last, the Porsche factory could compete against rival makes on level terms. Sure the 5-litre Ford GT40s could be, would be, a threat on the really fast circuits, and Porsche now had the responsibility of going for outright wins every time out, something that had not been the case before. It was a real challenge, and Porsche would rise to it.

To outsiders, it appeared that the change in Porsche strategy was more than purely mechanical. Dr. Piech introduced computers which could accurately predict car and driver performances on every type of circuit, after being fed information about track conditions, gradients and corners, engine power, roadholding ability and so on. Fortunately the drivers kept their sense of humour as they strove to attain the computer targets, which even on circuits like Le Mans could be within a second of actual performance.

To start the 1968 season the Porsche works team ran the 2.2-litre 907 models, running four at the Daytona 24-Hours early in February. Principal opposition came from the 5-litre, 425 horsepower Ford GT40s in John Wyer's team, but weighing over 1000 kilo-grammes they were only expected to be competitive on the faster circuits.

The two V8 powered cars of Ickx/Redman and Hawkins/Hobbs led the early stages of the race, but Ickx's car retired with a broken gearbox then, after 18 hours, Hawkins/Hobbs retired too with a split petrol tank leaving the way clear for a Porsche 1-2-3 finish. Vic Elford (fresh from winning the Monte Carlo Rally) was the winner with Jochen Neerpasch, but the winning car was also driven short spells by Jo Siffert and Hans Herrmann whose second place 907 had been delayed with throttle linkage trouble, and by Rolf Stommelen whose car had been crashed by co-driver Gerhard Mitter. Third place was taken by Joe Buzzetta/Jo Schlesser in another works 907.

At the Sebring 12-Hour race which followed, John Wyer's Gulf Oil sponsored GT40s again proved faster for a while, but both retired with mechanical problems leaving no real opposition for the 2.2-litre Porsche 907s. Jo Siffert/Hans Herrmann covered only one lap less than the winning 7-litre Ford had the previous year, a measure of how the prototypes were developing, and a second works car driven by Vic Elford/Jochen Neerpasch was second, delayed by needing to have a front wheel bearing upright replaced. Two more works Porsches retired early in the race, both as a result of over-revving, showing that the 270 horsepower flat-eight engines had to be treated with respect.

The next confrontation was in the BOAC 500 race at Brands Hatch in April, and after two disappointing outings the GT40 driven by Ickx/Redman scored a very narrow victory over the Porsche 907s, by a mere 22 seconds after more than six hours of racing. For all the teams and spectators, though, the afternoon was marred by news of Jim Clark's death in a Formula-2 race at Hockenheim. The result of the BOAC 500 was a disappointment for Siffert/Herrmann who had led much of the distance, only to retire with a failure in a front wheel bearing, a problem that was to crop up repeatedly during the season and eventually cost Porsche the coveted World Championship title. Due to making only two fuel stops compared with Porsches' three, Ickx was able to keep a safe distance ahead of Mitter in the closing stages of the race. In third place were Elford/Neerpasch in another 907.

At the Le Mans trials the same weekend two brand-new Porsche 908 cars made their debut, driven by Rolf Stommelen and Herbert Linge. The chassis was almost identical to that of the 907, in which the steel tubes were pressurised so that any crack in the frame could be detected immediately simply by checking with a tyre pressure gauge. Real interest centred on the new 3-litre engine, which co-incidentally had the same bore/stroke dimensions as the future 2.2-litre production six-cylinder engine, 84 x 66mm, giving a capacity for the eight-cylinder of 2,926cc.

The 908 engine was derived from an experimental (type 916) unit run at Mugello the previous year in a 910, thus shortening the development period. It was as simple as the 907's flat-eight engine was complex, following the production six-cylinder idea of driving the twin overhead camshafts by chain from the crank. A two-plane crankshaft was used (rather than a single-plane crank in the 2.2-litre), and the vertically mounted engine cooling fan shared a cogged belt drive with the alternator (repeated belt failures at the Le Mans trials however forced the design team to fit vee belts, and later twin vee belts). Dry sump lubrication was used, and as in the 2.2-litre engine, titanium con-rods and bolts were fitted. Engine weight was kept down to 178kg (394 pounds) through using a magnesium crankcase and alloy cylinder barrels, with chrome-plated bores. As in all the Porsche engines, two valves per cylinder were specified in order to keep cylinder head temperatures at an acceptable level, even though other manufacturers were getting more power with the help of four-valve layouts; but what Porsche lost on power — the 908 engine originally developed 335bhp at 8,500rpm — was more than compensated by the light weight of the car, right down to the 650 kilogramme limit which existed until the end of the 1968 season. (The minimum weight limit was removed by the CSI for 1969 to give the 3-litre prototypes a better chance against the heavier 5-litre cars, but too late — the 917 was already nearing completion!). Coupled to the new engine was a dry sump lubricated six-speed gearbox, developed for hillclimbing and used latterly on the 907s. A Borg and Beck four-plate clutch connected the drive, and Bosch direct fuel injection fed the cylinders.

The debut of the 908 was very disappointing. It raced for the first time at Monza, having long-tail bodywork almost indistinguishable from the 907's and very comparable performance too. Two 908s were entered for Siffert/Herrmann and Mitter/Scarfiotti, plus a 907 for Stommelen/Neerpasch. For a while Siffert kept pace with Ickx's GT40, but then part of the air ducting to the rear brakes caught up in a driveshaft and flailed the oil pipes leading to the gearbox. It was patched up to enable Siffert/Herrmann to finish 19th, while Mitter/Scarfiotti had fuel injection and alternator problems dropping them to 11th place at the end. Ickx's Ford went out with exhaust pipe breakages, leaving Hawkins/Hobbs in the second GT40 to beat the Stommelen/Neerpasch 907 by less than two minutes.

Following the teething troubles at Monza (where engine vibration seemed to be one of the worst problems) the 908s were withdrawn from the Targa Florio and four 907s were run instead for Siffert/Stommelen, Elford/Umberto Maglioli, Herrmann/Neerpasch and Scarfiotti/Mitter. Elford, who was on top form that year and later earned himself a place in the Cooper Formula-1 team, was quickest in practice, though Porsche's form book was upset when Scarfiotti crashed and destroyed a 907 during practice.

In another car, though, Scarfiotti led the early laps of the race while the two quickest men in the team met trouble: Siffert had a front hub bearing seize and lost an hour, while Elford had a front wheel come loose, then the tyre burst, and he arrived at the pits 12 minutes late on his Goodrich space-saver spare wheel. He lost a total of 16 minutes, then began a truly amazing climb back into contention, driving as he had never driven before. At half distance Mitter's leading Porsche was badly delayed by a broken driveshaft and two Alfa Romeos held the leading positions followed closely by Herrmann/Neerpasch.

It was Elford's day, though, the Englishman driving eight of the 11 laps and lapping consistently inside the course record, carving 67 seconds off Muller's previous record. Quickly he overhauled his team-mate Herrmann, then the Alfa Romeos, and with two laps still to run Elford overcame his handicap and was pulling away to record one of Porsche's most famous victories, his race time eight minutes quicker than the 907's winning time the year before.

Victory came to the new 908 second time out, at the Nurburg 1000Kms, in May, when Siffert and Elford teamed up in the winning car. Most of the teething problems had been sorted out, and the 908 now ran on 15-inch wheels instead of 13-inch, allowing bigger brakes to be used. Stommelen claimed pole position in the works' back-up 907 but Siffert and Elford held the lead almost from the start, except when Ickx's GT40 went ahead during the Porsches' first pit stops. Ickx was a real threat but his co-driver Paul Hawkins was a bit slower, and at the end Siffert/Elford had a three-minute advantage on Herrman/Stommelen, with the GT40 just behind in third place. Snow fell during the race, and at Spa a week later it was pouring with rain. Conditions were ideal for Ickx, ably backed again by Redman, and their GT40 lapped the second-placed Porsche 907 driven by Mitter/Schlesser, with Stommelen/Herrmann following up in third place in the 908.

Le Mans was delayed until September that year due to elections in France, so the next round of the 1968 championship was at Watkins Glen in July. By now the 908 engines had been increased to 2,997cc by increasing the bore to 85mm, and power was up to 350 horsepower. New, and much lighter 5-speed gearboxes had been developed, and the engine vibration problem had been alleviated, though not overcome. Furthermore a new chassis, 012, had been made up with aluminium tubes like the chassis of the previous year's 910 hillclimb car, saving 20 kilogrammes weight. Everything looked fine for the race when Siffert made pole position, but everything went wrong when once again the front wheel bearing broke up and caused two cars to retire during the six-hour race, while

American driver George Follmer in a works car missed a gear change and damaged his engine. The Gulf GT40s ran away with the race followed by the interesting Howmet turbine car, while two Americans finished fourth in a Porsche Carrera 6 and the factory salvaged sixth place with a 908 driven by Hans Herrmann/Richard Attwood/Tetsu Ikuzawa, delayed by numerous electrical and throttle linkage troubles.

Wheel bearing troubles had plagued the team all season, Watkins Glen being the fourth consecutive failure, and Porsche's reputation for reliability was being tarnished. The big 'inquest' which followed revealed that the grease specified for the bearings was inadequate, and a change of specification brought about an immediate solution on the test track. To make sure, small roller bearings were replaced by larger taper bearings, and no further trouble was encountered.

Minor problems cropped up on all four cars entered for the Austrian race which followed (the last race on the Zeltweg airfield, and allocated only half points due to the shorter race distance). Rather to the relief of the team John Wyer did not send his GT40s and Porsche gained a rather hollow 1-2 victory, five laps ahead of Paul Hawkins' privately entered GT40 — then on the slowing down lap Siffert's winning car broke its transmission, and coasted silently to the waiting band of officials! The Swiss driver looked amused and rather sheepish as the garland was put round his neck.

On to Le Mans, where four long-tail 908s were entered for Stommelen/Neerpasch, Patrick/Buzzetta, Siffert/Herrmann and Mitter/Elford, plus three privately entered 907s which were to prove useful. It was a wet race, which handicapped the streamlined Porsches (the long tails reduced the drag, but put less downforce on the back wheels), and the race turned into a disaster for the 908s as one car after another suffered alternator problems tracing back to the engine vibrations. Siffert's car went out early with a cracked gearbox casing, and after 24 hours Pedro Rodriguez/Lucien Bianchi scored an easy win for John Wyer's Ford team, ahead of Rico Steinemann/Dieter Spoerry in the Hart Ski sponsored Porsche 907, with the surviving 908 of Neerpasch/Stommelen close behind.

The result of the race, and the season as a whole, was a bitter disappointment for Porsche. To lose Le Mans was bad enough, but the championship lost to Ford as well. Only the five best results counted, and Wyer's team had five wins but little else: a gross score of 51 points, nett 45. Porsche had four wins but a string of good places, a total score of 67½ points but only 42 nett. The British newspaper *Motoring News* commented: "Nothing but the best has been good enough for Porsche this year, and the men at Stuttgart must be feeling pretty badly about the FIA at the present time, for in most people's opinion it would be only fair to allow the best seven results out of ten, giving Porsche 54 points to Ford's 51."

Two years later the points rule was indeed changed, but such was Porsche's domination that it did not make the slightest difference to the overall picture. The year 1968 did close on a good note, for Gerhard Mitter won the European Mountain Championship for the third consecutive time in his 909 bergspyder — the forerunner of the 908 spyder track car — and in the Paris 1000Kms held at Montlhery in October the 908s scored a runaway victory with perfect reliability, Siffert/Herrmann leading Elford/Rudi Lins.

After a reign lasting a decade as competitions manager, Huschke von Hanstein moved on to the field of public relations with the new VW-Porsche company in 1969, not entirely happy with the 'computer era' and the passing of the spirit of gentlemanly competition. His place was taken by Rico Steinemann, a useful competitor in Porsches and the former editor of the Swiss magazine *Powerslide*.

With the minimum weight limit abolished, the 908 was given a spyder body for 1969 resembling that on the bergspyder, including the retention of suspension operated flaps at the rear of the bodywork; long-tail coupes were retained however to take part in the endurance races, being easier on the drivers and faster, too, on high speed tracks like

Daytona and Le Mans. With aluminium tube frames, the 908/02 model as the spyder was called weighed only 590 kilogrammes, but some of the weight advantage was offset due to the need to fit large front spoilers. Titanium hubs and stub axles were now fitted at the front and rear, reducing unsprung weight.

Numerous modifications were done to the engine, and in the course of development the best units now gave as much as 370bhp, though 360bhp was average. Single-plane crankshafts were adopted to alleviate the engine vibration problem, although more complicated exhaust systems had to be fitted. Unfortunately a long distance test at Monza during the winter was inconclusive, because both cars crashed and were burned out, and due to this alone the first outing of the 908 (coupe) at Daytona in 1969 turned into a rout. The cars were clearly faster than their opposition during practice and the race, but by the 17th hour all five factory Porsches were out for the same reason. An alloy gear designed to reduce vibration on the camshaft drive broke up, causing complete engine failure. Even before this happened, the cars had been delayed by broken exhaust manifolds so it was a dark hour for Porsche, and almost unbelievably the Donohue/Parsons Lola won the race after spending 80 minutes in the pits.

The 908 spyder made its debut at Sebring, and again an unforeseen problem broke up the works effort. A weakness in the chassis tube holding the rear suspension in place struck four cars out of five entered. First Herrmann's car was retired, then Siffert's, but when Mitter had the same problem the chassis was repaired and the car was despatched again. Stommelen's car also had to be repaired but it picked up again to third place overall, only four laps behind the Ickx/Oliver GT40 and the new 3-litre V12 Ferrari driven by Chris Amon/Mario Andretti.

The Ford GT40s had been a problem the previous year, and would be again at Le Mans, but the Porsche team had new opposition when the Ferrari team returned to endurance racing in 1969 with the V12 312P prototype, Amon threatening to be fastest at Brands Hatch practising for the BOAC 500. It was decided to let Siffert practise on Firestone tyres (the first time a Porsche had raced on anything but Dunlop equipment), and he was immediately 1.7 seconds faster to claim pole position. His time of 1 minute 28.8 seconds was six seconds faster than he had gone the previous year in the 907, and was even faster than the 1 minute 29.7 seconds record lap that Siffert himself established when winning the 1968 British Grand Prix in Rob Walker's Lotus 49. Several times in 1969 the 360bhp Porsches were quicker than the previous year's Formula-1 times using 400bhp-plus open wheelers, and it was generally reckoned that the better aerodynamics of the sports cars, and Siffert's on-form driving, accounted for the performance.

Using the soft-compound Firestones in the BOAC race, it was realised that three tyre changes would have to be made (fronts twice, rear tyres once), but it was thought that Siffert and Redman could make up for that. Brian Redman, the Lancastrian driver, had been signed from Wyer's team during the winter, and was to prove a perfect match for Siffert as together they steam-rollered five victories during the season. At Brands Hatch they dominated the race from the fifth lap to the end, keeping ahead of the Amon/Rodriguez Ferrari despite a fault in the ignition which reduced the power slightly and lost them 400rpm on the straights. In a demonstration of perfect reliability, long sought, the three factory Porsche 908s filled the first three places, as the Ferrari fell back at the end with a stretched throttle cable which reduced its power. Siffert and Redman covered 227 laps averaging 100.22mph, Elford/Attwood covered 225 laps and Mitter/Schutz covered 223 laps. A minor modification to the chassis at the rear proved perfectly satisfactory, and from then on the 908s proved to be among the most reliable Porsches ever raced.

The Monza 1000Kms saw one of the most exciting races in years, until tyre trouble caused by high speeds and the banking slowed the pace. Ferrari entered two 425bhp 312P models for Amon/Andretti and Rodriguez/Schetty, and these proved faster in open form than the four longtail coupe 908s entered for Siffert/Redman, Elford/Attwood, Mitter/

Schutz and Herrmann/Ahrens. Amon held pole position but Andretti started the race (he was to fly to America immediately after his stint), and the early laps produced a tremendously exciting slip-streaming battle between Andretti, Siffert, Rodriguez and Elford, blasting their way between the slower GT cars in a ferocious manner.

Averaging 133mph, Siffert soon took the lead with two Ferraris on his tail. Then Rodriguez took the lead and Andretti had to make a pit stop to have his rear tyres changed, and after an hour Siffert made his first pit stop and had a hole in the windscreen taped over. After two hours Andretti handed his car to Amon, who lasted only another two laps before the hot engine expired with no oil pressure, and not long afterwards the Rodriguez/Schetty Ferrari had two more tyre failures, the first of which dropped it from the lead and the second caused it to crash into the barriers at high speed, fortunately without hurting the Mexican driver.

The Porsches proved equally fast, and more reliable although Elford had a blown tyre late in the race which caused him to crash. At the finish, Siffert/Redman were a lap ahead of Herrmann/Ahrens with Koch/Dechent third in a privately entered 907; of the Porsche onslaught, only the Mitter/Schutz car had any mechanical problems, the gearchange linkage breaking and leading to over-revving which damaged the engine.

On then to Targa Florio, where the Porsche 908s took all four leading places against poor opposition, and might have been fifth as well had not Richard Attwood's car retired with a broken driveshaft. Alfa Romeo opposition faded quickly, and Elford helped the process and dispelled some of his local popularity by nudging Giunti's Alfa into a barrier. The English driver was trying to make up time after having a fan/alternator vee belt breakage, and despite setting another lap record almost a minute quicker than the previous year's, he and Maglioli finished nearly three minutes behind Gerhard Mitter/Udo Schutz. Oddly enough although it was Porsche's ninth Targa Florio victory, it was only the second time that two German drivers had helped the marque to win this race.

All eyes were on the new Porsche 917 when it made its debut at Spa, and Siffert earned pole position with it though it was very much a trial run before Le Mans and retired after one lap with a broken valve. More about this in the next chapter. The real race was between the 908 coupes and a single Ferrari 312P for Rodriguez and David Piper, plus the Lola T70 of Paul Hawkins who had practised second fastest.

Siffert decided to race the 908 in preference to the unproven 917, and just as well he did for he seemed to be the only Porsche driver who could really compete with the Ferrari. The early laps at Spa were again enlivened by their duel, and Siffert was just ahead when Karl von Wendt moved across in front of Rodriguez at Eau Rouge and made contact. The Ferrari carried on after making a precautionary stop, while the German's 907 crashed harmlessly. Rodriguez kept up the pressure, but Piper was not quite so effective when it was his turn, so Siffert and Redman scored their third victory of the season, 3½ minutes in front of the Ferrari with Elford/Ahrens following in third place a lap behind.

A revised body form was seen on three of the six 908s entered for the Nurburg 1000Kms, with a flatter body profile and a narrower, 'single-seater' windscreen surround. The drag was appreciably less and the revised spyder, nick-named 'Sole' at the factory, was shown to be nearly 10mph faster in a straight line. However the downforce was not so good, and Siffert badly damaged one of the cars during pre-race trials on the south circuit; another was wrecked by Elford, who found that his 'Sole' would take off at the Flugplatz but would not come down again, at least where he intended. The three Soles were entered by the Porsche Salzburg factory, Herrmann/Stommelen driving the third, only surviving example in the race.

Again it was Siffert versus the Ferrari. The brilliant Swiss driver practised in 8 minutes 0.2 seconds, Amon at 8 minutes 0.3 seconds in the Ferrari, with Mitter close behind on 8 minutes 1.3 seconds followed by Stommelen on 8 minutes 4.2 seconds, Elford (slower   **211** after his experience) on 8 minutes 11.0 seconds, then Attwood/Lins on 8 minutes 11.1 seconds, and Kauhsen/von Wendt on 8 minutes 15.7 seconds. Even Jacky Ickx's renown as a 'Ringmeister' could not overcome the weight handicap of his 830kg Gulf-Mirage, now equipped with a Ford-Cosworth DFV engine, and he was out of the hunt with a time of 8 minutes 24.1 seconds. It should be noted that Siffert's practice time was 33 seconds faster than the previous year, when he was driving the new 908 coupe, and five seconds faster than the outright circuit record set by Jackie Stewart in a Formula-2 Matra some weeks before. But it was Chris Amon who went home with a new outright circuit record after the 1000Kms, set in 8 minutes 03.3 seconds despite having clutch hydraulic trouble right from the start of the race.

At quarter distance Siffert was 20 seconds ahead of Amon, but Rodriguez had an off day in the Ferrari with the clutch trouble and an out-of-balance wheel, and Redman was able to pull away easily in the leading Porsche to command the race. Amon pulled back later on, but with 29 laps run his race ended with electrical failure. Five Porsche 908s took the leading five places with Siffert/Redman, Stommelen/Herrmann and Elford/Ahrens all completing the 44-lap distance.

Together, Jo Siffert and Brian Redman had now scored four outright victories and done enough to earn for Porsche the World Sports Car Championship. At last, the coveted title had come to Zuffenhausen and it was done in the best possible way, with fast and reliable cars against good opposition.

Many people believe that it is as prestigious to win Le Mans as all the other races put together, title and all, so a tremendous effort was mounted for the 24-Hour race in June. Two of the new, rapidly developed 917s were entered for Elford/Attwood and Stommelen/Ahrens, while four long-tail 908s were entered for Siffert/Redman (an open spyder version), Hans Herrmann/Gerard Larrousse, Rudi Lins/Willi Kauhsen and Gerhard Mitter/Udo Schutz.

A fierce controversy raged around the moveable tail-flaps on the 917s and the 908s, critics alleging that they contravened the CSI's ban on aerodynamic wings since the Monaco Grand Prix, but Stommelen bravely went out with the flaps fixed and proved that the 917 was virtually undriveable in that condition. The 917s were allowed to compete in that race with the suspension operated flaps, but the 908's aerodynamic aids were to be fixed.

The 917s were clearly faster, but their reliability was unknown; the 908 long-tail Sole driven by Siffert/Redman was favourite, having practised fourth fastest at 3 minutes 29.9 seconds. Even on the opening lap there was a tragedy when John Woolfe fatally crashed his new, privately owned 917, involving Chris Amon's Ferrari which burned out, so it was already a contest between the works Porsches and one Ferrari, plus the Gulf Ford GT40s — Ickx made his protest against the Le Mans start by *walking* across the road while other drivers ran, and deliberately fastening his seatbelt before moving off.

As expected the 917s made the early running, but Siffert was right behind and after the first pit stops the Swiss driver moved into the lead, looking set to stay there. But after two and a half hours his race was run. There was inadequate cooling for the gearbox with the long-tail, and the high temperatures had welded the external plastic oil pipes and caused the transmission to seize.

Then the Herrmann/Larrousse 908 lost 20 minutes in the pits having a front upright changed after the bearing had turned and overheated, and this was a most critical loss of time for the car. Udo Schutz completely demolished his 908 at the Mulsanne kink during the night, misjudging the apex at 170mph and being extraordinarily lucky not to be hurt in the accident.

With only four hours to run the Elford/Attwood 917 was comfortably six laps ahead of the Lins/Kauhsen 908, but both cars retired and threw the race wide open again — the 917 had dire clutch trouble and the 908 had a failure of the differential pinion. So with three hours remaining the GT40 of Ickx/Oliver was just, but only just ahead of the Herrmann/Larrouse 908, and for the next three hours the two cars ran as if tied together, sometimes the Ford ahead and sometimes the Porsche.

In the final hour Herrmann saw his brake pad warning light come on, and because there was no time for a pad change he had to use his brakes as lightly as possible. Four times in the closing laps Herrmann went ahead on the Mulsanne Straight, and four times Ickx passed him again before the pits....twice while braking for the new Ford Chicane, to the wild delight of the spectators who appreciated a wonderful motor race. With two minutes to run, Ickx was in the lead as the cars went by the pits, and Herrmann could only keep up as they covered the last eight miles, the GT40 flashing across the line 200 yards ahead of the travel-stained Porsche. Ironically, the brakes on Herrmann's car were not worn out, the warning system being faulty.

The Porsche directors could only shake their heads in disbelief. The old GT40, which started the race so slowly, had been trouble-free while each of the Porsches had been in some sort of trouble, only one works car surviving to the finish. It was a traumatic experience, and immediately afterwards it was finally decided that the works team, Porsche System AG, would officially withdraw from racing.

That would have been sensational, but it was not the end of Porsche's programme by any means. Development costs on the 917 had been prohibitive, and it was decided midway through 1969 to hand over the running of the team to John Wyer's rival outfit, with handsome sponsorship from the Gulf Oil company. The factory would supply full assistance and development facilities, in fact still owning all the cars, and for the remainder of the year the 'factory' 908s were entered by Porsche Salzburg.

Sadly, Gerard Mitter died a couple of months later of injuries sustained in an accident at the Nurburgring, and his loss was deeply felt at the Porsche factory. At the time he was practising for the German GP in a Formula-2 BMW, possibly crashing because of a mechanical failure.

At Watkins Glen in July Siffert/Redman and Lins/Buzzetta were paired up in the two Porsche Salzburg 908s, and Elford/Attwood in another 908 which Tony Dean had bought from the factory.

Again Siffert dominated the race, though strong opposition came this time from a Matra 650 V12 driven by Johnny Servoz-Gavin/Pedro Rodriguez, and Siffert had the advantage when, after 33 laps, the Matra pitted to have a new fuel pump fitted. Now the way was clear for another Porsche sweep, and Siffert/Redman recorded their fifth win of the season with Elford/Attwood on the same lap, and Lins/Buzzetta in third place just headed home before the Matra 650.

For the final championship sportscar race of the season, on the new Osterreichring circuit, Porsche Salzburg entered three 908 spyders for Herrmann/Stommelen, von Wendt/Kauhsen and Lins/Larrousse, while Siffert/Ahrens and Attwood/Redman drove a pair of 917s, which were nominally privately entered though with full factory assistance from brown overalled mechanics. Herrmann, very upset by Mitter's death a week before, withdrew from the race so his car was used as a spare, and practised briefly by Siffert.

The grid looked unusual with Ickx/Oliver fastest in the Ford-Cosworth powered Mirage spyder, then Bonnier/Muller in a Lola T70, Rodriguez/Servoz-Gavin in a Matra, and only fourth fastest were Siffert/Ahrens in the 917. The quickest Porsche 908 was a privately owned car driven by Richard Brostrom/Masten Gregory, still painted in Porsche Salzburg colours and only seventh quickest; it seemed that all along the 908s had been only as quick as their drivers, and the Zuffenhausen team had been employing some extremely good drivers over the years!

Up to and beyond half distance Ickx and Oliver led the race but after 99 laps their Mirage had steering trouble, and after a fierce duel with Bonnier's Lola, Siffert gave the 917 its first race win. The Attwood/Redman 917 was third, and the next three places were filled by the 908s driven by Brostrom/Gregory, Lins/Larrousse and Kauhsen/von Wendt.

It was cut and dried that the 917s would be run officially by John Wyer's team in 1970, and another two cars would be run by the Porsche Salzburg team. But that was not the end of the 3-litre 908 story, because it was felt that the 908 or an even lighter development of it would fare better on the handling circuits, like the Targa Florio and the Nurburgring, and Porsche's experimental department accordingly set to work to develop the 909 bergspyder with the 3-litre 908 engine. Apart from that, around 25 of the 31 908s were sold to private owners, and would continue to run well for several years to come. Their successes in private hands are far too numerous to detail here, but they continued to give a good account of themselves in long distance championship events.

At Sebring in 1970 a Porsche 908/02 almost pulled off a sensational victory. Peter Revson and actor Steve McQueen were outpaced by the 917s and the new Ferrari 512s, but as the 12-Hour race progressed all the leading cars had reliability problems and with an hour to go, the 3-litre car was narrowly ahead. Andretti took over the second place Ferrari and drove desperately hard to go ahead, but five minutes from the end he had to stop for a churn of fuel and as he roared out of the pits Revson was in sight. But the superior speed of the Ferrari was enough to pull out 22 seconds at the end, and a surprise win was denied the privately run Porsche.

At the BOAC 1000Kms a Porsche 908 entered by the Finnish Porsche and VW distributor Aarnio Wihuri finished fourth behind the 5-litre cars, driven by the very promising Finnish driver Hans Laine with Gijs van Lennep.

Porsche's new 3-litre car, the 908/3, was ready on schedule for the Targa Florio race in Sicily, and proved untouchable on the mountain circuit. Basically it was similar to the 909 bergspyder in having an alloy tube frame, but the 2-litre engine was discarded in favour of the 3-litre 908 unit and the differential was mounted *behind* the gearbox, improving the polar moment of inertia and making the car more manoeuverable on tight corners. To compensate for this and put more weight on the front wheels, the driver's seat was moved further forward and his feet were ahead of the front wheels, protected from the elements by a spidery frame and translucent fibre-glass bodywork. Extensive use was made of titanium and the 908/3 was incredibly light, weighing 545 kilogrammes and saving 55kg compared with the 908/2. Even the cast iron brake discs were laterally drilled to save weight and improve heat dissipation, and with the usual 3-litre engine fitted (improved in having a fluid coupling on the cooling fan drive, to prevent any risk of belt breakages) the 908/3 had a power-to-weight ratio of over 680bhp per ton, identical in fact to that of the original and contemporary 4.5-litre 917 (520bhp/800kg).

Nine cars were made in the original batch, and two more the following year, and five were sent to Sicily; one was used for pre-race testing, three were entered by John Wyer's Gulf team for Jo Siffert/Brian Redman, Pedro Rodriguez/Leo Kinnunen and Richard Attwood/Bjorn Waldegard, each one vividly painted and with a heart, club or diamond symbol on the front for quick recognition. The fourth was entered by Porsche Salzburg for Vic Elford/Hans Herrmann, but not before Elford tried a 917 and found it to be competitive, but too heavy to drive quickly for more than a couple of laps.

Brave opposition came from a lone Ferrari 512S shared by Nino Vaccarella/Ignazio Giunti, from Autodelta's 3-litre Alfa Romeos and from a number of well driven Porsche 908/2s, and the scene was set for one of the most exciting Targa Florios ever held. Siffert and Elford had been the two fastest men in practice, but the road was wet on the opening lap of the race and Elford slid off, damaging his front suspension and retiring. Incredibly, Gerard Larrousse led the opening lap in his older, heavier 908/2 from Siffert, Kinnunen and van Lennep, the Dutchman in another 908/2.

At half distance only five minutes covered the first seven cars, Kinnunen having put his Porsche in the lead, but Rodriguez was not enjoying his drive that day and fell back

214

allowing Nino Vacceralla to put the heavy Ferrari ahead, 20 seconds in front of Hans Laine's 908/2. Wyer's cars were still well placed in third, fifth and seventh places, but things did not seem to be going according to plan!

Brian Redman was on brilliant form, luckily, and he forced his 908/3 into the lead as the two Italian drivers tired, and Kinnunen was closing like the wind as he drove the final spell. Laine, in third place, had the unnerving experience of losing a front wheel from his 908/2 at the start of the long straight by the sea on the tenth lap, but he found that by accelerating past 140mph the front of the car lifted and the brake disc rose clear of the ground. The Finn arrived at the pits in a shower of sparks still in fourth place, having broken the lap record twice during the race, and with a new wheel fitted accelerated away without losing his position.

Giunti took the Ferrari out for the final lap, still in second place, but Kinnunen caught the red car and passed it into second place, setting an incredible time of 33 minutes 36 seconds on that last lap — a new record which survived the '71, '72 and '73 races, and could stand for many more years if prototypes are not allowed to run again on the Little Madonie circuit.

Another Targa Florio win was in the bag, Siffert/Redman leading Kinnunen/Rodriguez by 100 seconds with the Ferrari nearly two minutes behind, Laine/von Lennep fourth and Attwood/Waldegard fifth; of the leading cars only the Lins/Larrousse 908/2 failed to finish, transmission failure halting them on the tenth lap. All three Alfa Romeos retired due to accidents, a sad fate for Carlo Chiti's team.

Unhappily Hans Laine died while practising for the Nurburg 1000Kms. He drove the 908/2 out of the pits knowing that one of the front aerodynamic fins had been knocked off, and on the long home straight the car lifted over the Tiergarten brow and turned on its back, the driver dying in the ensuing fire. This upset Kinnunen, his friend and fellow countryman, deeply, and possible accounted for his retiring during the next day's race, parked off the road after a spin.

The 908/3s, virtually unchanged except for changing from 13in. to 15in. diameter rear wheels, completely dominated practice: Siffert and Rodriguez practised in under 7 minutes 45 seconds, 15 seconds quicker than the 908/2 the previous year, driving Wyer's cars on Firestone tyres, and Elford and Herrmann were next fastest in the Salzburg cars on Goodyear tyres. The Alfa Romeos and Ferraris were not going to be a threat, failing to break eight minutes, and the fleet of little Porsches did indeed make all the running. Wyer's cars were well ahead at the first quarter of the race, the 11 lap mark when the first refuelling stops were made, but soon Kinnunen spun off the road and stopped, and Redman had to go easy because his oil pressure was low — the factory had not mentioned to Wyer that the 908 engines used quite a lot of oil, and none was added at the refuelling stop! At half distance the Siffert/Redman car was finished, the engine on the point of seizing, and the two Salzburg cars swept over the line a full lap ahead of the Surtees/Vaccarella Ferrari 512S. Elford and Ahrens took the flag ahead of Herrmann/Attwood.

The 908/3 cars were put away until the following year, the remaining races being run on faster circuits suiting the 917s better, but development continued on a more powerful version of the flat-eight engine because it was known that the 5-litre cars would be 'outlawed' at the end of the 1971 season. Speculation was rife that Porsche were planning a return to Formula-1, but the more powerful engine was in fact intended as a study for endurance racing. It broke with Porsche tradition in that the cylinder heads were water cooled, an expedient to allow the use of four valves per cylinder, and over 400bhp was seen on the test bench. The cylinder barrels were still air cooled but the engine did not fit into Porsche's general production policy, and when the CSI announced that the 650 kilogramme minimum weight limit would be restored in 1972 the project was dropped. Any manufacturer could make a car weighing 650 kilogrammes, and the new 3-litre formula would therefore be simply a power race.

Porsche's philosophy was always to achieve the lowest possible starting weight, and to concentrate on power afterwards. Piech told his team: every kilogramme of excess weight is another kilogramme to be accelerated, braked and taken round corners. The dictum proved right, year after year.

There was still life in the 908/2, as was proved at Le Mans in June; Rudi Lins and Helmut Marko showed that their car (run by Hans-Dieter Dechent in Martini and Rossi colours) was absolutely reliable and remained in touch with the big Porsches and Ferraris, helped by terrible weather conditions which handicapped the more powerful machines. After 24 hours of gruelling racing, Lins and Marko finished in third place in their spyder, only eight laps behind the winning Salzburg Porsche 917 of Herrmann/Attwood and a mere two laps behind the second-placed 917 driven by Larrousse/Kauhsen.

Only two races remained for the works-backed 908/3 model, the Targa Florio and the Nurburg 1000Kms run in 1971. There were few modifications, but wider rear wheels were fitted and the aerodynamics were improved by fitting a narrow spoiler around the nose panel skirt, and two high longitudinal fins on the rear panel above the wheels. The weight increased to 565 kilogrammes due to the wider wheels fitted, a compulsory reinforced roll-over bar and the addition of an automatic fire extinguisher system.

The Porsche Salzburg team withdrew from racing at the end of the 1970 season, and the second-string factory assisted team was run by Hans-Dieter Dechent with Martini and Rossi sponsorship. Wyer's two Gulf cars were for Jo Siffert/Brian Redman and Pedro Rodriguez/Herbert Muller, and the Martini 908/3 was shared by Vic Elford/Gerard Larrousse.

At the Targa Florio the three Alfa Romeos were quickest in practice, all three Porsches having trouble. Neither Siffert nor Redman got a trouble-free timed lap, and Rodriguez was steady rather than spectacular on his single timed lap. Elford put a wheel off the road and damaged a radius rod, which he carried back to the pits on foot. When he approached his pit Piech asked him: "Vic, is that what broke, or is it all that's left?"

During a fateful first lap Redman crashed off the road, and his face was burned when the car caught fire, then Rodriguez also went off the road at Collesano, hitting a wall. John Wyer remarked laconically that the Mexican had skidded on a patch of wet paint on the road, which acclaimed 'Viva Pedro!' Elford and Larrousse took the lead and hoped to save the day for Porsche, but on the seventh lap Larrousse had a puncture which led to suspension failure, and the Alfa Romeo team was handed a popular 1-2 victory on a plate.

Two new 908/3 cars were prepared for Siffert and Rodriguez to drive at the Nurburg 1000Kms, the final appearance for the model with works backing, but surprisingly the cars were slower than they had been the previous year and the quickest times were set by Ickx and Stommelen in a Ferrari and Alfa Romeo respectively. Ickx went storming away in the race and made a new sportscar record lap, but after six laps his Ferrari stopped with high water temperature, and soon retired with a cracked cylinder head gasket. Siffert followed him into retirement with a broken chassis, and Rodriguez was also handicapped by poor handling; although he finished, his car's chassis was cracked too, and a post-mortem showed that the two new cars had not been made to the proper specification in one vital place.

To level the score, the Stommelen/Galli Alfa Romeo dropped out with engine failure and the Porsches filled the first three places, though the final victory had not been achieved easily. Elford/Larrousse won the race for the Martini team, this being the Englishman's third 1000Km victory at the Nurburgring in four years for Porsche; Rodriguez was second with Siffert's assistance, just holding off Helmut Marko's third-placed Martini Porsche 908/3 by weaving down the final straight!

Most of the 908/3 cars were sold to private owners after the 1971 season and one of them, Reinhold Jost, competed regularly and successfully from 1972 although his car was ballasted up to 650 kilogrammes, and he was giving away 100 horsepower to the Ferraris,

Alfa Romeos and Matras. At Monza in 1972 the weather was extremely wet and the Ferrari team literally floundered, letting Jost/Schuller into the lead. Ickx/Regazzoni saved the day for Ferrari, but Jost's Porsche finished a gallant second. Jost followed up with third place at Le Mans, helped by Mario Casoni and Michel Weber, driving a three-year-old 908/02 Coupe, and ended the year with a win in the Interlagos 500Km sportscar race ahead of Luiz Bueno (Porsche 908/02) and Muller's Ferrari 512M.

In his ageless 908/3, Jost continued to campaign throughout the 1973 season and ended the year with an unexpected but well deserved win in the Kyalami 9-Hours with Muller co-driving; their victory was achieved, ironically, at the expense of John Wyer's Gulf-Mirage prototypes which both had mechanical problems.

To all intents and purposes that was the end of the road for the 908s, though it was not quite the time to pay homage to the car which in 1968 and 1969 had transformed the fortunes of Porsche in World Championship long distance events, and made a useful contribution to the titles gained in 1970 and 1971 as well.

Jost was still running his 908/3 in 1974, and the following year he installed a 2.1-litre turbocharged engine lifted from the previous year's Carrera turbo racing car. Dr. Dannesburger and Martini sponsored a similar project for Muller and van Lennep, but it was the year of Alfa Romeo dominance and the best privateer Porsche result in the sportscar races was second at Dijon for Jost/Casoni.

The last World Championship victory recorded by a 908/3 was at the Nurburgring in April, 1976, when Reinhold Jost (his turbocharged car now rebodied with Can-Am carrosserie) profited from the failure of the Alpine-Renaults to complete a lap to take a splendid win, enabling Porsche to win every single race they entered that year. The other victories were taken by the works 936, itself a development of the 908, but we will come to that in another chapter....

4 The Porsche 917

EVERY so often in motor racing there is a great era in which new and more powerful cars dominate the circuits, bringing lasting fame to their drivers. Almost by accident the CSI created the opportunity for Porsche to manufacture the 917 model, a car which dominated its rivals and smashed lap records everywhere it went. It brought new fame, too, to the outstanding drivers of the period, Jo 'Seppi' Siffert and Pedro Rodriguez, whose outstanding handling of these monster sportscars will be discussed by generations to come, just as we talk now of Nuvolari and Carracciola and their rivalry in the 1930's.

In 'outlawing' the 7-litre Fords and Chaparrals, the CSI decreed late in 1967 that from 1968 onwards the World Sportscar Championship would be contested by 3-litre cars with a minimum weight of 650 kilogrammes, and homologated 5-litre cars with a minimum weight limit of 800 kilogrammes and of which at least 25 had been constructed. There was no thought that a racing car manufacturer such as Ferrari or Porsche would make 25 racing cars of 5-litre capacity. The CSI members could not see beyond such makes as the Ford GT40 and the Lola T70 which used production stock-block, pushrod V8 engines from Ford and Chevrolet, producing around 420 to 450 horsepower (not very reliably, in the case of the Chevrolet). When introduced in coupe form the Lola T70 weighed over 900 kilogrammes (2000 pounds) and the Ford GT40 over 1000 kilogrammes. Also, the 5-litres had to run with big windscreens, and in theory at least the 'pure' racing cars should have had every advantage.

As it turned out Ford had a number of victories in 1968, when the 908 effort was delayed on a number of occasions by the front hub bearing problem, and Roger Penske's Sunoco Lola T70 won at Sebring in 1969 when the Porsches again had trouble, this time with the chassis.

The whole scene was destined to change, though, when in the summer of 1968 Dr. Porsche gave his experimental department the go-ahead to develop and build in quantity a pure 5-litre racing car, which would produce a minimum of 500 horsepower from the beginning. At the time it seemed to be a curious decision for a Porsche to make, for at all times in the past the factory had concentrated on high efficiency, small capacity engines. However the transition to 3-litre capacity had been made successfully, and the homologation requirement ensured that constructors of racing 'specials' would not be able to compete in a power race. In fact only Ferrari and possibly Ford and Chevrolet if they were interested, could be regarded as potential rival competitors.

Although it seemed revolutionary, the fact that 25 917s were manufactured within nine months of the project beginning indicates that Porsche were drawing considerably on past experience. Incredibly, the car used an aluminium spaceframe chassis which was very similar to that of the 908, even having the same track and wheelbase (the wheelbase, 2300mm, was identical to that of every circuit car made by Porsche right through from the 904 in 1964 to the Can-Am model in 1971). However to accommodate the driver ahead of the flat-12 engine, the cockpit was moved forward several inches and the pedals were actually ahead of the front hubs, so although the weight distribution was about the same as the 908's, and hence the handling characteristics, the drivers would receive less warning when the rear wheels were losing adhesion. The chassis weighed only 47kg, and later on two chassis made of magnesium weighed only 33kg, complete with body mounting brackets.

Providing that no rival constructor pitched in early the 917 could be used purely for development purposes during 1969, relying on aerodynamics and light weight, on the limit, to make it competitive, and for this reason the chosen flat-12 engine configuration used a good many parts from the 908 flat-8, including the same bore and stroke (85 x 66mm), the same pistons, conrods, valves port sizes and even a similar Bosch petrol injection system. A magnesium crankcase was used, and the most noteworthy feature of the engine was the method of drive: the engine was effectively two flat-6 units with the power take-off in the centre, following the configuration of the Mercedes-Benz W196 in 1954. In this way the crankshaft would be effectively halved in length, and whipping vibration movements would be avoided. Beneath the crank, and running parallel to it, was a layshaft leading to the Fichtel and Sachs triple-plate dry clutch and a new, stronger version of the 908's wet-sump five-speed gearbox.

The total weight of the engine, which had titanium con-rods and layshaft, was 240 kilogrammes, so the engine and chassis components alone accounted for only half the dry weight of the car. Also in common with the 908, the 917's flat-12 engine had chain driven twin overhead camshafts, interchangeable aluminium cylinder heads and, of course, two valves per cylinder, though the valves were sodium filled to assist cooling.

For the 1969 season the engine was rated at 4,494cc, and although the early publicity material stated that it developed 520 horsepower this was a very conservative figure. The first time the engine ran on a test bed it gave 540 horsepower, and at Le Mans it had been uprated to 580bhp DIN.

Superficially the 917's body form resembled the 907 and 908 coupe at the front, except that the windscreen was now further forward, but a good deal of wind tunnel testing had produced an interesting new form for the glass-fibre body, and two tails were envisaged, one for ordinary circuits and a longer one for fast circuits like Le Mans — both employed the suspension operated spoiler flaps, well-nigh essential to provide stability whichever tail was being run. A considerable amount of work was done on the suspension to make provision for nine and twelve inch wide wheels, and much wider rims later on, although earlier on the 917 was endowed with a good deal of suspension travel which suited bumpy circuits but made it difficult to employ the ultra-wide racing tyres seen in Formula-1. Titanium road springs were fitted at the rear to give progressive damping without resorting to the steeply inclined springs at the front end, and laterally drilled cast iron brake discs were fitted, though a limited number of beryllium discs were made in America, these being as light as magnesium, but the £400 per disc price tag proved a deterrent.

Altogether the development cost of the 917 was estimated at £2 million (20 million marks) and the whole process leading up to the announcement was conducted in the greatest secrecy. It was a bombshell in the racing world when the 917 made its debut at the Geneva Salon in March 1969, with the news that 25 examples would be completed by the end of the month with a price tag of 140,000 marks per car. To conform with the CSI's homologation requirements a proper catalogue was produced, and a number of cars were made available to customers from the outset although the majority of the initial batch were reserved for development and racing on behalf of the factory. More than 60 cars were made altogether over a four-year period, the final turbocharged versions developing over 1,000bhp for Can-Am racing.

The 917 made its debut at the Le Mans trials at the end of March and although stability seemed to be a problem, Rolf Stommelen unofficially trimmed nearly eight seconds off Siffert's lap record, going round the Sarthe circuit in 3 minutes 30.7 seconds at an average of 143mph; speeds of over 200mph were achieved on the Mulsanne straight. Homologation was delayed because the CSI wanted to inspect 25 complete cars, not the components, and the formality was completed in April for homologation on May 1, too late for Monza but in time for the Spa 1000 Kms.

Siffert practised the car between rain storms and although it was in short-tail form, he turned in the fastest practice lap in 3 minutes 41.9 seconds, an average of 142mph. The car was difficult to handle on wet roads and it was jumping out of gear, so Siffert elected to race a 908 instead — a wise decision, for the 917 only completed one lap driven by Gerard Mitter and retired with a damaged valve, possibly the result of over-revving, while the Swiss driver went on to win the race in fine style.

Three 917s were entered for the Nurburg 1000 Kms a fortnight later but none of the works-contracted drivers were keen to drive them, for apart from anything else six of the very competitive 908 spyders were also entered. One 917 appeared in the hands of BMW drivers Dieter Quester and Hubert Hahne. Quester practised in 8 minutes 37.8 seconds, or 37 seconds slower than Siffert in the 908, and stability again seemed to be a problem as Quester needed the width of the road to drive along the straight! Overnight the BMW directors forbade their drivers to become Porsche fodder, and at very short notice the British drivers Frank Gardner and David Piper were invited to drive the car. After practising in the rain on Saturday, the irreverent Gardner asked if the car could be resdesigned in time for the race.

Fortunately it was dry on Sunday and the 917 proved trouble-free, finishing in eighth place behind a quintet of 908s, a Ford GT40 and an Alfa Romeo. It had been difficult to drive and Gardner remarked that if he had taken time to look at the instruments he would have flown off the road into the next country, but at least the trial had been immensely valuable for development purposes. When the cars next appeared at Le Mans two weeks later a great many improvements had been carried out: the chassis had been reinforced to improve torsional stiffness and to prevent gears jumping out of selection; the anti-drive geometry in the front suspension had been virtually eliminated, springs and dampers were changed, and the gearboxes were modified to prevent drivers from changing from fifth to second by accident.

But all this work might have been nullified by the CSI's decision to ban all wing devices, another controversial edict which was the talking point at Monaco a couple of weeks before. Rico Steinemann threatened to withdraw all the works cars, as well he might since Porsche had already clinched the World Sportscar Championship, but they were presented for scrutineering and in a 917 Rolf Stommelen became the first man to break the 3 minutes 30 second barrier for the circuit which now included a chicane before the pits.

Stommelen quickly worked down to 3 minutes 22.9 seconds, averaging 148.5mph, and was actually quicker than Hulme's record in a 7-litre Ford before the chicane was introduced! It was a most outstanding performance, but so was his run on Thursday with the tail flaps in fixed position, to prove to the CSI members that the car was dangerous without this safety feature. Again the young German was below 3 minutes 30 seconds but his progress down the Mulsanne Straight at close on 230mph was positively frightening, so the 917s were allowed to keep their aerodynamic aids just for the one race. Two works cars took part in the race driven by Stommelen/Kurt Ahrens and Elford/Attwood, while Herbert Linge was nominated to share the first customer car with John Woolfe, an English amateur who previously raced a Can-Am McLaren.

It was a fateful, stormy and controversial year at Le Mans. On the first lap Woolfe lost control of his car at the White House, crashed heavily and was killed instantly as his car broke in two. The petrol tank broke free and Amon's Ferrari slammed into it, catching fire at once, and for a while it seemed that the race might have to be stopped for the first time in history.

There was criticism that Porsche should not have sold this new, difficult to drive model to a private owner. That is easily answered, for Woolfe had plenty of experience of powerful cars — and was it not implicit in the homologation requirements that cars should be offered for sale? It is a fact that Woolfe was the *only* driver to be killed in a Porsche 917, although some 25 cars ran hundreds of thousands of racing miles in the next two years, and subsequent Can-Am models were tuned up to more than 1,000 horsepower.

Stommelen and Elford commanded the race initially, but the German's car soon began laying a trail of smoke from a leaking cam cover gasket, and during the evening the clutch began to slip badly and the plates were changed, this leading to disqualification. Elford and Attwood were driving their car sparingly, keeping the revs down and changing gear carefully, knowing that the clutch was suspect. At half distance they were in the lead, four laps ahead of the Mitter/Schutz 908, and after 20 hours Attwood was six laps ahead of the Lins/Kauhsen 908 when he reported that his 917's clutch was slipping too. He struggled along for another 55 minutes but the clutch bell-housing was cracked, and with three hours of the race to run the car was pushed away, leaving the stage clear for the memorable battle between Ickx's Ford GT40 and the Herrmann/Larrousse 908.

Subsequently it was announced that Porsche would withdraw from racing, and at the new Osterreichring circuit in August two 'factory assisted' cars were entered privately by David Piper and Karl von Wendt, one for Siffert/Ahrens and the other for Redman/Attwood. Borg and Beck clutches replaced the Fichtel and Sachs equipment, oil sealing and brake cooling had been improved, and most notably the wheel rim widths had been increased substantially, to 10.5 inch front and 15 inch rear. Handling still seemed to be a problem, though, and John Wyer whose team was to take over the entries for the coming year, suspected that insufficient aerodynamic downforce lay at the root of the problem.

The race was a tremendous scrap between Ickx's Gulf-Mirage prototype, the Bonnier/Muller Lola T70, the Rodriguez/Servoz-Gavin Matra, and the Siffert/Ahrens Porsche 917, and the Porsche was not getting the upper hand until the Mirage and the Matra retired. One of the problems was a vapour lock which made the 917 difficult to re-start after pit stops, and four minutes were lost on one occasion. Once he got the engine running again Siffert blasted his 917 down the pits lane like a dragster, two long black lines broken only for a few yards where he had snatched second gear. It was enormously impressive, but tyre technicians wondered why the black lines were only ten inches wide — obviously there was still too much travel on the suspension.

Eventually Siffert and Ahrens took the lead, beating the Lola by a mere 70 seconds with Redman/Attwood following up in third place. It was the first of fifteen Championship victories scored in the next 24 months, and from then onwards the only three defeats of the 917s were the result of isolated technical problems. Truly, it became a world-beater.

Straight after the race Wyer put his Mirage away and did some testing with the 917, and the first thing that engineer John Horsman did was to modify the tail section, cutting away the back window and building the wheel arches upwards to the tail of the car, making a wedge shape at the back. The drag factor was increased but the tail was 33

221

pounds lighter, and the downthrust was substantially improved. Immediately Siffert was four seconds faster per lap, a gain that would have won him Sunday's race without any strain at all, and it became clear that the 917 was about to realise its potential.

Full works backing was given to John Wyer's Gulf sponsored team on a two-year contract, for the 1970 and 1971 seasons, and the factory itself prepared an open-bodied version called the 917PA for Jo Siffert to run in the later Can-Am races, another valuable development exercise which we will refer to in the next chapter. For long distance races, the 917s had new tail sections prepared along the lines of John Horsman's experimental tail, the transmission casing was strengthened and a four-speed version of the gearbox was prepared (five speeds had proved unnecessary due to the enormous torque of the flat-12 engine); the cooling fan (which absorbed only 17 horsepower) had a modified drive, and the ATE brake calipers and pistons were modified to prevent the fluid from boiling and to give drivers more feel through the pedal.

For the 1970 season John Wyer assembled an extremely competitive driver team, Jo Siffert and Brian Redman paired in one car, and Pedro Rodriguez and Leo Kinnunen paired in the other. The team was co-operating with Porsche's experimental department, and a second team organised by Porsche Salzburg was serviced by the company's customer department which inevitably meant that there was a lag on this team's development programme. The Austrian team nominated Vic Elford/Kurt Ahrens for one car and Hans Herrmann/Richard Attwood for the second.

The Porsches were not going to win any hollow victories, for in only nine months — dating from the first appearance of the 917 in Geneva — Enzo Ferrari's chief engineer Mauro Forghieri had rushed through a new 5-litre car, the Ferrari 512S. The Italian company had plenty of experience in building cars up to 4.4-litre capacity, and the 5-litre V12 engine developed 550bhp from the beginning, assisted by four-valve per cylinder heads. Weight seemed to be the main problem, though; on Ferrari's admission the 512S weighed 840 kilogrammes, more than 80 pounds over the minimum weight, and the disadvantage might, in fact, have been as much as 100 kilogrammes.

For the first race, at Daytona in February 1970, Andretti put his Ferrari on pole position ahead of the two Gulf-Porsches and the single Salzburg Porsche. The race was a different story, for Andretti hung on to the two Gulf-Porsches but never headed them, and one by one the Ferraris met trouble in the tyre and chassis areas, caused by the loading on the banking. Siffert's car also had a puncture and dropped back, then was delayed again by a distributor problem, but Rodriguez and Kinnunen sailed through the 24-Hour race without any problems and won by no less than 372 miles, with team-mates Siffert/Redman narrowly fending off the Andretti/Merzario/Ickx Ferrari for second place.

The tables were turned on Porsche at Sebring in March, where the Gulf cars had larger front wheel bearings fitted, part of a front hub redesign to improve the braking efficiency. Unfortunately the new hubs had not been sufficiently tested and in each case the four retaining bolts stretched, dropping the Porsches out of contention. Again Andretti set the fastest practice time and this time he and Merzario dominated the race, aided by the Gulf-Porsches running into minor time-delaying problems and Elford's 917 colliding with a Porsche 911.

Siffert's car had an ignition fault, and then the cooling fan sheared off and sailed 200 feet in the air like a child's toy, though a new one was fitted and the engine had not been damaged. Then the front left hub bolts stretched and lost Siffert 34 minutes, and Rodriguez's car was savaged at the back by a Ford Mustang. In the latter part of the race the Mexican's car stopped twice with front hub trouble but each time it got going again, eventually finishing fourth only four laps behind the winning Ferrari of Giunti/Vaccarella/Andretti, which had been chased to the line by the Revson/McQueen Porsche 908.

That however was the last defeat for Porsche for more than a year. With a number of teething troubles sorted out Wyer's drivers fairly dominated one race after another, though not unchallenged. At Brands Hatch the Ferraris of Amon and Ickx were fastest in practice, Elford being third quickest in the Salzburg 917, and on this bumpy Kent circuit Siffert was only fractions of a second quicker than he had been the previous year in his 908. Conditions were appallingly wet at the beginning of the race, and after leading the early laps Ickx had to stop to have his windscreen wiper motor changed; Siffert needed a new rear tyre and Rodriguez was black flagged and lectured for overtaking under the yellow flags.

That day Rodriguez was untouchable though. He had one of the outstanding drives that made him so famous, and after 20 laps the Mexican had pulled up from mid-field to take the lead from Amon's Ferrari. From then on he pulled away as he wished, ably backed by Kinnunen, and after nearly seven hours of hard racing Rodriguez/Kinnunen triumphed by five clear laps over the Salzburg 917s driven by Elford/Denny Hulme and Herrmann/Attwood — Redman had been knocked out of the race as a result of a collision with Amon's Ferrari, which finished fifth.

Another hard race was seen at Monza a fortnight later, where the Porsches and Ferraris were again evenly matched. Siffert's engine was uprated to 4,907cc with the adoption of a new crankshaft and larger bore dimensions, the bore and stroke now being 86 x 70.4mm. With this modification the power was increased from 580 to 600 horsepower, with much improved torque in the mid-range. Siffert's new engine developed an oil leak from the cam cover during practice and he elected to run a 4.5-litre engine, which he knew to be reliable, so the spare 4.9-litre engine was allocated to the Salzburg Porsche driven by Elford/Ahrens. Both Porsche teams now fitted Girling instead of the troublesome ATE brakes, and the drivers found them to be substantially better.

Three Ferraris and three Porsches were extremely well matched as they slip-streamed around at 150mph in one noisy bunch, and it was one of the most exciting duels seen for a long time. Siffert dropped from the contest after spinning and damaging his rear suspension, losing sixteen laps, and approaching half distance the 4.9-litre 917 of Elford/Ahrens narrowly led the 4.5-litre version driven by Rodriguez/Kinnunen, with the Guinti/Vaccarella Ferrari pressing hard to keep up. Then Ahrens retired, a blown tyre flailing away the oil tank, and Amon was taken out of the fourth-placed Ferrari to help Giunti/Vaccarella capture the lead. But when Amon pressed the starter button a spark ignited some swilling petrol in the under-tray and in a flash the 512 was wreathed in flames.

It took only moments to douse the fire and Amon gingerly pressed the starter button again. The car was undamaged and the New Zealander took up the battle with Rodriguez, though he was now a lap behind. That is how it finished, with Rodriguez/Kinnunen virtually a lap ahead of Amon, and Ferrari cars in second, third and fourth places. During the race Elford broke the outright lap record, at a speed of 151.68mph.

Porsche sent 908/03 models to the Targa Florio to sweep up the first and second places, and with the Giunti/Vaccarella Ferrari placed third after a gallant run it seemed that Porsche had virtually clinched the 1970 World Sportscar Championship.

On then to Spa, where Rodriguez lopped more than 10 seconds off the Formula-1 lap record during practice, averaging over 157mph on the ultra-fast road circuit. Even Jacky Ickx had no answer, on his favourite track, and was only third quickest behind Siffert — both the Gulf cars now ran 4.9-litre engines, as did Elford's which was unusually slow; a cracked chassis tube was diagnosed after practice.

The road was wet for the early laps of the race and the rivalry between Siffert and Rodriguez led to a collision between the two blue and orange cars at Eau Rouge, both cars carrying on with evidence of side-swiping on their flanks; Rodriguez, Ickx and Siffert thundered away from the field in a classic duel, pulling out 98 seconds on Elford in only ten laps. Then Rodriguez pitted with a chunk out of a rear tyre, Ickx took the lead, and the lap record tumbled again as Siffert lapped in 3 minutes 17.8 seconds, then Rodriguez replied with a 3 minutes 16.5 seconds — 14 seconds inside the lap record, and an average of 160.53mph! That was a lap for the *Guinness Book of Records,* easily the fastest ever seen on a closed road circuit. Alas the effort did not bring results, as Kinnunen retired later with a broken gearbox.

For a while Ickx kept Ferrari's hopes of victory alive, but co-driver John Surtees was not on top form that day, and with a string of 3 minutes 20 seconds laps Brian Redman regained the lead and pulled away, the Gulf-Porsche winning the race by almost three minutes. It was the third successive Spa victory for Brian Redman, who had helped Ickx to win with the Gulf-Mirage in 1968 and Siffert in 1969.

Three-litre cars again spearheaded Porsche's effort at the Nurburgring, and mighty efforts were mounted both by Porsche and Ferrari at Le Mans in June, the biggest and most important battle-ground of all — but Porsche had already clinched the 1970 title, a wonderful achievement for the Stuttgart company.

No fewer than 11 Ferraris lined up in combat with eight Porsche 917s, many of them in private hands, of course. The four works Ferraris had longer tails and the engines were uprated to a competitive 595 horsepower. Representing Porsche were three short tail (Kurz) 917s in Gulf livery, with 4.9-litre engines for Siffert/Redman and Rodriguez/ Kinnunen and a 4.5-litre engine for Mike Hailwood/David Hobbs. Porsche Salzburg had one car with a 4.9-litre engine and a long, streamliner tail for Elford/Ahrens, and a short-tail 4.5-litre model for Attwood/Herrmann, while Hans-Dieter Dechent's Martini and Rossi team had another long-tail 4.5-litre model for Gerard Larrousse/Willi Kauhsen. During practice Elford unofficially lowered the lap record to 3 minutes 19.8 seconds, with Vaccarella's Ferrari only a fifth of a second slower.

The majority of the race was run in rainy conditions which suited the short tail cars better, they having more downforce on the rear wheels. It was, though, a race of attrition. Within an hour Vacceralla's Ferrari retired with a broken con-rod, and three hours later another *four* Ferraris were eliminated in a multiple accident! Wisell slowed with a smeared windscreen as light rain began to fall, and seconds later the slipstreaming cars of Bell, Regazzoni and Parkes were spinning and banging into each other at Indianapolis corner. Bell's car, the only one not hit in the accident, ran no further as the driver depressed the clutch and burst the engine during the excitement. After that only the Ickx/Schetty Ferrari remained in contention.

Mike Hailwood redressed the balance between the makes when he was caught out by a sudden rainstorm and slid his Gulf-Porsche into the embankment at the Dunlop curve. Rodriguez was already out of the race with a broken distributor drive. During the night Siffert retired from the lead with a broken engine resulting from over-revving, handing the lead to Herrmann/Attwood, and four hours later as a wet dawn broke at the Sarthe the Elford/Ahrens 917 also retired with valve damage resulting from over-revving. Ickx spun off the road at the Ford chicane and retired his Ferrari, and none of the 'official' works Porsches or Ferraris were left in the running. Victory went to the 4.5-litre Porsche Salzburg entry of Herrmann and Attwood by six laps from the long-tail 917 of Kauhsen and Larrousse, with Rudi Lins and Helmut Marko placed third in a Porsche 908/02 spyder. Elford established a new lap record at 3 minutes 21.0 seconds, averaging 149.68mph, but for Herrmann the victory was consolation for his narrow defeat the previous year, and on that note he ended his 20-year career as a racing driver, having become a professional when he drove for Porsche and then for the Mercedes Grand Prix team in 1954.

Despite his set-back at Le Mans, Enzo Ferrari sent two cars to Watkins Glen in July, pitted against two Gulf-Porsches and two Salzburg 917s, all running with 4.9-litre engines. Only 1.4 seconds covered Siffert, Andretti, Rodriguez and Ickx at the end of practice,

The hillclimb derived Spyder, with an 8-cylinder engine, was driven by Colin Davis/Gerhard Mitter to second place in the 1965 Targa Florio

A rare outing for the 6-cylinder Porsche 904 (model 904/6) in the hands of Umberto Magliol/Herbert Linge on the 1965 Targa Florio, where they finished third

The 906 model first appeared at Sebring in 1966 in the hands of Hans Herrman/Joe Buzzetta, who finished in fourth place overall

The Porsche 910 at Daytona in 1967, driven by Hans Herrmann and Jo Siffert to fourth place overall

The 908 Coupe first ran at Monza in 1968, and its first victory was in the hands of Siffert and Elford at the Nurburgring

A triumph for the Porsche teams at Daytona in 1968, when the three 907s finished the 24-Hour race in perfect formation in the leading positions

Recovering from a puncture on the first lap of the Targa Florio in 1968, Vic Elford in a 907 drove an incredible race to snatch the lead and a new lap record before the finish

Brands Hatch, 1969 - Elford and Mitter in 908 Spyders sandwich Trevor Taylor's Lola-Chevrolet, and lead the Alan Mann Ford P69 prototype

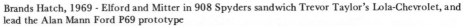

A long-tailed Porsche 908 was chosen by Jo Siffert/Brian Redman for Le Mans in 1969, in preference to the unproven 917, but it retired early in the race due to a split oil pipe to the gearbox, the result of overheating

Jo Siffert lapped Brands Hatch, in the BOAC 1000 Kms in 1969, faster than his Formula 1 record set the previous year, driving the new 908 Spyder. He and Redman won the race easily

For the Targa Florio and Nurburgring events in 1970 and 1971, Porsche prepared some lightweight 908/3 models. Brian Redman (pictured) and Jo Siffert won the Targa Florio in 1970

Reinhold Jost and Mario Casoni continued to race the Porsche 908/3 after the factory withdrew from the 3-litre formula, and pulled off a surprise win in the South African Kyalami 9-Hours in 1973

World debut of the Porsche 917 was at the Geneva Salon in March 1969, where it took the racing world by surprise

Leading the Le Mans 24-Hours in 1969 after 18 hours, Vic Elford and Richard Attwood had to retire their 917 with transmission problems. The tail flaps were 'legalised' for that race

After years of waiting, the top prize in endurance racing fell to Porsche in 1970 when Hans Herrmann and Richard Attwood won the 24-Hours of Le Mans

One of Pedro Rodriguez's most remarkable drives was in the rain at the BOAC 1000 Kms in 1970, sharing the car with Leo Kinnunen. Rodriguez is pictured preparing to pass Vic Elford's 917 which finished second

Following their victory at Le Mans in 1970, Porsche succeeded again in 1971 with a 917 driven by Dr Helmut Marko/Gijs van Lennep, the car running in Martini and Rossi colours

Pedro Rodriguez ended his career with a brilliant win at the Austrian 1000 Kms (Osterreichring) in June 1971. Sadly he died a fortnight later in a non-championship event, driving a Ferrari

Jo Siffert established his name in the record books with a road circuit lap record of 162.087mph at Spa in 1971, driving the 5-litre Gulf-Porsche 917

Porsche's experimental department prepared a wide-bodied, snub nosed 917 for Kauhsen and Jost to drive at Le Mans in 1971, and the styling department gave it a paint scheme to match its appearance! Jost butchered the pig in the latter stages of the race!

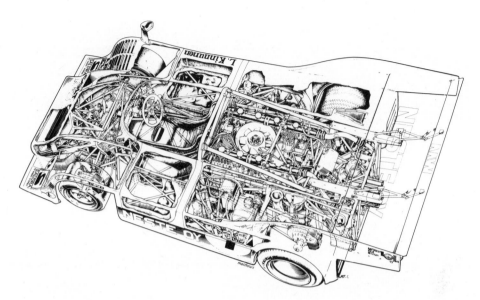

Leo Kinnunen's 4.5-litre turbocharged Porsche 917 (1972 model). Twin Eberspacher turbo-chargers boost the power output to 900bhp

Interserie Racing - which did not draw big crowds - represented at Silverstone in 1973 by triple champion Leo Kinnunen leading the similar Porsche 917-10 turbo of Willi Kauhsen

1973 Can-Am Champion Mark Donohue (917-30) leads 1973 Champion George Follmer (917-10) at Watkins Glen, July 1973

George Follmer, 1972 Can-Am Champion, pictured in 1973 in the same 917-10 in Bobby Rinzler's Crown Cola colours

The Martini-Porsche team of 1976. Left to right, M Schurti, R Stommelen, M Jantke, J Mass, and J Ickx. The cars are a 935 and a 936

The Group 6 model 936 was prepared in great secrecy for the 1976 World Sportscar Championship, and on Dr Fuhrmann's orders was painted black for mid-winter development. It was still painted black for the first race at Nurburgring, where it fell back with throttle trouble, but thereafter - in white livery - it won every race for which it was entered

Jacky Ickx and Jochen Mass won six of the seven events of the 1976 World Sportscar Championship, trouncing the French Alpine-Renault team which began the season favourites

Highlight of Porsche's 1976 programme was victory at Le Mans with the 936 sportscar driven by Jacky Ickx and Gijs van Lennep. This was Porsche's third victory at the Sarthe

During the 1976 season the 935 model was given a new nose panel with faired headlights, a controversial modification in view of the regulations. The engine cover had to be modified mid-season, involving a change in the engine specification which led to a bout of unreliability

The Group 5 car, model 935, which won the 1976 World Championship for Manufacturers ran as a basically standard 2.8-litre flat six engine modified to produce in excess of 600 horsepower, depending on boost pressure.

A privately entered VW-Porsche 914/6 on the 1971 Monte Carlo Rally. Three works cars took part, that of Waldegard/Thorszelius finishing third overall

A cross section view of the mid-engined Porsche 914/6

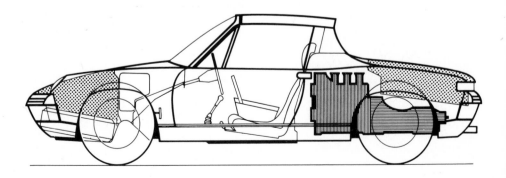

and Andretti led the opening laps of the race until first Siffert, then Rodriguez passed him and pulled away. The 'terrible twins' then proceeded to dominate the race, weaving in and out of the back markers in spectacular style and even managing to side-swipe each other as their rivalry got the upper hand, Rodriguez having a tyre mark on his door and Siffert pitting with a flat rear tyre. Later Redman had to pit again with his oil catch tank spilling over, and that was enough to give Rodriguez/Kinnunen their fourth victory of the season, half a lap ahead of Siffert/Redman and three laps ahead of the Andretti/Giunti Ferrari which was slowing with an overheated engine. The next day the Porsches rocked the Can-Am scene when Siffert, Attwood and Elford finished second, third and fourth behind Denny Hulme's 8.1-litre McLaren — despite making refuelling stops!

Early in September Porsche had another bonus when Tony Dean won the Road Atlanta Can-Am in his 908/02 spyder — by default of the larger engined cars it must be admitted — and the same weekend Brian Redman romped away with the Imola 500 Kms non-championship race in his 4.9-litre Gulf-Porsche, after Rodriguez had got involved with a spinning back-marker and backed his 917 into the guardrail.

The final Championship round of 1970 was at the Osterreichring in October, and here Ferrari fielded a new, much lightened 512M version of the 5-litre V12 model for Ickx/Giunti. Rodriguez practised in 1 minute 40.5 seconds, some eight seconds quicker than Siffert had gone a year before which gave some idea of the improvements on the 917, and Ickx was three-tenths of a second slower. In the race Ickx stormed away, creating a new lap record in 1 minute 40.0 seconds on the third lap (with full fuel tanks), and Rodriguez retired after only five laps with valve failure in his engine.

Unluckily for Ferrari the 512M had a dud alternator, and Ickx forfeited a 20 second lead after 50 laps when he needed a new battery. Twenty laps later Giunti retired the car, and Marko/Ahrens held the lead in the Porsche Salzburg entry while Siffert and Redman coped with poor handling on their Gulf car. Then the Austrian team manager made a costly mistake when he miscalculated the amount of fuel needed for his leading car, and he paid the penalty when Marko ran out of fuel on the far side of the circuit.

Suddenly Siffert, three laps clear of the best placed Alfa Romeo, slowed as one of the four camshafts broke in the flat-12 engine, and the Swiss driver had to tour around for the last half-hour of the race hoping that the engine would not fail completely. Pescarolo speeded up in the second placed Autodelta entry but, just as he got onto the same lap as Siffert, his engine blew up and the French driver rolled into the pits with a pool of oil gathering under the car. Siffert was safe, and won the final championship round of the season by two laps from Pescarolo who was credited with second place, having retired only five minutes from the finish.

The last works-assisted appearance of the 917 in 1970 was at the well supported Kyalami 9-Hours in November, where Siffert and Ahrens teamed up in the Martini racing 4.5-litre version which had finished second at Le Mans. The lightened Ferrari 512M of Ickx and Giunti was too much for the smaller engined Porsche, though, and the Italian car scored a two-lap victory despite the great efforts of Siffert; the Martini team also picked up third and fourth places with 908/02 spyders driven by Marko/Lins and Larrousse/van Lennep, while in fifth place was the 1.8-litre Chevron of Brian Redman, who had emigrated to South Africa (but only for a few months, as it turned out).

During the winter the CSI decreed that the 5-litre cars would be outlawed from the end of 1971 in favour of the 3-litre prototypes, so the next 12 months were going to finish the costly but successful endurance racing career of Porsche's super-car. For the 1971 season Wyer's team comprised Jo Siffert with Derek Bell and Pedro Rodriguez with Jackie Oliver, since Kinnunen had not learned English and did not fit in with the team despite his undoubted driving ability. The Salzburg team was disbanded for cost reasons, and the cars and equipment were taken over by the Martini and Rossi team managed by Hans-Dieter Dechent, who employed Vic Elford, Gerard Larrousse, Helmut Marko and

Kurt Ahrens to drive for him, with occasional appearances of Rudi Lins and Gijs van Lennep.

At Porsche's splendid new test track facility at Weissach a good deal of development work was carried out, concentrating mainly on suspension developments to cope with even wider tyres, aerodynamics on the long-tail cars for Le Mans, and a full 5-litre engine which made its first appearance in the BOAC 1000 Kms. The bores were increased to 86.8mm which raised the capacity to 4,998cc, but more important, the chrome-plated bores were changed to a nickel-silicon carbide specification which reduced friction and increased the power output to 620bhp.

If the Porsche effort seemed stronger for 1971, Wyer's task was eased as the Martini prepared cars were rather less reliable than they had been the previous year, and Ferrari reserved his effort for the new flat-12 three-litre prototype on which he would base his programme in 1972 (with outstanding success as it turned out, although his 1971 programme was dogged by ill-luck).

At the first championship race to be held at Buenos Aires, Wyer's cars swept to a one-two victory, Siffert/Bell leading Rodriguez/Oliver. The race was marred early on when Beltoise, whose Matra had run out of fuel, pushed his car across the track before the pits and Ignazio Guinti collided with it and was fatally injured; until that moment the new Ferrari had been amazingly fast, and Giunti had just taken the overall lead when the 5-litre cars stopped for fuel. Elford led briefly in his debut for the Martini team but retired with fuel pump trouble, while Marko's race lasted only one lap before engine trouble intervened. The Autodelta Alfa Romeos showed improved speed and reliability in finishing third and fourth, both within three laps of Siffert's Porsche after 164 laps.

Wyer's team was extraordinarily lucky to win the Daytona 24-Hours at the end of January, for Rodriguez/Oliver took the flag despite losing a 45-lap lead during a 92 minute pit stop to have the gearbox rebuilt. Pole position was claimed by Mark Donohue in Roger Penske's immaculate Ferrari 512M, and it was Donohue who made the running until just before the three-hour mark when minor electrical problems cropped up. A rare engine failure ventilated the crankcase on the Siffert/Bell 917, and Rodriguez/Oliver assumed a comfortable lead over the Martini Porsche of Elford/van Lennep at quarter-distance, with Donohue/Hobbs third in the Ferrari.

Just before midnight, tyre failure caused Elford's car to spin into the wall on the banking, and Donohue's Ferrari became involved in the accident and was badly damaged on the left side. The Martini car was out of the race, but after 70 minutes in the pits the Ferrari rejoined the race with its suspension rebuilt, having fallen only to fourth place. The chase was now taken up by the North American Racing Team's Ferrari 512S driven by Adamowicz/Bucknum, and the lead was theirs when, in the last quarter of the race, the Gulf-Porsche locked into top gear and would not downshift. The gearbox was rebuilt in an hour and a half, then with two hours to run the fiery Mexican driver was able to rejoin the race three laps in arrears.

Intermittent rain showers suited Rodriguez perfectly, and with another of his maestro performances he made up the deficit on the rather sick Ferrari and regained the lead 45 minutes before the end of the race.

If that race caused John Wyer and team manager David Yorke some anxious moments, Sebring was even more fraught and victory in the 12-Hour race was eventually gained by the lone 4.9-litre Martini Porsche driven by Elford and Larrousse. Omens were bad for Porsche when Donohue put the Ferrari 512M on pole position from Andretti in the 3-litre Ferrari 312P, with Rodriguez only third fastest, and for the first three hours of the race Andretti and Ickx pulled out a four-lap lead which seemed invincible until the gearbox broke.

Elford was delayed early on by a minor collision, and Siffert ran out of petrol on the far side of the course losing a total of 23 laps. Then Rodriguez and Donohue had a controversial collision (three collisions, according to Donohue!) which delayed both cars badly with body damage, and at half distance the Alfa Romeo team held first and second places. Soon Elford went charging through, and the second half of the race became processional as the silver Martini car established a three-lap lead from the Alfa Romeos, with the Gulf-Porsches taking fourth and fifth places.

Still things would not go right for the Gulf team at the BOAC 1000 Kms in April. Despite the introduction of full 5-litre, 620bhp engines the drivers were hard put to match their times of the previous year, and Ickx put the 312P on pole position followed by Stommelen's Alfa Romeo; Siffert made third fastest time but immediately afterwards spun around and damaged the back of his car.

Again on a damp track, conditions in which Ickx and Rodriguez shone best, the two pulled away from the field and Ickx was narrowly ahead when a spinning back-marker sent him skating across the grass; the Ferrari lost six laps there, and having a new nose panel fitted at the pits, leaving Rodriguez to lead the race comfortably. As the track dried Siffert caught him up, the two Porsches a lap ahead of the Alfa Romeos, and it looked as though Wyer's team had recovered its poise until, with 58 laps completed, Rodriguez's car spluttered to a halt with a blockage in the fuel system (a new gravity refuelling device was being used in the pits, and it turned out that some dirt had got into the churn). The lead Porsche was out, and when Siffert made his next pit stop it proved extremely difficult to change a front wheel — aluminium hubs were being tried out, and expansion made it impossible to remove the wheel until the whole assembly cooled down, and that took more than six minutes. Then Siffert's car dropped its spare wheel and another had to be fitted to comply with the regulations, and the Alfa Romeos moved up to secure first and second places. The engine in Hezemans' Alfa broke shortly before the end, but de Adamich/Pescarolo gave the Italian make its first World Championship victory for 20 years, three laps ahead of the Ickx/Regazzoni Ferrari and six laps ahead of the Siffert/Bell Porsche, which struggled home with third and fourth gears out of commission.

Things were going badly for Wyer's team, but fortunes turned at Monza where the principal opposition came from the Martini team; the Ferraris and Alfa Romeos could not be fully competitive on this 150mph circuit with 3-litre engines, although wet practice conditions upset everyone's calculations and Elford made the fastest time followed by Ickx. The Gulf and Martini teams both used new tail sections, with less upsweep at the back but with very large perpendicular tail fins to give lateral stability.

On a dry track, Rodriguez and Siffert pulled away from the field easily while behind them Ickx had a serious collision with a back-marker, and Elford's Porsche was handicapped by a misfiring engine. During the race Siffert dropped two laps because of a puncture, but Rodriguez/Oliver won easily at an average speed of 146.54mph — including three refuelling stops — and Siffert/Bell took second place ahead of a trio of Alfa Romeos.

Wyer's team scored another crushing victory at Spa, the two 5-litre 917s strolling away from the opposition and finishing nose-to-tail four laps ahead of the Pescarolo/de Adamich Alfa Romeo. The works Ferrari 312P crashed again, Regazzoni this time colliding with a back-marker (the same Dulon that made Ickx leave the road at Brands Hatch!), and the two Martini cars retired, Elford's with a cracked chassis and Marko's with a petrol leak.

The win was another one for the record books, Rodriguez and Oliver averaging 154.772mph; Siffert and Rodriguez took turns to smash the lap record, Siffert ending up with that honour at 3 minutes 14.6 seconds, an average of 162.087mph. Although it was not a very competitive race the 917s were tremendously spectacular everywhere around the course, incredibly fast and utterly reliable.

The 3-litre cars were wheeled out for the next two races, the Targa Florio and the Nurburg 1000 Kms, and the big effort was again saved for Le Mans where the Gulf and

243

The Porsche 917

Martini teams relied upon the 600bhp 4,907cc engines in the interest of reliability. Aerodynamics were an important feature as usual, virtually every Porsche having some different combinations of nose and tail sections, and the most unusual of these was a buff-nosed, short tail 917 which the styling department worked on before its arrival at the Sarthe — it was painted pink and the bodywork was divided up into various cuts of pork; the 'schwein' was entrusted to Willi Kauhsen and Rienhold Jost, and it was Jost who butchered the beast in an accident on Sunday morning.

Short, concave nose sections were needed to counterbalance the long-tails and provide more downthrust at the front wheels, and although the cars looked less sleek they were undoubtedly more efficient, as proved when Pedro Rodriguez unofficially lowered the lap record to an amazing 3 minutes 13.9 seconds during practice, averaging 155.4mph. A third car was run by Wyer's team for Attwood/Muller, this having the Monza nose/tail panels. The works Ferrari team kept well out of the 1971 race, and the only real opposition came from the Penske 512M handled by Donohue/Hobbs, but it did not run all that well and retired early with engine failure.

It was then virtually a foregone conclusion that a Porsche 917 would win, but which one? Elford/Larrousse were the first to retire when the cooling fan went into orbit and the engine cooked, and after six hours John Wyer's three cars held the leading places. This happy state was not to last very long, for Siffert's car broke a rear shock absorber and the upright was damaged, losing 70 minutes in the pits. Then at the darkest hour of the night Rodriguez pitted with a hub bearing seizing up, losing 20 minutes, and Attwood lost 40 minutes having a gear synchro ring replaced.

A Ferrari led — the privately entered 512M driven by Vaccarella and Spaniard Jose Juncadella was ahead at half distance, with Marko/van Lennep half a lap behind in the Martini Porsche (this car unique in having a magnesium chassis). Soon Juncadella had to retire with broken transmission and Rodriguez followed the Ferrari into retirement, the 917 having a broken oil pipe which almost seized the engine. Then, during the morning, Siffert's 917 retired with a split gearbox casing, and the prestigious race became a straight contest between the 'reserve' works cars of Marko/van Lennep and Attwood/Muller.

Although the Gulf Porsche made up two laps, it was still two laps in arrears when the clock hands reached four o'clock: Helmut Marko and Gijs van Lennep had written their names into the history books having averaged over 138mph for the duration, while Pedro Rodriguez had the consolation of a new lap record at 151.81mph which should stand for some years, as a new section of twisty track was built in to bypass the White House the following year.

Only two championship races remained for the 5-litre cars before they passed into history, and at the Osterreichring in June, Pedro Rodriguez drove one of the finest races of his life. It was also the last race he completed.

Siffert started in third gear by mistake and soon retired with clutch damage, leaving Rodriguez (paired with Attwood this time) to battle with the still competitive Ferrari 312P of Ickx and Regazzoni. Rodriguez was pulling away by 23 seconds when his battery went flat due to a broken alternator, and the Gulf car lost three laps in the pits having a new battery fitted. Ickx took the lead pursued by Marko/Larrousse, and as rain began to fall Rodriguez made a fantastic come-back drive through the field, again in his element on the slippery track.

Marko, who had experimental anti-skid brakes fitted, found that they were anything but suitable and fell back from Regazzoni, while by half distance Rodriguez had pulled back 1½ laps and was now in third place. David Yorke took full advantage of the regulations, putting Attwood into the car for 20 minutes to give the Mexican driver a short rest, then Rodriguez took the car over again for the remainder of the race.

Larrousse spun into retirement as a result of a puncture and then, with 30 laps still to run, Rodriguez got his 917 on to the same lap as the Ferrari. Calculations showed that he could, just, catch the 312P in the time available and tension grew as he pulled back three seconds on Regazzoni every lap. Alas, the contest ended when Regazzoni got carried away and spun into the guardrails, leaving Rodriguez with the easy task of beating the Alfa Romeos by two laps.

It was an amazing drive, worthy of the king of sportscar racing. Rodriguez, who set a new outright record for the circuit, covered 158 laps (934 kilometres) of the distance himself. A fortnight later the Mexican driver died in an accident at the Noris Ring at the wheel of Herbert Muller's Ferrari 512, in an unimportant non-championship race, and the great career of a colourful, brilliant driver had ended.

There remained only the Watkins Glen 6-Hour race in July to finish the works-assisted programme. Gijs van Lennep joined Wyer's team to partner Siffert, Bell and Attwood driving the second car, and ill-luck returned to the Gulf team for its final major outing. Two punctures delayed Siffert's car while Bell lost 15 minutes with broken throttle linkage out on the circuit, and although he drove brilliantly to make up ground, and set the fastest lap of the race, it was not enough to catch Siffert or the winning Alfa Romeo of Andrea de Adamich and Ronnie Peterson.

For Porsche, the third World Sportscar Championship in succession. For sports car racing, the end of a great era of *power* racing, with machinery which could often outpace the best Formula-1 cars of the day. Neither Rodriguez nor Siffert, the supreme drivers in these demanding cars, survived their era, for the Swiss driver was tragically killed in a BRM at Brands Hatch in October. The 917s carried on in another sphere, Can-Am, to reach new heights of achievement.

For the record book, Porsche won 24 of the 31 World Championship races in 1969, 1970 and 1971, fifteen victories falling to the 917 and nine to the 908. There were sixteen one-two results, eight 'triple' wins, three 'quadruple' wins and once, at the 1969 Nurburg 1000 Kms, Porsches took the five leading places. Porsche also scored three consecutive victories at Monza, at Spa, at the Nurburgring and at the Osterreichring.

Fifteen drivers contributed to these victories, Jo Siffert scoring ten wins, Pedro Rodriguez and Brian Redman eight each; a total of 36 drivers earned points for Porsche in the three years. Of the races Porsche did not win, Alfa Romeo scored three victories, the Ford GT40 scored two, Ferrari was ill-rewarded for a big and costly programme with just one victory, and Lola also had one victory at Sebring in 1969.

5 The Can-Am trail

IN SOME ways the Canadian-American Trophy trail represented a pinnacle in motor racing, in that it had fewer restrictions than either Formula-1 or USAC. Apart from the stipulation that two-seater 'sports car' bodywork must be used, the designers were free to construct virtually any car they liked with as large an engine as they felt necessary, and without any limitations on weight, fuel capacity, materials, aerodynamic devices and so on.

Apart from the first year, 1966, when John Surtees won the Trophy, the Can-Am series had been dominated by Bruce McLaren's team running specialised, lightweight cars powered by Chevrolet stock-block engines of 7-litres and more. Until the advent of the Porsche 917 the series could have had no more than an academic interest for the German company, but the combination of a very light spaceframe chassis and a powerful flat-12 racing engine gave Porsche a new aspect.

Officially Porsche withdrew from active competitions after Le Mans, but the company felt that the 917 would benefit from further development in racing before the 1970 season came along, and that a limited programme would also be a useful pointer in case they wanted to take Can-Am seriously a year or two later. Also, Porsche sales needed a boost in America because the new exhaust emission rules curtailed the export of the 911S model, and a bit of image-building for the lower powered 911 would do no harm. A deal was done with Californian Porsche-VW and Audi distributor John von Neuman to run one specially prepared spyder 917 for Jo Siffert, with retired Formula-1 driver Richie Ginther in charge of the team.

Only two months after Le Mans a new bodied spyder was ready, dubbed the 917PA (Porsche-Audi). The styling resembled that of the 908 spyder which had made its debut three months earlier, and the flat-deck tail cover was found to improve the handling straight away. Without a windscreen and roof, the 917PA scaled 775 kilogrammes, part of the weight saving offset by the twin fuel tanks fitted enabling the car to run a 200-mile race non-stop. The complete car, chassis number 917/027, was built in only three weeks, and it was powered by a regular 4.5-litre engine developing 580 horsepower.

Giving away more than 100 horsepower to the McLaren team, Siffert qualified seventh fastest at Mid-Ohio (the season's fifth Can-Am round) five seconds slower than Denny Hulme, and assuming the two orange cars of McLaren and Hulme were as reliable as usual the race was for third place. That is the way it turned out, with Hulme and McLaren in the leading places; Chris Amon was third, a lap behind in the 6.3-litre Ferrari V12 prototype and Siffert was fourth, only one lap behind the winners and not badly outpaced by Can-Am standards. Eighth place was claimed by Tony Dean in a Porsche 908/02, ahead of a variety of 6- and 7-litre cars.

Siffert was delighted with the handling of his 917PA, which on Goodyear tyres proved a lot easier to handle than the original Group 4 917. If Porsches high standards for reliability could be maintained — and they were! — the limited programme was worth going on with, for the majority of locally prepared Can-Am cars were anything but reliable.

At Elkhart Lake a fortnight later Siffert qualified eighth fastest but after seven laps he missed a gearchange and damaged the engine, but Porsche's pride was saved by Tony Dean who (also with Porsche-Audi backing) finished in a remarkable fifth place in his 3-litre 908.

Before the Bridghampton race in September the Porsche was fitted with an experimental four-speed gearbox to overcome gearchange difficulties, and this time Jo Siffert drove a really impressive race to finish in third place on the same lap as the dominant McLarens. Siffert's fighting display impressed the Americans enormously, bringing colour to the rather drab series, and although the Swiss driver had to swing the car from side to side on the last lap to get fuel to the pumps from the empty tanks, he hung on to collect 12 points and place himself seventh in the Championship, with only two finishes! Tony Dean again put many much more powerful cars to shame by finishing sixth in the race.

At Michigan Dan Gurney entered a McLaren M8B with a similar specification to the works' cars, and succeeded in giving McLaren and Hulme a hard time. This time the race was for fourth place, and Siffert again did what was expected of him. What was remarkable was that the 917's cooling fan drive sheared on the 25th lap, so Siffert had to slow his pace a bit and give up the chase of the McLarens. Even so, he stayed ahead of all the privately entered cars and, driving on the temperature gauge, finished the 195-mile race with his engine intact. Again, Tony Dean finished with credit in seventh place, and by this time his winnings had almost paid for the 908.

A collision with Gurney's McLaren at Laguna Seca meant a short pit stop for Siffert and this time he could only manage fifth place, a lap behind the leaders, while Dean's 908 finished seventh after an unusual episode in which the British driver was black-flagged for cutting corners, and again for driving out of the pits with a steward's walkie-talkie radio set caught on the bodywork!

An oil leak dropped Siffert out of the penultimate round at Riverside, but the final round in Texas brought his 917PA back into the limelight with a fighting fourth place, a performance which lifted him to fourth place in the final points standings behind only the two works McLarens and Chuck Parsons' Lola. Considering that this was achieved in only six of the eleven rounds, it did not say much for the opposition, and Siffert's prize money amounted to more than 50,000 dollars.

There was no official Porsche participation in the 1970 Can-Am trail, but two performances by the German make made a laughing stock of the prestigious series. The Watkins Glen round in July followed the 6-Hour endurance race and a number of Porsche 917s and Ferrari 512s took part in the event: in Porsches were Pedro Rodriguez, Jo Siffert, Vic Elford, Richard Attwood and Brian Redman with 600bhp 4.9-litre cars (complete with windscreens and weighing 800 kilogrammes), Gijs van Lennep in a 4.5-litre 917, and Mario Andretti and Jacky Ickx in 5-litre Ferraris.

Sadly Bruce McLaren had been killed a month earlier while testing a Can-Am car at Goodwood, and Dan Gurney joined Denny Hulme in the McLaren team. The Watkins Glen surface was badly broken up after the endurance race and it soon took its toll, as cars spun out and retired. Ickx went with a broken oil line, Rodriguez with a broken gearbox, Jackie Stewart with suspension trouble in Jim Hall's revolutionary new Chaparral, and Gurney fell back with an overheating engine. The real show was provided by the European cars, which chased after Hulme's McLaren as he had rarely been chased before.

Siffert was rarely more than 30 seconds behind Hulme, and despite a fast refuelling stop the Swiss driver was soon back in contention, driving one of his really inspired races. With 15 laps to run Siffert was a mere nine seconds behind Hulme, whose McLaren was overheating and handling badly. But the McLaren driver had plenty in hand, and pulled away easily when the challenge became serious. In the end Hulme won by less than 30 seconds, Siffert was second, Attwood third, Elford fourth, Andretti's Ferrari was fifth, van Lennep's Porsche sixth, Redman seventh, then two 700 horsepower McLarens filled the next two places before Gerard Larrousse came home tenth in the Martini Racing 908.

Team McLaren's record run of 19 successive Can-Am victories was finally broken at the Road Atlanta circuit in September 1970. A Porsche took the chequered flag, not one of the powerful 917s but Tony Dean's privately entered 908/02 Spyder. It was a calamitous day for the established Can-Am teams with one car after another eliminated by spins, crashes or mechanical failure. Only one car was on the same lap as Dean after 190 miles, and none of the other finishers was less than 7-litre capacity! At the end of the season Dean was placed sixth in the points standing after a string of impressive places, ahead even of Dan Gurney who drove the second Team McLaren car to two victories during the season.

A new Porsche 917 Spyder, called the 917-10, was prepared for Jo Siffert to drive in the 1971 Can-Am series, though again he would not make his debut until Watkins Glen, the fourth round of the ten-race series. By now the works-assisted endurance racing programme was drawing to a close and Porsche had a tremendous amount of experience with the 917. The new Can-Am car had a spyder body, the nose section developed from the snub Le Mans car with a lot of downforce, and many titanium and other lightweight parts which reduced the dry weight to 740 kilogrammes. As in the endurance cars, the 5-litre engine developed 620-630 horsepower, still hardly in the same class as Team McLaren's 7.5-litre 720bhp aluminium Chevy engines, but enough to deal with the majority of regular competitors.

Third place behind the McLarens of Peter Revson and Denny Hulme was a suitable reward for the new car, which ran very well to finish just ahead of Mario Andretti's 7-litre Ferrari, a V12 car based on the 512M. A month later at Mid-Ohio the McLaren team cracked up again, Hulme's car being knocked in a start-line fracas and Revson's retiring with engine failure. A Scots driver called Jackie Stewart, and a new model called the Lola T260, prevented Siffert from scoring his first Can-Am victory, but second place was his again.

Although the 917-10 was a significantly better car than the 917PA (which was still being campaigned in America by Milt Minter), the opposition had improved too, and Siffert was usually four or five seconds slower than the McLarens at the end of practice. More power was still needed, and until it could be found the 917-10 would not be a race-winner, except in lucky circumstances. The victory that Siffert wanted so much eluded him again at Elkhart Lake, for after pole-man Hulme coasted to a standstill with a broken engine, Peter Revson powered past from the back of the grid, and went on to score an easy victory. Second again, for the Porsche 917-10 which now had sponsorship from the STP oil additive corporation – the pit crew looked very distinctive, with blazing red trousers and candy striped shirts.

At Donnybrooke, Siffert could only finish fifth behind a quartet of McLarens, slipping back a place on the final lap as his car ran out of fuel. Another fourth place result followed at Edmonton, and then at Laguna Seca Jo Siffert was placed fifth in the final Can-Am he took part in, this being the gifted Swiss driver's last completed race. A week later Siffert, the man who had been the backbone of Porsche's sportscar team throughout four winning seasons, died at Brands Hatch when his Formula-1 BRM had some sort of mechanical failure and crashed in flames. Everyone at the Porsche factory grieved, for Seppi's death came so soon after the death of Rodriguez and it seemed that a glorious page in Porsche's history had been closed cruelly. For the record, Siffert was again fourth in the Can-Am points list after taking part in six of the ten rounds.

During the winter Porsche concluded an agreement with the leading American private entrant, Roger Penske, to run a new version of the 917-10 throughout the 1972 Can-Am series for his driver, Mark Donohue. Penske's preparation and development had proved impeccable time and again, Donohue himself being a talented engineer and race driver, and of the Americans Penske stood out head and shoulders above the rest as an ally for German efficiency.

More power would be needed, and this problem was solved by the application of two Eberspacher exhaust driven turbochargers in conjunction with the Bosch petrol injection. With careful tuning, turbocharging could improve the power output by 50% and although petrol consumption suffered, this was more than enough to take on the best Can-Am teams in the field. Such was the power increase that the whole chassis needed developing, and to start with a 4.5-litre flat-12 producing 'only' 850 horsepower was used.

The biggest problem was a lag in throttle response, but continuous development in the early part of 1972 solved this as a complicated system of valves was incorporated into the design. Donohue took part in the development work at the Weissach test track and all the problems were gradually overcome, and early in the series the turbocharging system was applied to the 5-litre engine raising the power output to 950 horsepower.

Bodywork was further developed to provide still more downforce, for sheer speed was no longer a critical factor and the important thing was to keep the car firmly glued to the road. Out of interest, the turbo-Porsche accelerated from rest to 60mph (97kph) in 2.1 seconds, to 100mph (162kph) in 3.9 seconds and to 200mph (344kph) in 13.4 seconds. Only specialised dragsters could accelerate faster than that, and their cornering potential is rather limited!

The twin turbochargers were boosting the engine at 20psi, the wheelbase was lengthened by 16mm, just over half an inch, and although the fuel capacity had to be increased to 300 litres (66 gallons) the weight of the first Penske car was kept down to 735 kilogrammes. The turbochargers added 70 pounds to the weight of the engine, but the adoption of the second magnesium frame pulled back 33 pounds.

The turbo-Porsche was an extremely expensive project, and to keep private customers happy a number of similar cars were made with normally aspirated flat-12 engines enlarged to 5.4-litre capacity by increasing the bore dimensions to 90mm, keeping the stroke at 70.4mm. Power was increased to 660 horsepower, a useful though not winning output, and from the start of the '72 Can-Am series two cars were available to Vasek Polak's team for Peter Gregg and Milt Minter to drive.

It was no surprise when Donohue, in a machine soon dubbed the 'Panzer Porsche' shattered the lap record while practising for the opening Edmonton Can-Am race in June, clearly ahead of Denny Hulme's new McLaren M20 with a little over 730 horsepower from its 8.1-litre Chevrolet engine. Donohue looked as though he would win the race easily until a valve played up in the turbocharging system, and a quick pit stop dropped him back to second place in the results. Minter was placed fourth in the 5.4-litre Porsche, behind Revson's works McLaren.

A near disaster stopped Penske's efforts in their tracks when Donohue's Porsche crashed heavily while testing for the second round at the hilly Road Atlanta circuit. The rear bodywork flew up and sent the car out of control, and Donohue emerged from the wreck with badly torn leg ligaments which put him out of racing for four months.

At short notice Penske recalled George Follmer to his team, the American driving the

249

alloy chassis back-up car, and such was its superiority that he was able to win the race. His luck was in, and Hulme's out, for while the New Zealand driver was chasing Follmer and shaping up to pass, an air current lifted his McLaren and turned it over. Hulme was unhurt, and considered himself very fortunate.

Against all odds a new car was readied for Hulme to drive at Watkins Glen, and he drove to a fine victory ahead of Revson while Follmer dropped back with an off-form engine and finished in a lowly sixth place.

Follmer and his Porsche were right back on form for the next race at Mid-Ohio and were strolling away from the McLarens until a heavy shower of rain created havoc with the field. The McLarens fell back, Follmer spun twice without hitting anything, and he was chased to the flag by Jackie Oliver's UOP-Shadow. In third place was Milt Minter, out for the first time in a 4.5-litre turbo-Porsche.

Now Hulme led the table by just two points, but Follmer went into the lead with a comfortable win at Elkhart Lake. Hulme started from pole position and Follmer was well back on the grid, troubled by rainy conditions, but the race was dry and Follmer stormed through the field and was chasing Hulme when the McLaren's ignition failed. In their efforts to find more power the McLarens seemed to be getting less reliable, and Team McLaren failed to win another race after the Watkins Glen success.

Follmer was only third at the Road America race in September, having run short of fuel near the end, and Cevert's winning McLaren was followed home by Minter's turbo-Porsche. Then Mark Donohue made his comeback at Laguna Seca and although his left knee was still strapped up, he put his Porsche on pole position and was able to overtake Hulme to win the race, with Follmer placed third after stopping to have a wheel changed.

At Laguna Seca Penske's L&M sponsored, white and red Porsches were comfortably first and second, Follmer taking the flag after being waved past by Donohue; this victory made Follmer the 1972 Can-Am Champion, and another win at Riverside in the final round lifted his points total to 130, exactly twice as many as former champion Denny Hulme scored. In fact Minter might have been runner-up with 69 points, a terrific performance by this privateer, but he had to discard four points under the scoring system and was nosed out by Hulme, who had more wins to his credit. From five starts, Donohue lifted his total to 62 points to be placed fourth in the championship, so Porsche had really taken over in a big way.

Still more was planned for the 1973 season, and Porsche's secret weapon was a turbo-charged version of the 5.4-litre engine which lifted the power beyond the magic 1000 horsepower level for the first time. With the turbocharger boosting at 1.5 atmospheres the power rose to 1,140bhp, and in the test house an engine boosting out 2.2 atmospheres gave an astronomic 1,560bhp. Team McLaren tried to turbocharge the Chevrolet engine, but withdrew from the series on finding this exercise exorbitantly expensive and none too reliable. The UOP-Shadow team also spent a lot of money trying to boost the Chevy V8 but the car only made a couple of unrewarding outings late in the series.

The two winning Penske Porsches were bought by Bobby Rinzler's private team for the 1973 season, for George Follmer and Charlie Kemp; Vasek Polak also had a 5-litre turbo-Porsche for rising star Jody Scheckter, and a 5-litre 917PA for Brian Redman to race a couple of times at the end of the season. Then there were turbo-Porsches for privateers like Hans Wiedmer from Switzerland, and Hurley Haywood ... and anyone who did not have a turbo-Porsche could only compete as best they could and hope for some lucky breaks.

Apart from the advantages of Porsche development and Penske preparation, plus the extremely powerful engine, Donohue's 917-30 also had a longer chassis to improve the handling. The wheelbase was extended by seven inches, and the far-back rear wing was supported by a sub-frame. Time and again it proved faster than everything else in sight.

The first race did not go Donohue's way, for after qualifying for pole position at

Mosport and leading the race he collided with a back-marker and stopped to have the bodywork repaired, falling back to seventh place. This event was won against the odds by Charlie Kemp, with Hans Wiedmer following up in second place.

The second race did not go Donohue's way either, for after winning the first heat (the first Can-Am race to be split in this way) a fuel leak delayed him in the second, and he followed George Follmer's 917-10 to the flag.

But Donohue did win the third race ... and the fourth ... and the fifth ... and the sixth ... and the seventh ... and the eighth. What the pundits called Donohue's 'unfair advantage' became more and more marked as the series went on, until it became almost pointless to discuss who would win. Apart from anything else Donohue's car was perfectly reliable, except for a suspension breakage during practice at Watkins Glen which resulted in damage to the car. But still, the back-up car was equally effective. The privately maintained Porsches were not always so reliable, for the turbochargers needed delicate tuning, and at the end of the season Donohue amassed 139 points, Follmer in second place only 62, Hurley Haywood 47 and Charlie Kemp 45.

Porsche had taken over the Can-Am scene completely, just as Team McLaren and private owners had dominated before. This dominance was no longer welcome, though, and the energy crisis at the end of the year made the SCCA directors change the rules for 1974. Fuel restrictions were announced, stringent enough to reduce the advantage of the turbo-Porsches and give more advantage to smaller engined, less thirsty cars. So after two consecutive Can-Am titles had been recorded, the Porsche factory officially ceased to support the series and Roger Penske dropped out too, though retaining a 917-30 for his personal use!

Another era was over, and for the time being it seemed that Porsche's unbroken record of building two-seater sports cars had come to an end. The turbocharging exercise was continued on the 911 Coupe for the 1974 season.

Always overshadowed by the publicity and money in the Can-Am series, Europe's Interserie contest proved to be a Porsche benefit. Run on the same lines as Can-Am, and with identical Group 7 unlimited capacity sports cars, the title was claimed in 1971, 1972 and in 1973 by the Finnish driver Leo Kinnunen, the latter years with turbocharged 917-10 models owned by his longtime sponsor Antti Aarnio Wihuri. His principal opposition usually came from Willi Kauhsen, who sometimes beat Kinnunen, but again the opposition was rather sparse and the series never became popular enough to attract good sponsorship and high returns for the expense invested in machinery. A 5-litre turbo-Porsche cost £50,000, approximately three times the cost of a Formula-1 car, so it is not surprising that no more than four or five such machines competed regularly in Europe.

Mark Donohue won a series of races called the International Race of Champions devised by Roger Penske. Leading drivers from throughout the world, including Jackie Stewart and Emerson Fittipaldi, raced identical 3-litre 1974 model Porsche Carreras in a series of four races, all televised throughout America. Donohue came out a clear winner with three victories, the last one scored at the Daytona Speedway in February 1974.

6 Turbocharging, the 930 to 936

PORSCHE did not invent turbocharging, but was the first company to develop the exhaust driven supercharger for successful competitions programmes in the international sphere, and to install that system on a full production car. The rival German company BMW had turbocharged the 2002 for European racing in the late 1960's, and half-heartedly produced a turbo version of the road model in 1974/75, but few cars were produced and the project was quietly dropped.

Meanwhile Porsche actively developed the 911 turbo during the 1974 racing season, and launched the type 930 — or, in marketing terms, simply the 'Porsche Turbo' — in August 1974. Originally it was a product of Weissach, a necessity to gain homologation for the 1976 racing programme, but the marketing department soon awoke to the potential of this ultra high-performing machine and the original target of 500 cars was passed by the end of the year. Within two years the Turbo was happily referred to as the company's 'flagship', and the prestige model was in demand throughout the world, production in the first 24 months passing the 1,300 mark.

The turbocharger is an exhaust-driven supercharger, but whereas the superchargers favoured by many manufacturers before the war were engine driven, and absorbed power, the turbocharger makes use of 'free' exhaust gases and raises the engine power by means of forced induction without any inherent penalty. The engine is more efficient, therefore, exhaust pollution is minimised, and a by-product is a lower exhaust noise level. So apart from raising performance, turbocharging does offer tangible benefits of the type that would naturally interest a company like Porsche, where much of the emphasis is on engineering.

As with the Can-Am cars and the 1974 racing 911 turbo, the production type 930 turbo employed a KKK (Kuhnle, Kopp and Kausch) turbocharger, now in conjunction with Bosch K-Jetronic petrol injection instead of mechanical injection on the racing cars. Contact breakerless electronic ignition was incorporated, for the first time on a series production engine, but basically the power unit remained the same as on the 3-litre Carrera. The Turbo engine developed a fairly modest 260bhp DIN at 5,500rpm (comparing with the Carrera's 210bhp at 6,300rpm) and an impressive 253 lb.ft of torque at 4,000rpm (Carrera, 188 lb.ft at 5,100rpm). Compression was lowered to 6.5:1, so that

96 octane lead-free fuel could be used, and a turbo boost pressure of 0.8 atmospheres, or 11.75psi, was originally adopted. This however gave a rather fierce 'bite' to the mid-range performance, and during 1975 the boost pressure was raised to 1 atmosphere and a by-pass valve was introduced to the system to give a smoother transition to boosted power, starting at around 2,500rpm.

One of the beauties of the system was that the Turbo would run happily in thick traffic, and remained vice-free even on wet roads. It could be driven quietly without any fuss, but a tremendous reserve of power became available whenever the throttle was floored at 3,000rpm or more. Acceleration from rest to 100mph in some 13 seconds is really in the racing car class, and of course the Turbo was by far the quickest production car ever made by Porsche, having a maximum speed in excess of 155mph.

Many mechanical modifications were made to suit the Turbo to that level of performance. A larger diameter, 9.5 inch Fichtel and Sachs clutch was fitted, mated to a beefed-up four-speed manual gearbox — the five-speed box was not designed to cope with that much torque, and would in any case be totally unnecessary in view of the engine's characteristics. The Carrera's ventilated disc brakes were fitted, and the MacPherson strut front suspension geometry incorporated some anti-dive. Aluminium trailing arms were fitted at the rear, incorporating larger wheel bearings, and the track was widened through the use of wider (7-inch front and 8-inch rear) wheels. These, incidentally, were shod with Pirelli's P7 tyre specially developed for the Turbo, having virtually race-track performance characteristics despite an all-weather tread pattern. The Pirellis had a 50 per cent aspect ratio, meaning that the tyre sidewall was half as high as the tread was wide. A deep air dam at the front, in conjunction with a large spoiler on the engine cover, reduced maximum speed lift from 180kg (397 pounds) to a mere 17kg (37.5 pounds), substantially improving the stability and handling in all conditions save for ice and snow, when there would be insufficient speed to gain aerodynamic benefits. These devices do however bring demonstrable benefits in cross-winds, and in the rain when aquaplaning is reduced.

Porsche now had a road car that was sensational by any standards, and the absence of any competitions activity during 1975 allowed breathing space for some even more sensational racing developments in 1976, when the FIA Appendix J regulations were re-written. Although the 1.4 equivalency factor for turbocharged engines was retained, the weight of the car was now related to engine capacity, so that in Group 4 modified GT cars a 3-litre car could weigh as little as 945kg but a 4.5-litre model must weigh at least 1,175kg. Twin-plug heads were barred, rendering the Carrera RSR model obsolete, and after careful consideration Helmut Bott and the engineering division decided to homologate the 930 into Group 4, re-designating this model the 934. The Group 5 version (935) would be eligible for the newly instituted World Championship for Makes, and a late decision by the factory saw a new prototype built for the Group 6 World Sportscar Championship (type 936).

All, of course, employed turbocharged engines, so that all normally aspirated power units were now history so far as Porsche was concerned.

Taking the Group 4 934 first, Porsche retained the nominal 3-litre capacity, so that the FIA rating would be 4,190cc. This required a minimum weight of 1,175kg, only 20kg less than the actual weight of the 930, so it could be raced with virtually all its luxurious road equipment! Type 917 brakes were adopted, but the suspension remained pure torsion bar front and rear. So far as the engine was concerned, the 2.1-litre engine's camshafts were fitted, but still retaining K-Jetronic injection, and the boost was raised to 1.3 atmospheres, or 19psi. Effectively the power was raised to a minimum of 480bhp, nearly double that of the standard car, and the most interesting modification was the adoption of water-cooled heat interchangers to lower the temperature of the exhaust gases by some 100-degrees Centigrade. Twin water radiators were fitted at the front, either side of the oil cooler, and the more compact water cooled interchanger allowed the standard engine cover to be used, as required by the regulations. A total of 30 cars were built and sold prior to the 1976 racing season, at 97,000 DM apiece, but rarely did more than a handful appear for the European Grand Touring Car races, and the Championship was won handsomely by the Dutchman, Toine Hezemans, driving for the wealthy German privateer Georg Loos.

Group 5 allowed more latitude, as befitted a World Championship, though basically the cars were supposed to look something like their production origins for the so-called Silhouette Formula; it was through interpretation that Porsche were fouled-up by the FIA/CSI midway through the season. For the Group 5 type 935, Porsche decided to go for the 4-litre engine class and a minimum weight of 970kg. The biggest drawback to the new formula was the stipulation of 14-inch maximum tyre width, which would impair the handling, compared with 17-inch rear tyre widths used on the 1974 911 turbo. In order to raise the tread contact area, 19-inch diameter wheels were fitted for the first time. Torsion bar suspension was now dispensed with, coil springs replacing the familiar bars as on the 1974 racer, and the bulky air-cooled heat interchanger for induction air was retained, necessitating a non-standard engine cover. The differential was dispensed with, and type 917 titanium driveshafts were fitted.

The 92mm bore was chosen in order to keep the total engine capacity down to 3,990cc, but with 1.6 atmospheres (23psi) of boost, twin-plug ignition and mechanical fuel injection, power was raised to no less than 590 horsepower, and probably more than 600bhp in fact. This car would accelerate from rest to 200kph (125mph) in a mere 8.2 seconds, and although the cornering power was slightly reduced by the tyre restrictions the 935 was considerably quicker in lap times than the 1974 turbo, thanks to the 100 horsepower advantage. At Le Mans, the works 935 had a maximum speed of 336kph (208mph).

In the World Sportscar Championship arena (Group 6), Alpine-Renault expected to have a clear field for supremacy with the turbocharged, V6 A442 with nominal 2-litre engine capacity. Racing experience had been gained over the past two seasons, in 1974 by winning the European 2-litre Sportscar Championship, and in 1975 with a turbocharged, beefed-up version of that car. Late in 1975, however, Porsche management made the decision to go ahead with a rival, and a rapid development/build programme was implemented based on the 908/3. It retained the aluminium spaceframe chassis, and inherited the turbocharged flat-six engine of nominal 2,142cc, developing 510bhp, and type 917 brakes, gearbox and driveshafts. Additionally, it had safety cells behind the front wheels, as required by the new regulations to reduce the risk of fire in a crash. Also in line with new regulations, it ran on wheels with a maximum rim width of 15 inches, so that the tyre width would not exceed 16 inches.

Porsche factory drivers Jochen Mass and Jacky Ickx won the opening round of the Group 5 series at Mugello, in Italy, without any difficulty, then all three championships had a fixture the first weekend in April, the Group 5 series at Vallelunga in Italy, the Group 6 and Group 4 series at the Nurburgring. Ickx and Mass had no difficulty winning in Italy, but in Germany the emasculated Sportscar series (races now had to be a maximum of four hours in duration) got off to a shaky start. The CSI delegates were more than a little upset when the Group 4 GT cars — that is, half a dozen Porsche 934s — were amalgamated with the Group 6 cars due to lack of entries for the EGT round; several more 934s were competing in Italy. Alpine-Renault claimed pole position, but on the second corner of the race, at the 'Ring's North Curve, Depailler and Jaussaud had a controversial collision on the wet track and both French cars were eliminated, virtually handing Porsche the race. Rolf Stommelen, in the 936, was leading by miles when the car's throttle link broke, dropping him back to fifth place overall. Reinhold Jost, the German privateer, was an easy winner in his Can-Am bodied 908/3 turbo beating a 2-litre

Lola-BMW. Second on the road, but classified separately, was Hezemans in his Porsche 934, a clear winner of the European Grand Touring Car Championship race.

At Vallelunga there was a good deal of discussion about the eligibility of the Porsche 935 concerning the shape of the engine cover, which was distinctly non-standard due to the air-charged intercooler. Porsche argued that this was part of the engine induction system, and therefore free, but the CSI ruled that Porsche would have to adopt the standard engine cover capable of accepting the standard (type 930) rear wing. The CSI gave Porsche just six weeks to alter the engine completely, for it meant throwing away the proven system and adopting the more compact water-charged intercooling, which had not been developed for the 935.

Having lost the opening Group 6 round (though with 20 points still going to Porsche thanks to Jost's effort), Mass, Ickx and Rolf Stommelen between them managed to win every remaining round in the series, often helped by Alpine-Renault's inferior pitwork and reliability. It was not a championship by default because the cars were very evenly matched, and the Renaults were often on pole position, but Porsche's low-key programme contrasted with Renault's in every way. The 936 was hastily developed, and a single car was entered in each championship round against two Renaults, and an occasional Alfa Romeo. Yet time and again, six times in all, the Porsche took the chequered flag and, having started as the underdog, eventually triumphed with a perfect score of 140 points.

The 935 was not having such an easy time, though. Victory over BMW's 3.5 CSL in the two opening rounds of the new series looked easy, but at Silverstone Jacky Ickx burned out the 935's clutch away from the standing start, and Ronnie Peterson was sensational in the new BMW, a turbocharged CSL reputed to be developing over 700 horsepower. Eventually the BMW's gearbox succumbed to the strain, as had been expected, and the race developed into a battle between Bob Wollek/Hans Heyer in Erwin Kremer's Porsche 934/5, and the normally aspirated BMWs. At the end of six hours John Fitzpatrick/Tom Walkinshaw gave BMW a deserved victory, a mere few seconds ahead of Wollek/Heyer.

Porsche would very much have liked to win that race, for at the next round, at the Nurburgring, the engine modifications would have to be ready. The alteration to water cooling for the induction air, necessary to save space in the engine compartment and thus to fit a standard engine cover, was by no means as simple as might be imagined. Altogether, the intensive development and test programme, not to mention the expense allocated to two World Championship races before the car was made reliable, cost the factory close on 500,000 DM, a terrific burden on the budget. Needless to say, the directors of Porsche were extremely critical of the CSI, and demanded that in future the regulations should be more carefully worded, and not subject to amendments during a racing season.

Pronounced throttle lag was the most obvious problem that Stommelen and Manfred Schurti had to cope with at the Nurburgring, after the engine modifications had been carried out, but the race revealed a much more serious defect. The engine was vibrating badly on part throttle, causing excessive wear on the distributor arm which eventually broke and stranded the car after eight laps, when it was far in the lead. Victory went to BMW, and the Munich company won again at the Osterreichring when the Porsches again proved unreliable: the works car, and two privately-entered but factory supported machines, all broke down when the throttle shafts broke, another effect of the hasty modification programme.

Stronger throttle shafts were still undergoing endurance testing at Weissach when the two works cars were air-freighted to Watkins Glen for the penultimate round of the championship, but at last the cars were reliable. After leading much of the way, Mass and Ickx were delayed in the pits when the rear brake pads wore out and proved difficult to replace, but the sister-car of Stommelen and Schurti took over the lead. The final result was 1-2-3 for Porsche, with the BMWs trounced, but the championship was still open when the teams went to Dijon for the final round in September, due to the scoring system which decided the series on the best five results out of seven.

Once again BMW wheeled out their fearsome turbocharged 3.5 CSL for Ronnie Peterson, partnered this time by Gunnar Nilsson, and in one of the most spectacular drives seen all year, Peterson led the race for 40 minutes ... until the BMW's rear axle succumbed to the strain. Mass and Ickx had no difficulty then in winning the race, and in fact Porsches filled the top five places taking the Championship in a very convincing fashion. It was at Dijon that the Alpine-Renaults had their most serious beating, on home soil, in the accompanying Group 6 event. Mass and Ickx won that race easily after the French cars were delayed by technical problems with their Michelin racing tyres, so the Germans went home to Stuttgart feeling extremely pleased with themselves.

It used to be said that victory at Le Mans is more important than winning the endurance championship, and though it may arguably not be the *plus grande course du monde* any longer, it still captures the attention of the world. The Automobile Club de l'Ouest had opted out of the World Championship series in 1975 with a 'fuel economy' formula, and did so again in 1976 through insisting on combining the Group 5 and Group 6 cars in one race against the wishes and dictates of the CSI. History will probably prove that the French club was right, and the governing body wrong — not for the first time! The 1976 entry was not exactly star-studded, but a lone Alpine-Renault driven by Jabouille, Tambay and Dolhem proved quickest in practice ahead of Jacky Ickx/Gijs van Lennep in the Porsche 936, Rolf Stommelen/Manfred Schurti in the factory Porsche 935, and Reinhold Jost/Jurgen Barth in a second 936 entered by the factory. Two 1975 Le Mans winning Mirages were entered (Gulf having given up team sponsorship), and a revelation of the race was the performance of Alain de Cadenet's Lola-DFV, shared with Chris Craft.

The Alpine-Renault led the first few laps but Ickx soon swept by, as it turned out to lead for the duration of the race. During the evening the French car retired with a holed piston, not unexpectedly, and through the night the two factory 936 prototypes forged ahead of the field. Sunday morning brought its usual crop of problems for many competitors, and the Porsche team was not free of incident. Jost's 936 lost power with damaged rocker arms, and then retired with a broken driveshaft between the engine and the gearbox — this was the *only* retirement by a Porsche 936 during the 1976 season — and the 935 of Stommelen/Schurti was delayed by repeated plug and distributor defects. Then with little more than four hours to run, Ickx/van Lennep made an unscheduled stop to have a split exhaust pipe changed, as this was affecting the turbocharger, but the 20-minute delay was insignificant as the top Porsche pairing still had an eleven-lap lead at the end.

Second were Lafosse/Migault in a Mirage-DFV, third Craft/de Cadenet in the privately-entered Lola (despite unbearably high cockpit temperatures which were blistering the drivers' feet) and fourth the factory Porsche 935 driven by Stommelen and Schurti, the first 'production' car to finish.

At the season-end the scoresheet for Porsche read: World Championship for Makes — Champions; World Sportscar Championship — Champions; European Grand Touring Car Championship — Champions; Le Mans — Winners. No-one could ask better than that. There had only been one turbocharger failure during the year on a factory car, and the 936 had been almost perfectly reliable. Early-season experience with the 935 had promised the same degree of reliability, and the mid-season failures were directly attributable to the CSI's insistence on technical changes, what amounted to a re-definition of the regulations.

None of the Championships captured the lustre of former years, and it was evident to most observers that the decision of the CSI to instigate two World Championships for

The body assembly hall. The cars appear to be fairly early 911s

Works II

The test and development centre at Weissach

Weissach on the ground

The VW-Porsche factory at Ludwigsburg, which subsequently housed Porsche's marketing department

The new generation of Porsche - the 924 in profile

Not always the best car to photograph - it is very handsome in the flesh

The 924 interior has all the finesse of the tradiational 911

Some would say that the 924 is a hatchback

The power train of the 924. The backbone tube forms a rigid unit. The engine is at the front and the transaxle at the rear

The 924 has pop-up headlamps after Porsche's experience with the VW-Porsche 914. Permanent driving lamps are also part of the equipment

This *Autocar* cutaway perhaps shows the 924 off at its best

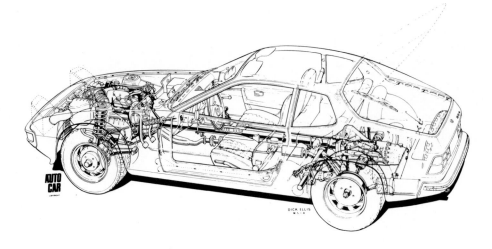

The 928, announced in 1977, has a water cooled V8 at the front. One of its styling and safety features is flexible front and rear impact zones

From the rear the 928 is a handsome car. Note the total absence of trim

Compare this photograph with the one of the power train of the 924. They are not alike but they do come from the same family

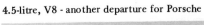
4.5-litre, V8 - another departure for Porsche

endurance racing had not been wise. But that was hardly Porsche's fault. There were two World Championships to be captured, the factory took them. What state would either have been in *without* Porsche's presence? The 1977 season would tell, with Porsche abstaining from the World Sportscar Championship.

7 The VW-Porsche, and future developments

FOR MANY years the Volkswagen company had relied upon its association with Porsche to provide some sort of sporting image, but there was no spare capacity to build a sportscar as such. However the VW directors felt that a market existed for a new sporting model and entered into an agreement with the Porsche management for a new joint holding company to be set up, to design and build an advanced mid-engined two-seater sports car.

Early in 1969 the company, VW-Porsche Vertriebsgesellschaft GmbH, was instituted, both partners having equal shareholdings, to produce the model with a choice of Volkswagen or Porsche engines in the Karmann factory. Initially the company, jointly managed by O.E. Filius and K. Schneider, took over the Motometer offices in Stuttgart, then two years later the company moved to a new parts warehouse and office complex (owned by Porsche) at Ludwigsburg, thus quadrupling the space available and accommodating more than 300 employees.

The design of the car was entirely Porsche's, and it retained many distinctive features such as torsion bar front suspension, the dashboard layout, and provision for a detachable 'Targa' roof. The VW-Porsche was strictly a two-seater although the generous 65-inch overall width meant that there was plenty of space inside the car for two people. A steel platform chassis was adopted and the metal body welded on in the usual way, an integral roll bar giving the monocoque extra rigidity. The glass-fibre roof panel could be detached and stowed away in the large rear compartment behind the engine, more luggage space being provided at the front where the petrol tank and spare wheel were located.

The VW-Porsche was given a wide, low look and a lot of attention was paid to wind-cheating, even the underside of the car being smoothed off. The advantages of mid-engine layout have been well known to racing car constructors for many years, it being much easier to achieve neutral cornering characteristics and higher cornering power, and both versions of the VW-Porsche felt incredibly secure on the road with far more cornering power than most drivers would want to use.

To keep the frontal area as small as possible, the headlights could be retracted into the bodywork by means of individual small electric motors. Disc brakes were fitted front and rear, and the most technically interesting feature of the models was the juxtapositioning of the engines, placing the gearbox and differential behind the engine, entirely ahead of the wheels. The wheelbase was 96.5 inches, and the overall length of the car 157 inches.

Customers had a choice of Volkswagen's 1,679cc Bosch injected four-cylinder engine from the 411 car, developing 80bhp DIN, or Porsche's 1,991cc six-cylinder engine with Zenith carburettors developing 110bhp DIN. Porsche's 5-speed gearbox was standard equipment on both versions.

The 914 with Volkswagen power was priced at 12,000 marks, and had a top speed of 110mph; it weighed 1,982 pounds (under 18 cwt) and would accelerate from rest to 60mph in under 13 seconds. The 914/6, as the Porsche powered model was designated, weighed 90 pounds more and had a top speed of 124mph, accelerating to 60mph in 9.7 seconds.

Both versions were unveiled at the Frankfurt Show in September 1969 and they received a good reception, although prices were felt to be rather high. The six-cylinder version, costing 20,000 marks, certainly had tremendously high performance on the road, due to its road-holding as much as anything, but it was not long before some customers wanted it to have a 2.2-litre engine, for they could be out-accelerated by the least expensive 911T in the Porsche range. Even so, the 914/6 accounted for over 20% of Porsche's sales in 1970 with 2,750 cars built, and many more were produced with the Volkswagen engine.

No production programme involving Porsche would be complete without reference to a competitions involvement, and there were three major achievements for the 914/6 in the early years. One car, privately entered but works prepared, appeared at Le Mans in June 1970 in the hands of Guy Chasseuil and Claude Ballot-Lena, and after a completely trouble-free run it finished the race in an amazing sixth place, beaten only by winning 917 models, a 908, and two 5-litre Ferraris. The two Frenchmen completed 284 laps of the Sarthe circuit, 58 fewer than Herrmann/Attwood, in weather conditions that were often appallingly wet, and many faster cars were disqualified for failing to complete a set distance in 24 hours.

Two months later the VW-Porsche factory entered three cars in the Marathon de la Route, now extended to an 86-hour rally-cum-race around the Nurburgring. All three cars had mildly tuned six-cylinder engines developing 160bhp DIN and one of them, for Claude Ballot-Lena/Gunther Steckkonig/Nick Koob was a standard Group 4 GT car. Two more, for Gerard Larrousse/Claude Haldi/Dr. Helmut Marko and Bjorn Waldegard/Ake Andersson/Guy Chasseuil were entered as prototypes, with wider than standard wheels, larger fuel tanks and other things to suit the conditions, like Porsche 908 brake calipers, a limited slip differential and some glass-fibre body panels.

In terms of reliability the VW-Porsches, managed by Rico Steinemann, trounced all the opposition. One peculiar rule of the event was that cars had to complete as many laps in the last 12 hours as they did in the first 12 hours, so to be on the safe side all the drivers were told to drive well within their limits. The three cars averaged 16 minutes per lap, although they could go round in under 12 minutes, and after six hours the field was led by two British Leyland entries, a Mini-Cooper and a Rover V8. Mechanical troubles forced both British cars out within 20 hours, and at half distance the three VW-Porsches held the leading positions ahead of a pair of Porsche 911s.

No troubles were reported, and it was 60 hours, 4,600 miles, before the tyres had to be changed. Everything was completely routine to the end, and the two 'prototypes' headed the GT VW-Porsche in formation across the line, more than 30 laps ahead of a BMW 2002.

A full factory team was entered for the Monte Carlo Rally in January 1971, and to some extent this was a mistake although there was a creditable result. Porsche had won the rally for three consecutive years with 911 models, and all the drivers were extremely keen to run the 911s again. They felt that the 2-litre VW-Porsche was underpowered, and did not like the neutral cornering characteristics, their technique being to 'hang the tail out' on snow or gravel. In fact the VW-Porsche team had early setbacks when Larrousse's car broke its clutch and Ake Andersson's broke its differential. Bjorn Waldegard, winner for the past two years, battled gamely against the lightweight Alpine-Renaults and in the end he was narrowly beaten into third place, only two minutes behind Ove Andersson's French car. By most standards that would have been full justification for running the mid-engined cars, but the drivers were openly critical of the choice and robbed the result of some of its value.

Due to adverse trading conditions in America, and the increasingly stringent emission rules, sales of the 914/6 dipped disastrously in 1971 to a mere 357 cars, or 3% of Porsche's total output. Early in 1972 prototypes were prepared with 2.4-litre Porsche engines, but this version did not reach the production stage as a top-level decision had already been made to phase the 914/6 out later in the year. Production then concentrated on the 1.7-litre 914S, and the much more successful 2-litre Volkswagen four-cylinder model, the 914SC, which developed 100bhp DIN and had a top speed of 115mph. This became a very popular version, particularly in America (though right-hand drive was never introduced) and it continued in production until 1975 when a new project, the 924, was nearing completion.

Porsche bought up Volkswagen's share of the joint holding company in 1973, effectively ending the VW-Porsche agreement, though at that time the Zuffenhausen company was still working on project EA425 for VW-Audi, and this is the model that later became the Porsche 924.

The public was given an opportunity to look into the future at Frankfurt in 1973 when Porsche showed a research project called the Longlife automobile. Unlike so many futuristic exercises from the Italian styling studios, the Porsche Longlife was an incomplete vehicle incorporating just some of the ideas which would become reality in future, based on the practical theory that a car designed to last 20 years or 180,000 miles need only cost 30% more than a model with a life expectancy of 10 years.

Aluminium and scratch-proof clear plastic were used extensively in this prototype, and in the future the Porsche designers saw the adoption of special alloy disc brakes, large capacity and lightly stressed engines, hydraulic torque converters instead of the normal clutch, ozone resistant silent bushes, contactless ignition systems, and more use of indestructible materials. Two years later all Porsche's car products were made with galvanised steel chassis pans bearing a six-year anti-corrosion guarantee, and the Turbo was the first model to have a contactless ignition system. And in 1976, the government sponsored Austrian Federation of Industries opened talks with Porsche to investigate the possibility of setting up car production in Austria, bearing in mind some of the Longlife principles.

Who knows what the future will hold? For a quarter of a century Professor Ferdinand Porsche's firm has concentrated on good engineering principles to produce high performing, sports oriented cars, developed extensively through works supported competitions. No amount of legislation will remove from man the desire to own a car which handles better than most others, accelerates faster, and has more inherent safety in the design than so-called safety models in which the occupants are restrained and protected from injury.

Even so, the increasing level of social awareness so far as pollution and safety are concerned is making all motor manufacturers take a hard look at the automobile of the 1980's and wonder if the projection of current concepts will serve the need of the motoring public in another decade. But if that sounds despondent, there is no reason why a company like Porsche could not combine new concepts and new safety standards with high performance, and the sporting tradition that has put the Zuffenhausen firm where it is today.

8 Dr. Ing. h. c. Ferry Porsche

IF Professor Ferdinand Porsche was the superb innovator, the creator of the illustrious name, his son Ferry is the man who turned the legend into a sound (but still family owned) commercial enterprise with world-wide ramifications. Professor Porsche was released from internment by the French in August 1947, a sick man, and although he participated fully in the foundation of Porsche GmbH at Stuttgart in 1950 it is doubtful that he would have had the strength or the time to forge the company into a flourishing manufacturer with retail outlets on every continent. For a quarter of a century Ferdinand (Ferry) Porsche assumed full responsibility for the growth of the company, until the time came in 1972 for him to sever all the family connections and move up to the post of chairman, leaving all day-to-day matters in the hands of the board of directors.

Ferry Porsche was born in Austria in September, 1909, and naturally inheriting his father's great interest in cars he joined the newly founded Porsche design company in 1933 as an engineer. Germany was in the throes of near revolution and change, but it was under the seemingly benign patronage of Chancellor Adolf Hitler that exciting projects came to the Porsche company. First the design of the Auto Union Grand Prix car, then the design of the small, rear-engine Kubelwagen 'People's Car' that years later became known internationally as the Volkswagen Beetle. With these projects Ferry assisted his father capably, learning the broad spectrum of automotive engineering most thoroughly. It was Ferry who did most of the test driving in the VW, it was Ferry who carried out the initial testing of the Auto Union Grand Prix car, having already proved himself to be a highly competent driver who might, with the necessary amount of racing experience, have become renowned. It was Ferry who saw the need to improve traction on the Auto Union and designed the limited slip differential which gave the mid-engined machine supremacy over the Mercedes-Benz in 1936.

In 1937 Ferry accompanied his father on a trip to Detroit, to see at first hand the advanced American techniques of mass production. Their experience enabled them to plan the Volkswagen plant at Wolfsburg, though fatefully the Beetle did not go into production until the Allies gave the go-ahead in 1945.

The war years, of course, prevented any development of passenger or racing cars and Professor Porsche's company played its part in the war effort, designing desert and snow versions of the Kubelwagen for use in the southern and eastern theatres of the war, going on to design the world's largest tank, appropriately named the Maus and weighing no less than 188 tons.

The beginnings of the post-war Porsche story were seen in 1943, when Ferry approached the German High Command in Salzburg (Austria) to see if the Porsche design company could be moved away from Stuttgart, which was being bombed with increasing intensity. Porsches moved to a sawmill at Gmund, in Carinthia, and the works was grandly named the Vereinigte Huttenwerke (United Smelting Works) to allay gossip and suspicion. The final major war project for Porsche was the design of a cheap jet engine for the V1 flying bomb, to replace its outdated pulse-jet motor, but fortunately for London the war ended before the design was finalised.

Post-war interrogation was comparatively light for Ferry Porsche (though he was detained by the French for several months), but the French took a special interest in the now ageing Professor, tricking him into prolonged captivity, and in the next 18 months the old man was compelled to help with the design and production of the Renault 4CV passenger car.

It was during this period, early in 1947, that Ferry Porsche was commissioned to design the Cisitalia Grand Prix car, in company with Engineer Karl Rabe and Professor Eberan von Eberhorst. Carlo Dusio, a wealthy Torinese businessman, commissioned this car and a large part of the advance fee (one million francs, to be exact) was paid to the French to secure the release of Professor Porsche and his son-in-law, Dr. Anton Piech. The Cisitalia was type number 360, so the first 'real' Porsche (356) must have preceded it slightly, though in the biography *We at Porsche* (John Bentley, published by G.T. Foulis) the exact dates are not specified. In any event, the four-wheel drive Cisitalia, powered by a 'boxer' flat-12 engine, was Ferry Porsche's first Formula-1 design. Upon Professor Porsche's release in August 1947, he studied the plans and gave the car his complete approval. That it was one of motor racing's most publicised failures, second perhaps to the early BRMs, was no fault of Porsche, for Dusio had merely commissioned the design, not the construction and development, and money ran out long before it was ready for competitions.

We can pinpoint the design of the Porsche 356 to the spring of 1947, and again it was Ferry Porsche's own brainchild. It had a tubular chassis, aluminium roadster bodywork, and the Volkswagen 1,131cc four-cylinder, air-cooled engine turned around to be in the middle of the car, with the gearbox at the rear. The car was completed on 8th June 1948, and initial trials on the steep Katschberg Pass proved it to be an extremely promising sports car. The bodywork was styled by Dr. Erwin Komenda, for long a colleague of Professor Porsche before the war, and it was Komenda who styled the coupe, as the next four prototypes were. At the suggestion of Professor Porsche, though, the engine was turned around to the rearmost position allowing some space for small seats behind the driver and passenger, thus improving its market appeal.

The four coupes which followed the roadster were commissioned by Herr von Senger, a Zurich dealer who was appointed the Swiss representative for Porsche cars.

A total of 50 aluminium bodied 356 models (49 of which were coupes) were built at Gmund in 1948 and 1949, most of which had been sold before they were built. All had steel platform chassis, and a number of chassis were sold to the coachwork company, Beutler, in Switzerland where they were equipped with convertible steel bodies.

Supply of components and aluminium was proving to be a handicap in Austria, which was not in the 'hard currency' circle, and in the spring of 1949 Ferry Porsche had initial talks with Professor Nordhoff, 'father' of the now flourishing Volkswagen company, to ensure the supply of mechanical parts. A further meeting, at which a contract was signed, was held in October 1949. Not only was VW's parts supply assured, but Porsche was signed to act as consultant engineer to the VW firm: This two-sided agreement prevented

Porsche from acting as consultant to any rival manufacturer for many years to come, but was probably the most astute move of Ferry Porsche's entire career because a royalty on every VW produced was paid to Porsche! Furthermore, the family of Piech was appointed VW distributors in Austria. In return, Porsche had to design, develop and offer all subsequent modifications for the Beetle, and these ran to thousands of changes before the contract eventually expired in 1970.

The financial base for the Porsche company had been established, and steady growth was seen through the years. Porsche GmbH moved to rented space at Zuffenhausen, a Stuttgart suburb, in September 1949, consisting of 600 square meters of space. Fewer than 100 men worked there initially, but the coupe bodies (now made of steel) were made by the Reutter coachwork company nearby. Originally, a run of 500 cars was envisaged, for neither Ferry Porsche nor his colleagues could see much possibility of selling more cars than that. As history now tells, between 1950 and 1965 no fewer than 78,000 examples of the 356 were built. The Reutter company was taken over and absorbed and three distinct 356 model changes (A, B, and C) were produced.

In 1952 Dr. Ernst Fuhrmann, one of Porsche's most promising designers, started work on the Carrera engine, the first unit which could be called 'Porsche' and which finally went into production in 1955. The work of Dr. Fuhrmann was clearly significant, for subsequently he designed the Fuhrmann camshaft, the 904 engine, and eventually became the managing director of the company in 1972 after a brief spell away from the company.

Ferry Porsche was a firm believer in the value of competitions, allowing the entire publicity budget to be spent on research and motor racing 'where results speak for themselves'. The research aspect of the company grew apace, culminating in the opening of the Weissach centre in the late 1960's and the fulfilment of many contracts with European manufacturers, and foreign governments for advice on anything from new car designs to road-building. In fact, car production today is little more than the tip of the iceberg, the House of Porsche having a firm base in consultancy.

History began to repeat itself when two of Ferry Porsche's four sons, Ferdinand Alexander ('Butzi') and Peter joined the company. Butzi started in 1957, and four years later became head of the styling department, taking responsibility for the remarkably successful type 911 body shape. Peter joined the firm in 1963, becoming head of the production department late in 1965 and taking responsibility, among other things, for the renowned quality and reliability of the road cars. From the Piech side of the family, Ferdinand joined Porsche in April 1963 and immediately set about designing the flat-six, ohc engine that powered the type 911 road car. Later, he was responsible for the 917 racing car that gave Porsche its outright wins at Le Mans in 1970 and 1971, and Ferdinand Piech also took over the development department in 1966. Dr. Michael Piech was with the company a mere 11 months, from April 1971 until March 1972, with responsibility for the general management departments at Zuffenhausen.

It was the growth of family influence, which is rudely termed nepotism, that finally led to the breakup of the system. Certainly it inhibited other staff members and limited their promotion, but worse, the two sides of the family were grating 'like sand in a well-oiled machine', to use Ferry Porsche's own words.

Upon Professor Porsche's death in 1952 the company became known as Dr. Ing. h.c.F. Porsche A.G., with Ferry Porsche and his sister, Louise Piech, having equal 50/50 shareholdings. Later, the entire shareholding was split into 10 parts: Ferry and his four sons, and Louise Piech and her four children, each took a 10% shareholding. Their financial interests are still maintained, but following a family meeting in 1971, when it was decided to ban members of the Porsche and Piech families from holding management positions, the company was renamed Porsche AG in August 1972. Ferry Porsche himself became chairman, Dr. Fuhrmann the managing director, and the younger members of the family severed their management connections.

9 A new image, the 924

THE relationship between Porsche and Volkswagen did not blossom in the way that might have been expected (possibly the progenitors of VW-Porsche AG did not have the maximum backing from their respective boards), and when the 914/6 slumped it became clear that the joint holding company would soon dissolve.

Kurt Lotz, who had been at the head of VW in 1969, retired and was replaced by Rudolf Leiding in October 1971. Leiding was less enthusiastic about the joint venture than his predecessor had been, and the revaluation of the Deutschmark, which led to the German manufacturers' recession in America, merely accelerated the demise of the 914. Even so, in its final form with the 100 horsepower VW engine, the 914 did enjoy renewed popularity in the States until it finally went out of production in 1975. Meanwhile, the Porsche family had handed over effective control of their company and in 1973 Porsche's new joint managing directors, Dr. Ernst Fuhrmann and Heinz Branitzki, decided to buy up Volkswagen's share of the joint concern making it wholly Porsche.

For a couple of years there was an odd situation whereby Porsche were responsible for a sportscar they had designed, but with a Volkswagen engine, and built in the Karmann factory. By 1975, when a total of 115,646 VW-Porsches had been manufactured, the offices at Ludwigsburg were occupied by Porsche management personnel, the 914 ceased production, and the Karmann company prepared to manufacture BMW's 630/633 Coupes.

Leiding, whatever his feelings about the VW-Porsche company, had wanted to see a sporting car in the Audi range and in 1972 had commissioned Porsche to design and develop a two-plus-two Grand Touring car, employing the Audi 2-litre engine and as many components from the VW-Audi range as would be compatible with such a model. Prototypes were already on the road in 1974, but by this time Volkswagen was undergoing a massive production and finance crisis in the wake of the oil shortage, leading to Leiding's early retirement in December 1974. His successor, Toni Schmucker, made a rapid reappraisal of the VW-Audi range and his first step, in February 1975, was to 'kill' project EA425.

Rather than wind up the project, Porsche bought back the rights to the car they had designed and renamed it the Porsche 924, bringing forward its production for readiness in February 1976. It certainly broke with tradition, having an Audi-based four cylinder engine — with water cooling! — at the front, a stiff backbone chassis encasing the propellor shaft, and a transaxle gearbox/differential unit at the rear. Sleek, rather wedge-shaped aerodynamic lines featured electrically operated pop-up headlights, and an expansive wrap-round rear window, top hinged in estate car fashion allowing easy access for luggage, heavy shopping, even children or dogs. The small 'plus two' seats at the back would fold flat, increasing the luggage area. Front suspension consisted of coil sprung MacPherson struts, while more traditional torsion bars were fitted at the rear, saving space. The 924 had disc brakes at the front, drums at the rear, and servo assistance, while rack-and-pinion steering made it a responsive car to drive.

Although based on Audi's 2-litre engine, Porsche carried out various modifications, adding Bosch K-Jetronic petrol injection, altering the pistons and combustion area, the oil pump, and a host of minor items. It now developed 125bhp DIN while retaining excellent fuel economy — 27 to 35mpg (Imperial) were normal operating figures, thanks partly to the high overall gearing of the car (the differential gear was 3.44:1). Thus the standstill to 60mph acceleration figure was reasonably good (9.6 seconds) yet the 924 had a genuine, and quiet, top speed of 125mph.

Purists — and Porsche 911 owners tend to answer that description — threw up their hands and said it was not 'a proper Porsche', forgetting perhaps the origins of the 356. The fact is that the 924 was designed, developed and eventually built entirely by Porsche, albeit on a production line in Audi's Neckarsulm plant for capacity reasons. It was built to Porsche's high standards, and through the years could be expected to undergo various avenues of development. For a start it had the galvanised steel platform chassis, in common with the 911 range, bearing a six-year anti-corrosion guarantee, and that alone marked it out from its competitors.

"We are not bound by any concept, we are just bound to make that any concept work better than others." Those were the words of Professor Porsche many years previously, but they proved apt in the introduction of the 924, which broke so many traditions.

When introduced in February 1976 the Porsche 924 was priced at 23,450 DM, and soon afterwards the car became available with VW's automatic gearbox at an extra 1,500 DM. Though still a little dearer than its nearest international competitors, such models as the Alfetta GT and the Lancia HPE, the 924 found a ready market and six months after the introduction the production rate was increased from 80 to 109 cars per day in order to meet the demand. Right-hand drive models began production early in 1977 for the British and certain other export markets.

Porsche did not rush to homologate the 924, but former racing driver Rudi Lins and his co-driver, Gerhard Plattner, made a remarkable journey early in 1976 to prove the car's reliability and economy. When Jules Verne wrote his classic *Around the World in 80 days* he foresaw adventurous, rather than political problems. Phineas Fogg had quite a straightforward itinerary, but Lins and Plattner set themselves the task of following a similar route, not in 80 days, but in 30. For political reasons Fogg's route could not be followed, so some odd-looking detours were made so as not to shrink the mileage. The undertaking was promoted by the Austrian Tyrol Tourist Board, so the route began in Innsbruck and visited Ankara, Teheran, Zahedan, Karachi, Brisbane, Melbourne, Sydney, San Francisco, Los Angeles, Phoenix, Salt Lake City, New York, Montreal, Amsterdam, Brussels, Geneva, Karlsruhe, Milan, Paris, and then back to Innsbruck.

This journey, which clocked 23,312 driving kilometres (13,864 miles) was actually accomplished in 28 days at a road average of 78kph (48.5mph). For the record, fuel consumption averaged 10.7 litres/100 kms (26.35mpg) from Innsbruck to Karachi, 9.9 litres/100 kms (28.48mpg) in Australia, and 9.4 litres/100 kms (30.00mpg) in America and in Europe.

10 The 928

JUST as the 911 had been a turning point for the Porsche company, so too would be the 928 which was introduced at the Geneva Salon in 1977. Its success was less critical in the immediate sense, for the 911 would continue in production at least until the early 1980's, but within Zuffenhausen and Weissach, the 928 was seen as the 911's logical and natural successor at such a time as international noise and pollution regulations eventually overtook the immensely successful six-cylinder range.

Increasingly, the noise and accident regulations tended to favour 'conventional' cars, those with the engine at the front, and no doubt after a great deal of heart-searching it was decided to abandon a 40-year tradition and place the engine at the front. The 928 would be a bigger car than any of its predecessors, having more passenger accommodation and luggage space, so it would have an engine capacity of 4.5-litres. In the interests of smooth power delivery this engine would have more than six cylinders, and at the critical stage it was decided to go ahead with a V8 water cooled engine.

V8? Water cooled? Would not the 928's configuration resemble that of just about every American car on the road? Possibly, except that nothing from the House of Porsche could possibly be big, sloppy and uneconomical. What eventually emerged was a futuristic, muscular, fast Grand Touring machine tailored to the needs of a wealthy and discriminating driver. To even out the weight distribution the five-speed gearbox was placed at the rear, just ahead of the differential and the axle. This 'transaxle' as it is called, enabled the 928 to have a near-perfect 50:50 weight distribution, affected very little by the load. Optionally, the customer could order fully automatic transmission, tailored to give rapid and responsive changes.

Completely new cars ... new engine, new body, new gearbox, new configuration ... are relatively rare in the world of automotive engineering, so in that sense alone the 928 followed the tradition of the 911. The styling, with rounded, conservative lines, looked neat and economical. Pop-up headlamps which faced the sky in daylight hours resembled those on the outmoded Lamborghini Miura, and attracted some critical comment. But the 'disc' alloy wheels with generous brake cooling, the rear hatchback allowing easy access to the luggage compartment, and the general level of comfort and refinement, all marked out the 928 as the Porsche for the 'Eighties.

To minimise weight, the doors, bonnet and detachable front wings were all made of aluminium, while the entire bodyshell was made of galvanised steel (rather than just the chassis of the later model 911s and the 924). Thus Porsche were able to offer a comprehensive six-year 'Longlife' warranty against corrosion, a significant advance in the pursuit of conservation.

Front and rear ends of the 928 were constructed entirely of polyurethane, a plastic which could take low-speed knocks without significant damage and help Porsche to meet the higher speed crash regulations. With a complete absence of chromium plating, the 928 was constructed almost entirely of galvanised steel, alloys and plastic, all of which could be kept in good condition for many years. Depreciation would not be a major factor, and low servicing and maintenance costs were also priorities during the design stage. Engine oil needed changing every 20,000 kilometres (12,000 miles), contactless ignition was employed, and despite having an overhead camshaft on each bank hydraulic tappets were adopted in the interests of saving maintenance and reducing the noise level.

The power unit itself might be orthodox, but it was designed as a thoroughbred. A conventional 90-degree vee formation was adopted, but with exceptionally wide-angle heads the engine was kept unusually low and compact. Even the cylinder liners were made of aluminium, specially hardened, while the alloy pistons themselves had a thin steel coating, a simple way of reducing piston/bore wear without introducing complexity at the manufacturing stage. The forged steel crankshaft ran in five main bearings, and the shallow sump pan was designed to eliminate oil surge even in the most strenuous cornering conditions.

Toothed belts drive the single camshaft on each bank, and induction was by means of the Bosch K-Jetronic petrol injection system developed by Porsche for the 911 range. This power unit, with a bore and stroke of 95 x 78.9mm, had a capacity of 4,474cc and an impressive power output of 240bhp DIN, torque peaking at 267.6 lb.ft at 3,600rpm. With a compression ratio of 8.1:1, the engine required 91-octane regular-grade fuel.

The switch to water cooling must have seemed odd to Porsche fanatics, the Zuffenhausen firm following the path trailed by Volkswagen with its new generation of family cars. Logically, once the engine has been placed at the front there is little to choose between water or air cooling, and water was the chosen medium for two reasons: first, for better heat dispersion without the power loss of a fan, and second, because it facilitates interior heating. A cooling fan was fitted, of course, of the viscous coupling type operating only at low engine speeds.

Unusually a twin-plate clutch was adopted, driving the gearbox via a torque tube running in two bearings, much the same method as in the 924.

Front suspension was by means of unequal length wishbones, but the rear suspension was particularly interesting as it incorporated geometry to prevent toe-in which normally follows deceleration in a curve. A good deal of experimental work was done with a dual control Opel Commodore, the second driver sitting in the back seat and making unexpected steering wheel movements to deflect the back wheels. This way, Porsche's engineers at Weissach built up a good deal of data on handling behaviour in adverse conditions, and the patented 'Weissach axle' was the result. The toe-in control of the 928's rear axle was accomplished by a steering element mounted in the lower diagonal trailing arms. Referred to as a controlling swing, its movements were defined and limited, virtually eliminating toe-out and thus making the car much easier and more relaxing to drive.

Another break with tradition was the elimination of torsion bars as a means of suspension (though front and rear torsion anti-roll bars were incorporated), relying instead on coil springs and telescopic dampers. Yet another break was the adoption of power steering, not an ultra-light system but one which gave decreasing assistance as the car's speed increased. Completing the recipe, ventilated disc brakes front and rear provided suitable retardation.

At the kerb the 928 weighed 1,450 kilogrammes (3,193 pounds), not exactly a lightweight compared with the heaviest 911 derivative, the Turbo model at 1,195kg. With 240bhp available the 928 was endowed with considerable performance, however, on a par with a 3-litre Carrera: the quoted top speed was over 143mph, with zero to 100kph acceleration in 6.8 seconds. Ultimate road-holding was assured by Pirelli's 50% aspect ratio P7 covers on the 16-inch diameter rims. Some 'novelty' items on equipment included a pantograph rear window wiper, a special reservoir of cleansing fluid for removing oily and silicone deposits from the windscreen, automatic locking of the passenger door with the driver's door, and finally, a splendid central warning system in case of malfunctions. If the engine oil or brake fluid should need topping up a warning light would show on the centre console panel, but this could be turned off. If, on the other hand, all the oil or fluid disappeared and rendered the car's operation dangerous, the warning light would blink on and could not be ignored.

The whole cockpit of the car could be tailored for the driver, with adjustable pedals, adjustable gear lever, steering column rake, seat height, even the armrest tilting to suit the driver. In so many ways the 928 was far, far removed from the simple, sturdy, economical 356 which was gaining in popularity a quarter of a century before; even the sunroof of the 928 was designed so that the wind would not ruffle the driver's hair! Yet throughout Ferry Porsche's career, and his father's before that, everything was dedicated to progress and improvement ... all these technical advances needed to be incorporated into new Porsche designs, and many would become trend-setters.

THE END.

Index

Porsche type numbers